The Timid Corporation

The Timid Corporation

Why Business is Terrified of Taking Risk

Benjamin Hunt

WILEY

Other Wiley Editorial Offices

John Wiley & Sons Inc., 111 River Street, Hoboken, NJ 07030, USA

Jossey-Bass, 989 Market Street, San Francisco, CA 94103-1741, USA

Wiley-VCH Verlag GmbH, Boschstr. 12, D-69469 Weinheim, Germany

John Wiley & Sons Australia Ltd, 33 Park Road, Milton, Queensland 4064, Australia

John Wiley & Sons (Asia) Pte Ltd, 2 Clementi Loop #02-01, Jin Xing Distripark,
Singapore 129809

John Wiley & Sons Canada Ltd, 22 Worcester Road, Etobicoke, Ontario, Canada M9W 1L1

Wiley also publishes its books in a variety of electronic formats. Some content that appears
in print may not be available is electronic books.

Library of Congress Cataloging-in-Publication Data

Hunt, Benjamin.
    The timid corporation : why business is terrified of taking risk / Benjamin Hunt.
        p.   cm.
    Includes bibliographical references and index.
    ISBN 0-470-84368-3 (cased : alk. paper)
    1. Risk management.   2. Business planning.   I. Title.

  HD61.H86   2003
  658.15'5—dc21   2003041084

British Library Cataloguing in Publication Data

A catalogue record for this book is available from the British Library

ISBN 0-470-84368-3

Typeset in 11/15pt Goudy by TechBooks, New Delhi, India
Printed and bound in Great Britain by Biddles Ltd *www.biddles.co.uk*
This book is printed on acid-free paper responsibly manufactured from sustainable forestry
in which at least two trees are planted for each one used for paper production.

For Val and Adrian Lewis

Contents

Acknowledgements

Many people deserve thanks for helping with this book. Since much of the book is based on primary research and numerous conversations over the last five years, I would first like to thank everyone who took time out to discuss ideas. Many people have been willing to offer insights in their particular field. I cannot possibly thank everyone by name. Thanks in particular to Mark Bernstein, Tracy Kugelman, Mark Rice, Satkar Gidda, Pierre Chao, Yuji Hatano, Toru Takenaka and Bill Scott.

A number of friends have been great in offering support, both practical and moral. Thanks to Hugh Peto, Deborah Pretty, Christopher Stoakes, Richard Woolfenden, Jeremy Henderson, Sarah Simonds, Fenno Outen, Ameet Malhotra, Tamla Small, Peter Kwong, Sarah Herman, James Matthews, Louise Burton and Jason Burton.

I have been very lucky to have had an excellent editor at Wiley, Diane Taylor. I could not have hoped for someone better. Diane was always willing to discuss and challenge ideas and move things onto the next level.

Finally, four people were especially generous with their time to read drafts and give valuable comments and insights. They have undoubtedly made this book a better product. Thanks to Daniel Ben-Ami, Phil Mullan, Joe Kaplinsky and James Woudhuysen.

Introduction: The Rise of the Cautious Manager

A hundred and fifty years ago, according to historian Eric Hobsbawm, the elites of society 'believed in capitalism'. They believed strongly in competitive private enterprise, technology, science and reason. The 'bourgeois society of the third quarter of the nineteenth century was self-confident and proud of its achievements' (see Hobsbawm, 1975, pp. 245 and 251).

Capitalism has always been driven forward by people with belief and a strong sense of purpose in shaping the future. Yet in recent times something seems to have changed. Those in charge of capitalism do not seem to be very self-confident, or very proud of their achievements.

As this book was being finished, the business world was engulfed in a mood of 'irrational pessimism'. Managers of corporations, fearful of the future, seemed scared to invest and take risk. In the United States, boards were busy regulating themselves in new ways, ostensibly in response to the string of business scandals known collectively as 'Enronitis'. The US president had called for greater accountability, responsibility and transparency. Public officials were busy attacking the 'excessive' pay of top executives.

This book attempts to highlight a new problem. It argues that managers have become increasingly cautious and risk-averse. This risk aversion is not just a temporary mood that, with luck, might go away in the near future. A peculiar development is that risk aversion has become more of a permanent mindset and mode of operation, independent of the business cycle. A sense of caution and restraint has become entrenched. The aim of this book is to show how and why this has happened, and why it represents such a problem.

Much of this book is based on primary research, and case studies gathered from a wide variety of interviews and conversations with people in the business world and the business and financial services sector surrounding it – executives, finance managers, risk managers, sustainable development managers, brand managers, engineers, consultants, lawyers, analysts, venture capitalists and finance and insurance professionals.

The focus is on 'Anglo-Saxon' capitalism – the United States and Britain. As the United States is the most advanced and dominant capitalist nation, it is well known that trends tend to begin there and migrate to the rest of the world, as political, cultural and economic institutions everywhere attempt to put American ideas into practice. While the focus is on the United States and Britain, however, large corporations tend to behave in a similar way around the world. It is striking how issues such as corporate governance, sustainable development, ethics, risk management, customer relationship management and brands, to name a few explored in this book, have found practical expression everywhere around the globe.

The timid corporation

The central theme of this book is the way that risk aversion has become *institutionalized* in business. The best way to understand this development is to understand a wider process of behaviour that has been unfolding over the last decade or so.

It is easy to forget today that throughout history business as an institution has always had a strong sense of purpose, galvanized by the dynamic of the market and strong belief systems. A strong pioneering spirit has always existed in commerce and industry. In the nineteenth century, there was considerable excitement about scientific and technological breakthroughs. Throughout the cold war, people working in industries such as aerospace, chemicals, pharmaceuticals, movies, electronics and information technology (IT) were excited about new technologies, experimentation and the prospects for doing big things.

Down the years captains of industry have made bold pledges to create new products and new markets. Henry Ford believed in a future where there would be a car in every garage. At least some industrial leaders – not everyone of course – felt they could 'bet the company' on large technological projects. In hi-tech industries, defined by their spending on research and development (R&D) and more radical innovation, industry leaders have not shied away from taking risk with resources. Boeing's creation of the 747 and IBM's spending on mainframe computing are two noticeable examples. The Japanese company Sony also springs to mind: it was a major pioneer in consumer electronics throughout the post-war period, introducing the pocket transistor radio, portable TVs and the Walkman, among other things.

The American academic Richard Lester suggests that the 747 project was never a narrow response to market or competitive issues. Boeing thought the 747 would lead to competitive advantages. But according to Lester, 'it was Boeing's sense of itself as an aviation pioneer, as a company that pushes the envelope of aeronautic technology, that "eats, breathes and sleeps" the world of aeronautics, that was a critical factor both in determining whether to proceed at all and in driving this historic project to completion' (see Lester, 1998, p. 247). The pioneering spirit of the people working at Boeing was important in driving things forward.

Traditionally, business leaders have been confident in the purpose and mission of business as a private institution. Business elites of the past had no qualms in believing that private profit was a justifiable reward for risk-taking. Many believed that society in general would benefit from the pursuit of private gain and self-interest. Milton Friedman famously said that the only social responsibility of business was to make a profit. In the post-war period, many business leaders would have shared this view. As long as business kept within the law, the freedom of business to operate with autonomy was valued (see Friedman, 1962, p. 133).

In the last decade or so, however, something drastic has changed. It is arguable that the traditional belief systems that used to drive business forward have broken down. For instance, many people across industry report that the excitement there once was about change and the future does not seem to exist in the same way. In the place of these beliefs, a more fearful mentality has emerged. The world, relatively suddenly, seems a more risky and unpredictable place. Rather than act on positive beliefs of what might go right, business leaders increasingly act on fears of what might go wrong.

At the same time, corporations seem to be in far more defensive relationships with the world. Finding it difficult to take a leadership role, corporations tell themselves they should 'listen to society' and 'listen to the customer'. The trouble is, the world around them has become more fearful of the future. The result is that more anxious and fearful corporations relate to and trade with a more anxious and fearful world. By understanding these wider themes, we can understand how risk aversion has become institutionalized in business.

This book shows that caution and restraint have been institutionalized in two main ways. The first relates to the dramatic rise of regulation and self-regulation in the last 10 years or so.

Governments have always regulated corporations. Today, a new dynamic for regulation has emerged, explored in Part One of this book. There is an increasing notion that big business – including the personal behaviour of managers – is more reckless, abusive and unethical, and in need of re-regulation. An ill-defined feeling has developed that corporate behaviour is more out of control, and in need of restraint in myriad ways.

A new regulatory language has suddenly popped up; words such as accountability, transparency, responsibility and disclosure now trip off the tongue. Although governments – which themselves have done much to encourage this new social climate – would not admit it, they have become 'moral crusaders', a development examined in Chapter 1. They are re-regulating business in all sorts of new ways.

The business world itself has tended to view regulation with considerable scepticism. Not so today, it seems. The last 10 years have been witness to an unprecedented bout of *self-regulation* or voluntary regulation.

Corporations have reacted defensively to broader fears about behaviour, explored in Chapter 2. Managers have considerable new worries. For example, never before have fears about 'loss of reputation' come so strongly to the fore in managing a corporation. Managers are far more anxious about damaging the reputation of the corporations they are managing 'on their watch'. But this is just the tip of the iceberg. Managers worry more that corporations may be seen as unethical, socially irresponsible, unsustainable, failing to manage risk, and in relations with shareholders, inefficient with capital. They are more concerned that they themselves may be seen as 'fat cats' or reckless 'empire builders'.

In the last decade or so managers have devised new frameworks for running corporations, based around notions of ethics, risk management, corporate governance, managing for shareholder value and, more recently, sustainable development and corporate social responsibility (CSR).

Under these frameworks, corporations have set in motion a huge number of self-regulatory initiatives. Unfortunately, they all tend to entrench caution and restraint. Worried about appearing to be unethical, managers filter many decisions through ethics departments that deliberate endlessly on the morality of particular decisions. A new ethics apparatus has emerged, consisting of ethics departments, ethical codes of conduct, ethics officers, ethical audits and ethics training courses.

Anxious about being perceived as 'fat cats', 'autocratic bullies' and 'empire builders', boards of corporations are now subject to the kind of self-regulation that previous generations would have found extraordinary. The idea of letting directors set their own levels of pay, or nominate other directors, without new committees and regulations is seen as far too risky and dangerous. The fear is this could lead to excessive or reckless behaviour of the Robert Maxwell variety. Elsewhere, the whole area of sustainable development and corporate social responsibility has led to a plethora of new self-regulations.

The rise of risk management is a striking trend in business, explored in Chapter 3. Managers share new, society-wide anxieties about risk. At the same time, defensive about appearing to be irresponsible and reckless, managers feel they need to show greater awareness of risk and take greater responsibility for managing it. Corporations have set in motion a huge range of initiatives under the banner of risk management.

So, employees now need authorization before making decisions, under the auspices of new risk controls. Worried about making a mistake, managers filter decisions through elaborate risk assessment exercises. Other managers spend considerable time in front of computer screens modelling every conceivable set of risks that could impact a corporation in the future. The insurance industry has been busy devising new hedging mechanisms for risks that previously would have been accepted as business risks.

The new voluntary regulation is most insidious in the way it affects finance and investment. Like all relationships with 'stakeholders', the groups that corporations relate to, managers are in more defensive relations with shareholders. These relations have become subject to considerable mistrust.

In these relations, company directors are more intolerant of risk. Institutional shareholders for their part are also more intolerant of risk and uncertainty, and request greater forms of accountability. Over time, this situation has led managers to put in place new rules and guidelines for running a corporation at the financial and strategic levels. Although obscure to those outside the business and financial worlds, a new 'management correctness' has developed in business. Relatively suddenly, corporations have told themselves they should abide by all sorts of informal rules and procedures, in order to be accountable to shareholders. Under notions of 'managing for shareholder value', managers exhort themselves to only invest above the 'cost of capital'; focus on 'core competences'; only grow if it is 'capital efficient' to do so; and return cash to shareholders if these conditions cannot be satisfied. Major corporations return huge amounts of cash to shareholders because they are more unwilling to take risk and invest in conditions of uncertainty, where returns cannot be guaranteed beforehand.

Through this process, managers have developed a kind of business version of the 'precautionary principle' increasingly used in the world of science. The precautionary principle – a new self-regulation in science – has emerged in response to considerable fears about new technologies and experimentation. It advises that scientists should only experiment if they can guarantee a safe outcome – effectively making science and experimentation impossible. In business, managers now tell themselves they should only invest if they can be sure of the risk and return – making bold investment difficult. Chapter 4 explores this development.

Self-regulation is arguably changing the nature of capitalism. On the other hand, the second major trend, explored in Part Two, is that managers now approach customers and markets, innovation and growth far more cautiously.

The global marketplace was once seen as an entrepreneurial playground. New markets could be created, and the world was there for the taking. Yet a new view of the marketplace has emerged, explored in Chapter 5. Managers and consultants seem to believe that markets are more risky, uncertain, turbulent, volatile, unpredictable, chaotic and complex. Competition is always said to be 'increasing'; customer behaviour is perceived as becoming more and more unpredictable; technological change is more intense; and the pace of change is somehow speeding up.

This book argues that these are one-sided perceptions of reality. Acting on these fears, however, it is striking how corporations have oriented themselves far more defensively to customers and markets. Rather than take a pioneering approach, managers gravitate toward all sorts of protective measures.

Since the early 1990s, corporations have become, self-admittedly, obsessed with 'the customer'. Does this obsession involve the creation of genuinely new products for customers? Unfortunately not.

The new obsession with the customer reflects a highly defensive approach to markets. Chapter 6 shows that a new obsession with building customer *relationships* of loyalty is now well underway, almost as an end in itself. By trying to foster loyal relationships, firms try to create a comfort zone of safety around them in order to survive in markets. Integral to this is the rise of brand building, concepts of brand loyalty, and something called 'customer relationship management' (CRM).

Chapter 7 looks at the dumbing-down of innovation. It explores a major paradox. Technology is getting better. Organizations are more sophisticated in how they can tap knowledge, organize and innovate. However, managers do not seem confident that long-term, risky innovation will pay off. They have become far less tolerant of risk and uncertainty. A marked retreat from radical innovation in R&D labs has taken place. A reluctance to use new IT tools to effect genuine change is also evident. In fact, what corporations often like about the Internet is that it helps them *avoid* risk in the physical world. By reducing risk in the supply chain, keeping costs low, and getting ever 'closer to the customer', firms aspire toward a kind of low risk, high return 'virtual' business model by using the Internet.

In addition, if corporations are more unwilling to take risk with innovation, they are also more unwilling to uphold a discriminatory approach. The whole concept of innovation has become relativized. Anything vaguely 'creative' seems to pass for innovation today, and anybody, with or without experience, can be an innovator.

Chapter 8 shows how the whole nature of 'growth' has become peculiarly defensive. In a world where competition is said always to be increasing, managers tell themselves they cannot 'go it alone'. Companies want to grow, but by investing in each other – mergers and acquisitions (M&A). At the global level, international economic activity has not taken the form of dynamic increases in greenfield investment – where new assets are created – but cross-border M&A activity, where existing assets change ownership. Global economic activity today has risk avoidance built into it. A kind of global business 'huddling together' process is taking place.

Greater regulation and self-regulation, and cautious commercial behaviour, co-exist as part of a whole, not in a cause-and-effect relationship. At a general level, one can say that if firms have placed new restrictions on themselves in how they are run, it is not surprising they will be more cautious in how they approach markets and grow.

For instance, because firms worry about appearing to be unethical, and have new ethical self-regulations, many do not invest in certain projects and refuse to enter certain markets. More substantially, because firms are run with new financial self-regulation, it is not surprising they prefer risk-averse forms of growth where they can be more certain of risk and return.

But it is important not to make hard and fast cause-and-effect connections where they do not exist. New financial self-regulations have not caused the rise of brands, for example. Rather, managers are more defensive when it comes to relationships with shareholders. They are more defensive when it comes to relationships with customers and competitors.

Finally, Part Three returns to explanations in more detail. Risk avoidance has essentially created a new type of capitalism, one that the writer Daniel Ben-Ami calls *Cowardly Capitalism* (Ben-Ami, 2001). In this new system, corporations still strive to make products, profits, innovate and pursue growth. But they go forward far more cautiously, wrapped up in far more regulation and self-regulation, and attempting to pursue profits, innovation and growth in the safest way possible.

The attempt to avoid risk is not being planned out by anyone. It is not happening in a conscious, organized way. There are no conspiracies. Similarly, risk aversion cannot be understood at a psychological level. It is not a new psychological condition. Nor does risk aversion reflect macro or micro economic conditions.

To return to the themes outlined at the beginning, it happens because older belief systems in society, that created a sense of confidence in experimenting and going forward, have broken down. A momentum that previous societies took for granted has ground to a halt. As institutions and individuals have lost traditional beliefs, and are not driven forward by strong ideas in the way they were, they have come to see themselves more as victims of external forces. The world and the future have come to be *perceived* as more risky. Because institutions lack a strong agenda, and see the world as more risky, they react far more defensively to the world around them and to change. Rather than take a lead themselves in upholding strong principles and shaping change, corporations attempt to 'listen to society' and 'listen to the customer'. But the world around them – including the business world and broader society – has also become more risk-averse at the same time, and newly demands caution and restraint in behaviour. Through this process, risk aversion has become institutionalized.

The conclusion throws down a challenge to the culture of risk aversion. Living in a regime of irrational caution and restraint is already frustrating.

Employees become frustrated because ethics departments, paranoid about the appearance of unethical behaviour, prevent them from doing normal activities. Managers of company divisions become frustrated when highly tedious, doorstopper-like risk management manuals land with a thump on their desk, and they are asked to wade through them before making a decision. Trained engineers become frustrated when their firms refuse to do radical innovation. Design consultancies become frustrated when their clients want every new idea to be researched to death in consumer focus groups. Caution and restraint will become more frustrating unless we challenge it.

This book offers a few proposals. We need to adopt a far more critical attitude to regulation, and professional and institutional self-regulation. In the past, regulation at least had a rational component. It was rational to try to prevent workplace accidents when they were prevalent, for instance. Today's bout of regulation and self-regulation is anything but rational. It feeds off one-sided perceptions that things are more out-of-control, that human behaviour is more unethical, and that there are many more risks and uncertainties out there. In reality, the morality of society, and our reactions to anti-social behaviour, tend to improve over time, not get worse. All we are doing with today's self-regulation is wrapping ourselves up in red tape, and entrenching an irrational caution and restraint.

As well as challenging regulation, we need to raise our expectations of the types of product and service that can be innovated, and take a more universal, rounded approach to innovation. One of the paradoxes about today's risk aversion is that it coexists with technological and organizational progress, and the ability to do more ambitious things.

PART ONE

The Re-Regulation of the Corporation

1

The New Dynamic of Regulation

Part One of this book examines the enormous rise of self-regulation in the business world. But before understanding self-regulation, it is necessary to backtrack several steps. The first port of call is to look at regulation more broadly.

Regulation, admittedly, is not the most exciting subject in the world. Unfortunately, it has become interesting for all the wrong reasons. Governments have always regulated the private sector. Today, however, there is a new dynamic for the regulation of professions and institutions in society.

A brief history of regulation

Regulation is nothing new. At least since the nineteenth century governments have regulated the private sector. Academics often break down this regulation into two main areas: economic and social. Rules that regulate trading behaviour and competition between firms fall under the former category, while social regulation refers to rules that dictate how firms should behave in their dealings with social groups and the environment.

The Interstate Commerce Commission (ICC) was the first regulatory agency in the United States, created in 1887. It was set up to outlaw discriminatory practices in the railroad industry. Different operators were found to be offering different rates and prices to different customers. Smaller competitors were losing out to large businesses and found themselves out of the loop. The US government stepped in to address the grievances of particular businesspeople and create a level playing field. The ICC was the first real attempt to oversee and regulate competition and the market, an example of so-called economic regulation. Similarly, the US government passed the Sherman Antitrust Act a few years later in 1890, which tried to outlaw restrictions of trade by monopolies (see Vernon, 1998, p. 262).

In the 1930s the regulatory apparatus of the US government burgeoned, in the form of new legislation and a plethora of new agencies. In the aftermath of the Great Crash of 1929, and in the context of Franklin D. Roosevelt's New Deal, new securities laws were passed to protect investors. The business world was forced to disclose more financial information to the investor community. The Securities & Exchange Commission (SEC) was created in 1934 to enforce these new laws. A whole range of other agencies emerged, such as the National Labor Relations Board. Its purpose was to protect the bargaining rights of labour and prevent unfair labour practices.

New social forms of regulation appeared in the 1930s, but academics view the 1960s and 1970s as ushering in a new era of social regulation. The Equal Employment Opportunity Commission came into existence in 1964, under the Civil Rights Act, and in the early 1970s, the Environmental Protection Agency, the Occupational Health and Safety Administration, and the Consumer Product Safety Commission were created (see Steiner and Steiner, 2000, p. 302).

An era of deregulation?

One assumption is that recent decades have experienced some kind of deregulation revolution, especially in the economic sphere. Yet this idea of deregulation has always been very misleading. Governments have certainly *privatized* and *liberalized* various industries. They have passed over government ownership of industries to the private sector, and/or introduced greater competition, by lowering barriers to entry in various ways. But they have not deregulated industries.

The academic Steven Vogel puts this in perspective. He notes that freer markets tend to lead to more rules by government. So, governments have tended to combine privatization, liberalization and new systems of *re-regulation*.

Take some examples. In the world of finance, the London Stock Exchange went though a move called the Big Bang in 1986. It abolished its antiquated system of rules and regulations. These rules, it was thought, offered too much protection to particular domestic institutions, and not enough choice to others, such as international investors. Investors had to pay fixed fees for buying shares, rather than having more of a choice between prices.

The idea of the Big Bang was to encourage greater competition in the trading of shares. It was hoped that while many domestic institutions would lose out from new competition, London as a whole would benefit from the greater business brought in by foreign investors and brokers. Overseen by the Thatcher government, this was an act of liberalization. Yet only two weeks later, Parliament passed the Financial Services Act (FSA).

The FSA subjected the City to a new web of rules and regulations, ostensibly in order to protect investors from fraud. Vogel (1996, p. 3) suggests that 'the FSA may have revolutionalized life in the City even more than the Big Bang, for in matters of regulation it replaced the informal with the formal, the flexible with the rigid, and the personal with the legalistic'.

This same pattern is replicated everywhere. The British telecom market is another example of how the government has overseen a process of liberalization, but has retained control over the market in significant ways.

In 1981, the government helped to introduce greater competition in the voice transmission market. A single competitor, Mercury, was allowed to compete with British Telecom (BT), the dominant player. Ten years later, all telecom services were opened to competition under the supervision of the regulatory authority, Oftel, which granted licences to new entrants. By 1996, around 90 cable operators had been given a licence to compete with BT in the domestic marketplace.

BT remains a regulated company, however. BT does not have the freedom to charge any old price to consumers for services. Under the rules, it endures price caps. It has to discount prices according to criteria, such as its efficiency in particular areas, and the rate of inflation. Here, competition has been introduced, but the government does not feel it can leave the market to its own devices. The government plays an important role in controlling the shape of competition, by limiting BT's flexibility in how it can price *vis-à-vis* its competitors. Companies such as BT have had to develop large regulatory affairs departments with hundreds of staff simply dedicated to complying with the regulator's demands on issues such as pricing, acquisitions, strategic issues and license issues (see Bonardi, 1999).

In the United States, attempts to liberalize industries have gone the farthest. Beginning in the mid-1970s, governments have overseen the introduction of new market challenges to existing firms in industries such as airlines, trucking, railroads, communications and banking. But this has not meant that governments have somehow stepped out of the way. The process of liberalization has been far from trouble-free. Governments have had to oversee and enforce the introduction of greater competition, and address new problems as they have arisen.

Take the Telecommunications Act passed by Congress in 1996. A major aim was to open up local telephone markets to competition. It was hoped that greater competition would lead to greater choice for the consumer and lower their bills, especially in the context of new services such as broadband Internet. A measure of liberalization began in 1984 when the national monopoly AT&T was broken up into the 'Baby Bells'. But the Bells went on to dominate local markets and faced no outside competition. The 1996 Act required the Bells to open up their local networks through the principle of 'unbundling', i.e. leasing their networks to competitors. If they complied, the US government would allow the Bells an extra outlet for expansion. They would be allowed to compete in long-distance markets.

But it has hardly been a smooth process. For a start numerous issues require government intervention. The Bells have been reluctant to 'unbundle' their local networks to competitors, and many have reneged on their original promises. They have already been fined hundreds of millions of dollars for non-compliance of the Act. In 2002, the Bells still had around 90% of business in local markets, and faced limited competition from the competitive local exchange carriers (CLECs). Also, there was a hope that customers would have lower bills. Yet in many areas that has not happened.

As regulation experts John Braithwaite and Peter Drahos observe, while the Act continues the policy of liberalization for telecommunications, deregulation 'is too simple a term to describe the US process. "Regulatory experimentation" approximates the truth more closely.' For instance, they note that 'State public utility commissions continue to have regulatory powers over the local networks' (see Braithwaite and Drahos, 2000, p. 325).

The attempt to introduce competition into the Californian energy industry in the second half of the 1990s, and the much-discussed 2000 Californian energy crisis, further illustrates the problems with the deregulation label. Not only did the process of liberalization, in its early stages, require an active process of regulation by the state, but when the process began to derail, the Californian state intervened even more strongly in the energy industry.

In 1996, legislation was passed to restructure and liberalize the Californian electricity industry. The aim was to encourage market competition, and lower electricity bills for consumers. Previously, the main utilities in the state had a monopoly over both the generation of power and the supply of power to the consumer. Under the new plan, this would change. Other firms would generate power, after buying generating facilities from the utilities. The utilities would become suppliers of power to the consumer. Unable to generate much on their own, the utilities would have to buy power in a new competitive wholesale market.

In 2000, new problems arose. Under the liberalization plan, price caps were imposed on the utilities, limiting what they could charge to the consumer. The idea was to protect consumers from high bills in a period of transition. However, prices in the wholesale market began to skyrocket – for reasons that have been heavily debated, amid allegations of improper market manipulation by the wholesalers. The utilities were squeezed in the middle, forced to pay out massively for wholesale power, but unable to pass on extra costs to the consumer because of the price caps. In 2001, Pacific Gas & Electric, one of the three state utilities, filed for bankruptcy after running up huge debts to pay for wholesale power.

The utilities, which wanted the liberalization plan to go ahead, initially appeared to benefit from it. They got a good price for selling off their power-generating assets for example. But then they were caught in a strange situation. They became more exposed to market forces in the form of a new wholesale market, but more regulated by the state in their dealings with consumers, perhaps for them the worst of all possible worlds.

In the aftermath, the Californian state government has decided to step in to buy wholesale power on behalf of the utilities. In fact, as *The Economist* reported on 21 July 2001, the whole affair has led to an 'astonishing expansion of public power'. The Californian state was attempting to buy the state power grid. Gray Davis, the governor of California, proposed that the state buy the grid assets of Southern California Edison for US $2.76bn, after plans to buy the grid assets of the utility San Diego Gas & Electric.

Conservative governments on both sides of the Atlantic in the 1980s and 1990s often tried to make deregulation – both economic and social deregulation – into a political theme. But their claims were often exposed. The writers

Christopher Booker and Richard North argue that there was always a 'curious air of unreality about this deregulatory chatter' in Britain. They note that 'in the very year that [British prime minister] John Major was calling at Brighton for the need to "hack back" the jungle of red tape and "bloody-minded petty bureaucracy", his own government was breaking all records for the number of new regulations pouring out of the machine. In 1992, the number of statutory instruments passed on the nod through parliament soared to a historic high of 3359' (Booker and North, 1994).

In America, Ronald Reagan went further than previous presidents in pursuing an agenda of deregulation. He subjected new regulation to systems of cost–benefit analysis. But Reagan's administration did not *reverse* the process of regulation in any significant way. Rather, the best it could manage was to curb the impetus towards greater regulation. And, in the latter phase of his government, regulation was on the rise again. To conclude, then: deregulation has always been a misleading term.

A final point relates to regulation and international activity. The internationalization of economic activity since the 1960s has not somehow led to less regulation at the level of the nation state. Many corporations may have internationalized their activities – which has overwhelmingly taken place in the triad of Japan, the United States and the European Union (EU) – but have faced greater state and international regulation.

For example, it is often assumed that the global financial system has become some kind of 'runaway' world, under-regulated and out of control. But in reality, international banks and other financial institutions have had to comply with a new complex web of international standards and regulations in recent years. They are more regulated than at any other time in history. Beginning in the late 1980s, regulators insisted that banks maintain special capital reserves as a form of insurance against risk. If customers run into financial problems and default on loans, a risk known as credit risk, the hope is that banks can protect themselves.

These regulatory requirements impact significantly on the running of banks, because they touch on central questions of how banks manage and allocate capital. A case could be convincingly made that *fear* of banking and financial collapses has actually led to too much international regulation and too much risk aversion on the part of financial institutions in recent years.[1]

Another point is that, as economic activity is internationalized (although only to a limited extent within certain regions), more regulation flows from international organizations. The United Nations (UN), for example, has a plethora of standard-setting agencies, such as the International Labor Organization, the World Health Organization and the International Telecommunications Union, to mention a few. Similarly, the Organization for Economic Cooperation and Development (OECD) creates international agreements that companies abide by. It is well known that the EU has spewed out many new regulations, and other trading blocs such as the North American Free Trade Agreement (NAFTA) set rules that affect companies.[2]

A new dynamic of regulation

So far regulation has been discussed in a fairly technical fashion, to give a brief historical overview of how governments regulate corporations and markets. The more important point is that a new social and political dynamic for regulation exists today. The rest of this chapter examines this dynamic.

In recent times a peculiar new development has emerged. There is now a generalized idea that big business – including the behaviour of managers and corporations more broadly – is more reckless, abusive and unethical, and in need of re-regulation. An ill-defined feeling has developed that corporate behaviour is more out of control, and needs restraining in various ways.

For instance, the fact that large corporations often make large profits provokes howls of outrage today. In early 2001, BP–Amoco, the Anglo-American energy company, announced record profits of £9.8bn. The reaction was one of disgust. The Labour MP for Chorley, Lindsay Hoyle, felt the profits were 'outrageous and obscene'. For one labour union, British oil companies had become 'modern-day highway robbers' (Cope and Grice, 2001).

The next month apparently brought a double insult. Energy rival Shell announced record profits of £9.04bn. The announcement provoked widespread revulsion. The British Automobile Association (AA) immediately sought an 'urgent explanation' from the company. Shell, it argued, seemed unconcerned that consumers were paying more at the petrol pumps while it enjoyed record profits. These kinds of reaction to profits announcements are becoming common around the world.

Reaction to large profits is possibly surpassed by outrage toward executive pay rises. During 2002 it was hardly possible to pick up a newspaper in the United States and Britain without reading about some supposed scandal about executive pay. The apparently outrageous news that directors receive pay rises is now the subject of intense moralizing on a daily basis – a trend that has gathered momentum over the past 10 years.

If a company suffers from poor profitability, a low share price, or has raised its product prices, but a director of the same company receives a pay rise at the same time, then the breast-beating seems to double in tempo. Also, the executive jet aeroplane seems to have taken on a symbolic importance. The revelation that some executives may pop into a personal jet to fly from London to New York is now interpreted as a sign of excessive greed, selfishness and – from the shareholders' points of view – inefficiency and waste.

In many of these moral reactions it is hard to know what is at stake. The issue of executive pay is peculiar to say the least. The starting point is not that everyone in the economy should be paid more, which might be an understandable demand. Rather, the starting point is far narrower. A tiny minority of people should 'exercise restraint'. Yet it is not clear who really benefits from this.

The tendency to see aspects of managerial and corporate behaviour through the prism of unethical and abusive behaviour has now become a generalized phenomenon. It is not just that corporations are viewed as making 'excessive' profits, or that directors have become 'fat cats', or that consumers are being 'ripped off', or that Asia is awash with 'crony capitalists'.

Media corporations such as Rupert Murdoch's News Corporation are accused of manipulating the media and threatening democracy. Oil companies such as Shell are frequently assumed to be destroying the environment. Tobacco firms such as American Tobacco are seen as murderers simply by producing and selling cigarettes. Life sciences firms such as Monsanto are assumed to be threatening people's health by dabbling in risky new technologies such as genetically modified organisms. Major retail chains such as Wal-Mart are viewed as destroying small communities through their monopoly of markets. Brands such as Nike are seen as manipulating children through marketing and leveraging their brands. And so the list goes on, including endless allegations of various other abuses, such as human rights abuses and political corruption.

The ill-defined feeling that management and corporate behaviour is more out of control, and in need of restraint and regulation, is shared by broad sections of society. These views can be heard everywhere, not just from demonstrators who smash up shop windows. Church leaders feel comfortable with such an agenda. Yet so do members of royal families, and both conservative and radical commentators, not to mention large sections of the media.

In this climate, governments everywhere – which have done much to encourage this climate – have redefined themselves as moral crusaders. In the US presidential election campaign of 2000, Al Gore, the ultimately unsuccessful presidential candidate, made numerous attacks on 'faceless corporations' a feature of his campaign. As he rampaged energetically through various states, Gore complained that oil companies, insurers and drugs companies were making 'excessive' profits. These profits, he pleaded, should be more 'reasonable'. Not everyone agreed with Gore at the time. But after the American business scandals of 2001–2002 (explored below), which appeared to confirm suspicions about corporate 'greed', Gore was reinterpreted as a man of great wisdom and insight.

In the name of protecting certain groups from various 'abuses', governments have stepped up their regulatory efforts. Governments draw on a new language of regulation: the holy trinity of accountability, responsibility and transparency.

At the same time, a new institutional framework for regulation has evolved. Corporations are now surrounded by a plethora of institutions that continually call for more regulation and self-regulation: shareholder rights activists, consumer watchdogs, environmental groups, and thousands of non-government organizations (NGOs). In this new social climate, trade unions have redefined themselves. Many trade unions may have little moral legitimacy to call for ambitious economic demands, such as higher wages for their members, or job security. Today, they tend to argue for greater regulation of the workplace and often see their members as kind of victims of workplace abuse.

Also, in this new framework the large global accounting and consulting firms play a key role in helping managers to implement all this new regulation. Finally, international organizations such as the United Nations and the OECD are keener to insist that multinational corporations adopt various voluntary codes and regulations.

The new dynamic of regulation can be seen in all areas today, but take examples in the arena of competition regulation and consumer rights. The United States has been witness to volatile gasoline prices in recent years. From 1999 to 2000, prices soared from around US $1 per gallon to US $1.60.

In the Mid-West region, consumers were paying up to US $2 per gallon at the gas station.

For a range of American politicians, something did not seem right. For Carol Browner, Administrator of the US Environmental Protection Agency (EPA), and Bill Richardson, US Energy Secretary, there was a suspicion that oil companies had secretly got together to push up prices, stitch up the market and abuse the trust of the consumer. This was an act of 'price gouging' no less, on a huge scale. In June 2000, they formally requested that the Federal Trade Commission (FTC), the competition regulator and protector of consumer rights, investigate.

Before long others shared the same suspicion. US Democrat congressman David Bonior queried, 'why is it that gas prices to consumers stay at record highs despite drops in wholesale prices? It looks, smells and feels like price gouging to me.'[3]

Senator Dick Durbin also accused the oil industry of 'gouging' the public. In reference to the price hikes, he was confident that 'it's an increase directly attributable to profit taking by the oil companies'.

In an interview on NBC's Today show, Bill Clinton, President at the time, felt he had to express concern. 'What we don't know is whether there was any price gouging', he said. 'I'm quite concerned about it.' Clinton reassured the public that a multitude of agencies were looking into it, including the FTC, the EPA and the energy department (Riechmann, 2000).

After a nine-month investigation, the FTC reported back on 30 March 2001. It found 'no credible evidence of collusion or anticompetitive conduct by the oil industry'. Oil companies were not found to be secretly colluding to push up prices. The FTC suggested they were putting up prices on an individual basis to pass on costs to the consumer, in response to particular problems, such as refinery breakdowns and pipeline disruptions.[4]

In Britain, a few years before, an uncannily similar kind of government investigation, with similar conclusions, had taken place. Many had come to believe that British corporations were 'ripping off' consumers with high prices. The Trade and Industry secretary at the time, Stephen Byers, had decided to go on a moral crusade, readily employing the buzz phrase of the moment, 'Rip-off Britain'.

Quite quickly, the large supermarket chains were somehow felt to be abusive. The UK Competition Commission, created in 1999 to replace the older Monopolies and Mergers Commission, began a special investigation into their behaviour.

After a 16-month investigation, the Commission reported back in October 2000. It found the supermarkets to be 'broadly competitive'. The supermarkets were not found to be 'ripping off' consumers. Supermarkets were not found to be abusing consumers, then. Yet they still found themselves subjected to greater regulation. In a special report, the Commission explored initiatives to prevent supermarkets from ripping off consumers.

The supermarkets, they suggested, should post their prices on the Internet. Supposedly myopic consumers could then easily compare prices and avoid being overcharged. Supermarkets should also adopt new codes of conduct for good behaviour, so small suppliers – another key 'stakeholder' – could be protected from abuse.

In December 2001 the supermarkets agreed to comply, adopting codes of conduct to provide guidelines in the relationships between themselves and suppliers. Commenting on this development, one perceptive academic suggests that 'regulation, like mistrust, has become divorced from actual experience' (Burgess, 2001). In other words, regulation – and as we will see, self-regulation – has taken on a dynamic of its own today, no matter what the reality of the situation.

The oil company and supermarket investigations are just two examples of the way that a traditional area of regulation – economic regulation – is being driven by a new feeling that management and corporate behaviour is more abusive and out of control. There are many other examples. In Britain, the Competition Commission has become missionary-like in relation to industry in general. In addition to supermarkets, car manufacturers, banks and mobile phone operators have faced a range of special investigations for alleged 'abuses'.

For instance, during May 2002, four glum-faced chief executives from the world of the British retail banking industry found themselves in a government Treasury select committee. They were there to answer questions about the levels of profits in the industry, and in particular, to face a government allegation that the industry was 'ripping off' customers.

The session was a sequel to one two years before. Then, executives were accused of ripping off consumers through cash machine, or ATM charges. Also, they had come under fire for receiving 'excessive' pay awards.

The latest session proved to be fraught. The British government, with a report by the Competition Commission to hand, argued that executives were exploiting a monopoly. Here, they could rip off customers, make excessive profits, and treat themselves to massive pay rises.

The executives suggested the methodology employed in the report was flawed. They questioned the notion of excessive profits. 'I don't know what excessive profits mean', said Matt Barrett, chief executive of Barclays. The government, however, remained unconvinced. The Office of Fair Trading was considering an unusual action. It was considering whether to implement price controls on the industry. That way, banks would be forced to limit the prices they could charge to customers (see Cameron, 2002).

In recent years a more stringent penalty culture has emerged in the field of economic regulation. When breaches are found to have occurred, the United States and the European Union have fined companies huge amounts. In late 2001 the European Commission (EC) handed out a record £529m fine on Roche of Switzerland, BASF of Germany and several other companies for a nine-year conspiracy to control the vitamins market. It followed a similar probe by US antitrust authorities, which led to a US $500m fine for Roche and a US $225m fine for BASF.

In the arena of environmental and health and safety protection, agencies are becoming more prone to 'name and shame', fine and prosecute more than ever before. The UK Environment Agency now runs a 'Hall of Shame'. This Hall lists companies that, rather dramatically, 'have let down the public, the environment and their own industry'.

A new trend is the direct regulation of individual company directors. Senior executives now find themselves more liable for the actions of the companies they are managing. So directors can find themselves being held under caution during investigations of breaches of environmental law for the first time.[5] Elsewhere, there have been lengthy debates about holding directors responsible for corporate manslaughter.

It is no coincidence that governments around the world have attempted to reform traditional company laws. In Britain, the New Labour government has grappled with the issue of forcing companies by law to care for the interests of stakeholders, such as employees, not just the interests of shareholders.[6]

To conclude here: governments have always regulated companies. But today a new dynamic for regulation has been set in motion. The underlying driver is an acute sensitivity to – and an inflation and exaggeration of – unethical, abusive, destructive, reckless and excessive behaviour. Corporations are exhorted to be more 'accountable, responsible, transparent' and 'disclose' more information about themselves to the public. Governments are stepping up their regulatory efforts. In addition, a new institutional framework, comprising representatives of particular groups, such as shareholders, consumers and environmentalists, has evolved. The rest of this chapter examines these trends in more detail.

Privacy: how the dynamic of regulation has become an end in itself

While protecting individual privacy is not a new regulatory issue, today's new concern for consumer privacy, known as e-privacy in the context of the Internet, is inextricably bound up with the new dynamic of regulation. As such it illustrates some of its problems and contradictions. Although it may seem a strange observation at first, new privacy regulation has very little to do with protecting privacy. It is motivated more by a feeling that corporations are being abusive and need keeping in check, and by the new political agenda of governments.

The issue of consumer privacy is one of the hottest public policy issues in the United States, the European Union and elsewhere. In the late 1990s, data protection legislation came into force in many countries around the world.

The aim, ostensibly, is to protect consumers from so-called privacy abuses by corporations and other institutions. The European Union Data Protection Directive took effect in October 1998. It means that within member states, institutions have to gain consent from individuals before using their personal data.

At the same time, data cannot be transferred to non-EU member states that do not meet an adequacy standard for privacy protection. The United States has decided to comply with the European Union by developing the 'Safe Harbor' framework, approved by the European Union in July 2000. US companies that want to comply with the EU directive can do so by complying with the Safe Harbor principles.

The Internet adds a new dimension to older discussions of consumer privacy. Here, it is said that consumers need greater protection. Consumers need assurances that when they give out personal information over the Internet, they will not receive unwanted marketing material such as spam emails. Also, they need assurances that companies will not collect information about them without their knowledge. Businesses can use a number of techniques to do this, although the 'information' is not necessarily that profound or personal. For instance, 'cookies' are files that are downloaded onto people's computers by companies operating websites. They are used to track the particular areas consumers visit on websites.

Discussions about how to legislate against breaches of 'e-privacy' have been feverish on both sides of the Atlantic. Legislation already exists to protect consumer privacy, but not specifically in the context of the Internet. The Federal Trade Commission in the United States, which enforces the laws of consumer protection, has been keen to take a lead on the privacy protection issue. It has increased its resources in the privacy protection area, and has announced all sorts of initiatives in the name of consumer rights. It announced something called a national Do Not Call List, which allows people to take their names off marketing databases.[7]

It is no exaggeration to say that, as a result of new privacy regulation, and various self-regulatory initiatives by companies, the whole interface between companies and consumers has been re-regulated. New rules and regulations overhaul traditional ways in which corporations collect, process, store and transfer personal information. Privacy regulation forces a new approach to marketing. A central debate in the privacy discussion is that consumers should have a choice to 'opt-in' or 'opt-out' of receiving marketing material. To prevent so-called abuses of privacy, corporations practise something called 'permission-based marketing'. That is, before marketing to consumers they have to gain their permission beforehand. In essence, a whole new etiquette of behaviour is created in the business–consumer relationship.

Corporations have also had to overhaul IT systems. Before the legislation, companies segmented data in databases in particular ways. An airline, for example, may have marketed to its most 'frequent fliers'. But now, these old lines of segmentation are useless, because half of frequent fliers may now decide to opt out of receiving promotional material. Airlines therefore cannot just send out material to their frequent fliers. In this new context, old databases, based on older lines of customer segmentation, need to be overhauled.

The privacy regulation and ongoing discussion has led to a spate of new rules and regulations affecting many other areas. Areas such as cross-selling have come under the microscope. Before, companies could swap information internally. One particular business unit could use customer information gathered elsewhere to do marketing. This area is now being considered afresh. Also, consumers have new rights to demand that corporations within a certain short time limit disclose the personal information they have on them. This requires further internal corporate change.

The privacy issue is just one of many creating a new internal bureaucracy within corporations. Firms have created permanent new board positions, Chief Privacy Officers (CPOs), to oversee these new changes. These directors keep track of new regulation, develop new policies and management frameworks, and set internal education schemes in motion, among other things. In the new millennium, household names such as IBM, AT&T and Eastman Kodak installed CPOs. By the end of 2000, it was estimated that at least 100 US companies had created new CPO positions (see Schwartz, 2001).

The new obsession with privacy abuse fits into the pattern discussed so far. It is motivated far more by an underlying suspicion of corporations, and an obsession with unethical behaviour, than it is a genuine desire to protect people's privacy. This must be the case, because the way that 'privacy' is conceived is extremely narrow. It is arguable that the new laws do not even begin to touch on genuine issues of people's privacy.

Even a cursory look at history suggests that states pose a much greater threat to people's privacy than corporations ever have. One does not have to be a paranoid conspiracy theorist to see that different agencies of the state have extensive powers to erode privacy. Under various laws, such as those under terrorist prevention, governments can investigate citizens and thoroughly sift through their personal lives. Other laws allow agents of the state to intervene directly in family lives. Elsewhere, different agencies of the state oversee systems of surveillance on streets through close circuit television cameras. States can monitor people in their homes through bugging devices, and can track people through identity cards. It is surely odd that in today's discussion of privacy, many of these issues are barely raised, if raised at all.

The reason is that the current discussion on privacy protection is not so much about privacy. Rather, it is more about behaviour that might be deemed unpleasant, insensitive, offensive or unethical. Today's discussion of privacy is more about ethics and etiquette.

For example, an insurance company might know that a customer has a terminal disease. It might pass that information onto a drug manufacturer, which then markets a drug to that customer. This is not standard practice in the insurance industry, but from time to time these kinds of incident occur within industry. Companies use personal and sensitive information without gaining the consent of individual consumers.

For some individuals, that may be insensitive and offensive. For others, they may not be too bothered. But whichever way, this is not a genuine issue of privacy. Today's discussion of so-called privacy is driven far more by a kind of generalized suspicion that, left to their own devices, and behind closed doors, corporations are probably up to no good, and need re-regulating in various ways. But the actual substance of the privacy debate is very shallow indeed.

In this context, the new privacy regulation is more like a new series of ethical codes of conduct on how to handle personal information. But it actually has little to do with genuine issues of privacy. Rather, it is more accurate to say that new anxieties about offensive or unpleasant forms of behaviour are masquerading in the clothing of a concern about privacy.

While privacy is an important right to defend, there are serious problems with today's discussion of 'privacy'. First, the whole concept of privacy is trivialized. It is reduced to an issue of consumer whingeing, where people are encouraged to get angry about the issue of junk email. This, rather than being empowering in any sense, is deeply dis-empowering. It tends to reinforce the notion that people are victims of horrible corporate abuse, and need protecting in various ways.

Second, institutions will simply become even more regulated, defensive and anxious about the way they interact with the world. Huge resources have already gone into protecting so-called privacy. The interface between companies and consumers has become subject to a plethora of new rules and guidelines. Those resources could have gone on something far more in the consumer's genuine interest – such as the pursuit of genuine innovation.

The privacy issue also illustrates another characteristic of today's new regulation, explored throughout Part One. Corporations tell themselves that abiding by privacy regulation is really an *opportunity* for competitive advantage. This is because, the hope goes, they can gain society's *trust*. Trust, it is now said, is an important intangible asset that leads to advantages over other companies that do not have as much of it.

The privacy issue illustrates an irrational development in microcosm. An ill-defined notion has developed that corporations are unethical and abusive. At the same time, governments have become moral crusaders for their own reasons. They have sought to investigate companies and pass new laws. Simultaneously, managers and consultants, rather than adopt a more questioning approach, have told themselves that, all of a sudden, consumer trust is an important intangible asset, and secures a competitive advantage. In essence, subjecting behaviour to all sorts of guidelines and forms of restraint leads, in their view, to opportunities, because society trusts them more.

A new institutional framework for regulation

Over the last decade or so, the new dynamic of regulation has helped to create a new institutional framework that has essentially replaced the old industrial relations framework.

In the post-war period, business was conducted through tripartite agreements between labour, government and business. That framework was based around economic concessions to labour. Governments would provide welfare and social security to citizens. Corporations would provide a job for life and security, in return for the loyalty of workers. Trade unions would argue for higher wages for their members and various labour rights.

The 1980s was a transitional phase where the old framework began to break down. In its place emerged a new regulatory framework, which started to shape up over the 1990s. The new framework involves governments at centre stage as new moral crusaders. But at the same time, increasingly influential institutions argue that corporations abuse their power and trust in various ways. New checks and balances are needed on corporate power. Corporations need to become more accountable and transparent, behave more responsibly, and disclose more information about themselves.

Institutional investors argue that managers and companies abuse their power, and that companies should be managed in the interests and rights of shareholders. Consumer rights activists and watchdogs argue that managers and companies abuse their power, and pursue rights for consumers. Environmental activists and non-government organizations (NGOs) pursue an agenda of environmental rights and various notions of sustainable development. Other NGOs, of which they are now tens of thousands, each have their own self-interests. They pursue their own agendas.

At first glance these institutions appear to have different interests. But they share a regulatory agenda. They all use exactly the same language and argue for the same regulatory mechanisms. So, they all employ the language of accountability, responsibility and transparency. Institutional shareholders call for financial audits and new forms of financial reporting. Environmental groups and NGOs call for ethical audits and new forms of ethical reporting. Many groups favour increased risk management. Many speak the language of corporate governance and, increasingly, sustainable development.

So, an institution arguing for shareholder rights might see itself as very different to an environmental pressure group. But they actually share strikingly similar assumptions. Both argue that managers and corporations are abusing power and trust in various ways. Both propose checks and balances on management and corporate behaviour. Both stake a claim to be recognized as legitimate stakeholders in the process of management decision-making, and the allocation of resources.[8]

Finally, not to be left behind in this new world, trade unions have redefined themselves. They argue that corporations abuse power and trust when it comes to employee relations and the rights of employees. Unions have been especially important in pushing the idea that the workplace is a zone of greater stress, and that managers behave irresponsibly. Here, it is now assumed, employees' work–life balances are out of kilter. Although not articulated as such, the workplace is reinterpreted as a place where destructive things happen to people.

For example, the Trade Unions Congress (TUC) in Britain issued a report in 2000 called Work Smarter – An End to Burnout Britain: the case for sensible regulation to tame the modern workplace. It called, among other things, for new and more effective laws to protect people from issues such as stress, long hours and work pressure.

Feeding vampire-like off regulation: the role of consultants

Consultants have not been slow to benefit from the new regime of regulation. In fact, they have become 'policy entrepreneurs' on a grand scale. Consultants see regulation and self-regulation as providing them with huge new revenue opportunities. They now play a key role in helping firms implement new government regulation and voluntary regulation.

At the same time, consultants have become very adept at arguing that corporations should go far beyond the letter of the law in implementing new regulation. To boost their own revenues, consultants innovate all sorts of new regulatory initiatives that use the original regulation as a springboard for yet more regulation – which by that time takes the form of self-regulation.

The most obvious expression of this is the way consultants tend to pitch their ideas to corporations using a standardized language. So, the biggest crime of all, say the consultants, is to adopt a *tick-box approach* to new legislation. This is far too relaxed. Managers definitely need a *policy*. But this is just a basic requirement. Managers should definitely take a *strategic* view of regulation. They almost definitely should embed the regulation into their *culture*. Ideally, firms should institutionalize a new *architecture* or *framework* around a regulation. It is often incredible how zealous consultants become in wanting to install huge new layers of internal bureaucracy within corporations.[9]

The way that consultants operate can be seen through the issue of privacy, explored before. When governments were busy passing new data protection legislation, consultants were busy developing 'e-privacy practices'. Here, consultants from the major professional service firms work closely with regulators around the world in the pursuit of private sector compliance.

Before long, consultants began to mobilize their familiar language. Companies were advised to go far beyond a tick-box approach. A privacy statement, where a company's attitude to privacy is spelled out, would be a start – but only a start. Ideally, companies need to develop company-wide privacy policies, with the whole gamut of technological and organizational reform this requires. Of course, ideally speaking, companies should create new positions of CPOs. If they have already, then perhaps the CPO needs a new course of training or education? But ultimately, companies need to create a culture of privacy protection. The concept of culture is often the holy grail of consulting. Developing some kind of culture, in this case a culture where consumer privacy is protected, is a platform for all sorts of juicy new reforms and fees, especially in the arena of internal training and education.

The consulting and accounting firm KPMG, like every other, began to develop a privacy framework for companies to adopt in the late 1990s. In one paper, written in 2001, they lay out what they call the 'privacy risk management life cycle', an elaborate framework for managing privacy issues.

So what does this include? Readers unfamiliar with consulting speak should now prepare themselves. Firms should start off with Strategy and Risk Identification. That means an environmental analysis, a business risk analysis, a privacy business strategy, and something called a gap analysis. Then, next in the life cycle, comes Design and Planning. That entails policy development, business processes and controls. Then we have the Development stage, including considerations of human resources, information systems modification, security architecture, relationship management and functional procedures. After that, Implementation, involving business process changes, information systems modification, security implementation, a customer contact programme and compliance. Finally, we have Monitoring and Control, which refers to compliance testing programmes, issue identification and resolution, third-party assurance and environmental updates.[10]

Once new regulation comes into force, therefore, consultants are very competent at running with it, and urging companies to go much farther than the original regulation requires – just to be on the safe side.

Take the approach of one consultant. Using the privacy legislation as a springboard, he goes into boardrooms and asks directors to ask themselves: 'Are you hassling the customer?'[11] Because if you are, he suggests, you have a problem.

This is an imaginative interpretation of the legislation. The starting point is not, Are you breaching the law in the way personal information is used? Rather, the much broader notion of hassling the customer is brought in, which then smuggles in a whole variety of other issues.

A final point is that consultants have been quick to exploit relations of mistrust between corporations and governments. Corporations often are very fearful of approaching regulators even for advice. In one particular case, a major British corporation had zero confidence in being able to approach the data protection regulator. Why? The fear was that even raising a question could prompt an investigation, and a moral crusade of the type seen earlier on. They were very worried that the regulator could single them out in public as an example of an irresponsible company failing to take the legislation seriously. In these circumstances, consultants neatly insert themselves as 'facilitators' between companies and governments to promote 'dialogue'.[12]

A generalized 'culture of suspicion'

So far, this book has argued that while governments have always regulated the private sector, today a new dynamic for regulation exists. This is a dynamic that feeds off a new, ill-defined feeling that the professional behaviour of managers, and the behaviour of corporations, is more unethical, abusive, corrupt, reckless and destructive than in the past. Governments – which have played an important role in creating this new culture – try to exploit it for their own reasons. A new language for regulation has sprung up, and a new institutional infrastructure. An integral part of this process is that corporations have attempted to translate regulation into the commercial language of opportunity.

It is worth asking the question: Why is this happening? For a start, the idea that professional and institutional behaviour is more out of control and in need of regulation is hardly confined to business. The philosopher Onora O'Neill suggests that, 'every day we read of untrustworthy action by politicians and officials, by hospitals and exam boards, by companies and schools. We supposedly face a deepening crisis of trust. Every day we also read of aspirations and attempts to make business and professionals, public servants and politicians more accountable in more ways to more stakeholders.'[13]

Perceptions of 'untrustworthy action' seem to have reached epidemic proportions. So, police forces are regularly accused of racist behaviour. The social services and the Church are regularly accused of fostering child abusers. Doctors are accused of abusing patients in various ways. The Justice system is accused of miscarriages of justice. Scientists are accused of being reckless in their experimentation.

In this new world, scandals have become so ubiquitous that it is becoming very hard to work out the real scandals from the false ones. Given that scandals have become so trivialized, literally every institution and profession in the Western world can expect to be involved in one at some point, whether it likes it or not.

It is hard to think of an institution that has not been mired in scandal in recent times. From the White House, to the US Catholic Church, to the European Commission, to the International Olympics Committee, to Oxford University, to numerous corporations – virtually all institutions are suffering under the weight of scandals. In such a culture, what could be called 'M-words' seem to surface more than in the past. This is a world, apparently, of endless malpractice, malfeasance, miscarriages, mismanagement, mis-selling, misdemeanour and misconduct.

Onora O'Neill puts forward the useful observation that we live in a new 'culture of suspicion'. The notion of a culture of suspicion captures well the gap between perceptions – or suspicions – and reality. It is not really the case that the moral behaviour of professions and institutions has suddenly taken a turn for the worse. Rather, society tends to *suspect* this is taking place.

Of course, there are always isolated cases of genuine anti-social, unethical behaviour. In these cases it is very important that justice should be served, and innocent people protected. Yet what is new about today is that isolated incidences of shocking behaviour are somehow seen as symbolic of a wider breakdown in moral standards. There is an underlying feeling that, somehow, society can no longer tell right from wrong, and that there are few rules in society for guiding people in making moral judgements. In such a society, there is a fear that individuals will run rampant in an uncontrollable way, essentially damaging other people in the process.

This generalized sense of moral breakdown and out-of-control behaviour leads to a situation where it becomes acceptable to regulate everyone's behaviour, even if they are not guilty of any crime. All professions and institutions are now exhorted to be accountable, responsible and transparent. They must continuously disclose information about themselves to 'restore trust'. They must adopt 'codes of conduct' to keep their behaviour in check. Everyone is obliged to abide by new rules and regulations, irrespective of their behaviour in the past or present.

In such a culture it is interesting how the 'whistleblower', relatively suddenly, has become some kind of heroic figure. A whistleblower is an employee of an institution who comes forward to report underhand or abusive behaviour. Of course, it is always important for individuals to act on principles and conscience. But the peculiar thing perhaps is that in today's climate of suspicion, such figures actually become celebrated and put on a pedestal. In recent decades, governments everywhere have put in place new legislation to protect whistleblowers and give them new rights.[14]

The current obsession with unethical behaviour distorts reality. Society tends to perceive behaviour as being out of control. In reality, the morality of society tends to improve over time. For instance, there is now an idea that discrimination is on the increase. Every institution is said to be racist and unfair to particular minorities and women. But this arguably reveals a lack of perspective. Society's attitudes towards racial groups and women have come on by leaps and bounds in recent decades. Society no longer finds discrimination acceptable in the way that it did even a few decades ago. We no longer think it acceptable that women should be stuck in the home and be confined to doing the worst jobs in society, or should be discriminated against in the workplace. Racist behaviour is no longer seen as acceptable. Yet somehow there is a feeling that discrimination is always increasing.

In today's new social climate of suspicion, the underlying assumption, although rarely articulated as such, is that individuals, institutions or professions should not be left to their own devices to interact organically without a plethora of new rules and regulations. In a world that continually exaggerates the downside of human behaviour, freedom of choice and freedom of action quickly become viewed as threatening. There is a perceived danger in allowing people to interact on their own. Interaction between people therefore becomes subject to all sorts of new moral codes and guidelines. Perhaps the most obvious expression is the spectacular rise and proliferation of the code of conduct. These codes, which were rare a decade ago, have now been adopted by a huge variety of different institutions and professions. But as the next few chapters will illustrate, such codes are the tip of the iceberg in a new process of self-regulation.

A culture of suspicion has arisen because of a breakdown in the strong beliefs that individuals used to hold, and a breakdown in the strong relationships they had with institutions in society. These beliefs and relationships used to cohere society and give people a sense of trust in each other, social institutions, and a confidence in the future. It is easy to forget that people once had strong ties to institutions such as the church, the corporation, political parties, trade unions and the extended family.

Today, individuals in society tend to feel more vulnerable and the victims of external forces beyond their control. Not only have relationships with institutions broken down, with little to replace them, but over time, such institutions have become viewed with suspicion, as harbouring undesirable forms of behaviour. As a result, there is a general feeling that they need new forms of regulation, such as codes of conduct, and need to become more accountable, responsible and transparent in their dealings with the world.

At the same time, individuals that feel more isolated in the world and see the future as more uncertain tend to react to change in a more defensive manner. Today, society lacks a framework that might provide a sense of perspective on how people actually behave. What tends to happen today is that isolated examples of immoral behaviour are interpreted as somehow symbolic of a wider problem in society (see Furedi, 1997, for an excellent broader discussion of these themes).

Enronitis: the reaction of an anxious elite

By understanding the new culture of suspicion and dynamic for re-regulation discussed so far, it is possible to grasp why there was such an extraordinary reaction to the recent spate of business scandals in the United States. In a world that now inflates and exaggerates scandal, corruption, unethical, abusive behaviour, real cases of misdemeanour tend to be blown out of all proportion.[15]

The Enron saga began in Autumn 2001. The SEC demanded that the US energy firm disclose the true extent of its debt to the outside world. Enron had hidden its debts in 'special purpose vehicles'. These were mini-organizations that were set up to raise finance and make investments. Crucially, they were off-balance-sheet and did not register in the liabilities of the company. When Enron accounted for this debt, it reported a loss of US $618m, owing to a special charge of US $1.01bn. In the week afterwards, the stock price slid by 40% as investors digested the news and lost confidence in the company.

The collapse of Enron was the start of an extraordinary period in US history. In the year after, the world awoke to a seemingly astonishing array of scandals and cases of impropriety. The announcement that US telecom firm WorldCom overstated its operating cashflow by US $3.8bn proved to be the second major bombshell. WorldCom resorted to a simple accounting trick. It had paid out a lot of cash as expenses, but decided to account for these expenses as capital investment. The cash would not show up as an immediate hit on profits, but could be spread out over time, therefore impacting profits in gentler fashion.

If Enron provoked a range of 'corporate governance' questions, from the role of the board to the role of the auditor, WorldCom sparked further questions. And, that summer, more and more allegations emerged of accounting fraud, tax evasion, and insider dealing. Names such as Global Crossing, Xerox, Adelphia Communications and Tyco International found themselves investigated by the regulators for improprieties. As each scandal hit the headlines, the stock market plummeted even further.

Commentators were shocked when even the doyen of American housewives, Martha Stewart, found herself embroiled in allegations of insider trading. Stewart was investigated for selling shares in ImClone, a drugs company run by a close friend, Sam Waksal. She sold her shares one day before ImClone announced that its cancer drug had been rejected by the regulator, which sent the share price down by 86%.

At the same time, allegations of unethical behaviour soon embroiled the financial sector. The investment bank Merrill Lynch was investigated by the New York Attorney-General, Eliot Spitzer. In the investigation, Spitzer had subpoenaed 30 000 internal emails. Some of the bank's celebrity analysts, such as Henry Blodget, were castigated for privately rubbishing the shares of particular companies while publicly recommending that investors buy them.

After negotiations, Merrill Lynch reached a settlement in May 2002 to pay a US $100m fine. It also agreed to tie analysts' pay to the quality of research; review all stock ratings more stringently; monitor the flow of emails between analysts and bankers; and appoint a compliance monitor to police the agreement.

During the summer of 2002 the world seemed to enter a strange twilight zone where stock markets twitched at the slightest hint of further scandals. At one point it seemed that every institution in the economy was under suspicion for its accounting practices, governance structures and ethical credentials. The search for scandal seemed to take on a logic of its own.

Enronitis provoked one of the most serious bouts of soul-searching in American history. For a huge variety of commentators this was clear evidence of a crisis: a crisis in morality and ethics; a crisis of corporate governance; a crisis in corporate America. As the television beamed pictures of sad-looking executives being handcuffed and taken away by the authorities, magazine columnists asked: Is capitalism sick? Elsewhere, one television journalist perhaps summed up the mood by stating, in official tones, that 'lying, stealing and cheating is at the heart of the US financial system'.[16]

The 1990s, which already seemed tarnished when markets slumped in Spring 2000, looked even unhealthier from the perspective of Enronitis. More discussion took place on the bubble conditions. The dominant response was cynicism. Commentators asked themselves how everyone could have been so stupid during those times. More to the point, they suggested, how could people have been so 'greedy'?

In the summer of 2002 a serious discussion on 'greed' emerged. The problem was that a whole range of professions and institutions had succumbed to greed. Executives were certainly greedy. But so were analysts, investors, lawyers, accountants, investment bankers, consultants and auditors. Everyone had become too greedy.

Chairman of the US Federal Reserve, Alan Greenspan, announced, in his official way, that 'infectious greed' had gripped much of America.[17] Paul Volcker, former Chairman of the Federal Reserve, backed him up, opining that during the 1990s 'we went from "greed is good" being said as a joke, to people thinking that "greed is good" is a fundamental fact'.[18] *The Economist* chipped in, asking itself, 'is greed good?'. After pausing for thought, it replied, rather inexplicably, 'only if it is properly governed'.

The soul-searching extended to chief executives themselves. They felt something drastic had changed. Many came forward to express their disgust and sadness. Andy Grove, chairman of Intel, stated that 'I've been in business for 40 years . . . and I find myself feeling embarrassed and ashamed by what I see in corporate America' (see Race, 2002).

The regulatory response to Enron and others was astounding. Legislation gushed from the US government, the most significant since the Depression era. Under the Sarbanes–Oxley Act of 2002, executives have to personally certify that financial statements are accurate, and face jail sentences if the statements are found to be false. The Act also requires disclosure of all sorts of financial information, and other information such as whether companies have specific codes of ethics for senior financial officers. Other reforms include greater oversight of the accounting profession.

The New York Stock Exchange put forward unprecedented reforms for the governance of corporations. These proposals surprised and delighted even the most hardened corporate governance advocates. In June 2002 it announced the most significant set of reform measures since the Depression, a 17-point plan. Elsewhere, a range of other institutions and independent experts did not hold back, and put forward a plethora of guidelines and recommendations.

The media was keen to get in on the act. Magazines such as *Business Week* and *Fortune* offered up various reform proposals of the ten-bullet-point variety, with subtitles such as 'how to fix corporate America'. Meanwhile, governments outside of America announced plans to review their accounting professions, and examine, yet again, the question of corporate governance.

Enronitis revitalized the decade-long discussion on the role of boards and the role of independent or non-executive directors. Those with a keen interest in corporate governance issues took to their computers yet again to write articles on how companies should be run in a more ethical fashion.

The issue of non-executive directors involves how directors should best be monitored by outsiders. For some, the problem was that independent directors had become too close to the chief executive. How could they call themselves 'independent'? For others, the problem was a lack of proper information. One remedy, perhaps, might be that independent directors simply distrust everything they are told from the top. Perhaps they could scurry around the company themselves to do intelligence work. For others still, the crux of the matter was pay and incentives. Independent directors should be paid more. But will that make them do a better job, inquired others? Some with more radical leanings, perhaps sick of the whole debate, advised that independent directors should be scrapped altogether.

Interrogating the response

There were plenty of reasons to be angry about Enron, WorldCom and the other corporate frauds. Ordinary people's lives were uprooted and their future upset by powers beyond their control. Employees lost the value of their pensions bound up with the value of companies that collapsed. Enronitis caused a great deal of grief to employees and investors.

Yet the response to Enron and others was deeply problematic. It hindered a rational approach to problem-solving. As this chapter has suggested, a search for scandal, corruption, excessive, unethical and abusive behaviour has taken on a logic of its own in Western societies. Therefore, it is not surprising that when genuine examples of unethical behaviour and crime do occur, they are quickly blown out of all proportion. Very quickly, they are viewed as symbolic of some kind of deeper moral malaise. Fears are expressed that people have lost their ability to differentiate between right and wrong. This makes it difficult to sift through the issues and adopt a clear strategy on how to solve problems.

What became highly revealing about the reaction to Enronitis was the fact that even those investigating the scandals found themselves embroiled in – yes, scandals. Harvey Pitt, chairman of the SEC, found himself facing accusations. He was accused of not responding ethically to the scandals. This was then seen as scandalous.

Pitt's supposed crime was to meet personally with the executives of the companies the SEC was investigating. Pitt's argument was simple: this was his way of operating. He would make a personal plea to the executives to put their houses in order. For critics, however, this appeared that Pitt was 'too close' to big business. A number of American politicians called for Pitt to resign.

It was not long before Eliot Spitzer, the New York Attorney-General who was investigating the Merrill Lynch saga, also found himself embroiled in scandal. It took friends to point out that Spitzer was unlikely to have skeletons in the closet. For a start, they suggested, he was probably a bit too ethical for his own good.

During the period in question, president George W. Bush attempted to show leadership by making speeches and proposing regulatory reform. He too, however, was called a hypocrite. Bush found himself embroiled in accusations that, a decade before, he was involved in improper relationships with business.

Similarly, it was revealing that many commentators found it necessary to suspect *all* institutions that had some kind of connection with Enron. Thus, there was an attempt to blame American consultants McKinsey for recommending financial engineering practices to Enron. The US pension fund, CalPERS, was blamed for doing little about Enron. It too found itself embroiled in allegations about unethical conflicts of interest.

So, what was going on here? Put bluntly again, the suspicion of abusive behaviour has now taken on a logic of its own, regardless of reality. And this hinders a rational approach to problem-solving. Today, those in positions of authority seem keener to perpetuate their obsession with scandal than address more intractable problems.

In reality, Enron, WorldCom, Arthur Andersen, Merrill Lynch and the other scandals raise a number of different issues that cannot easily be lumped together. Take straightforward fraud. As one perceptive commentator on Enronitis put it, 'cooking the books is hardly new to capitalist enterprises'.

He notes that, in the early 1930s, the case of Middle West Utilities involved allegations of stock fraud, crooked accounting and (like Enron) the setting up of multiple companies to deceive. He also notes that the Equity Funding Corp of America collapsed in 1973 when it was found to be riddled with fraud, even though the accountants (like Andersen) signed off on the books. In the 1980s, he adds, there were the infamous insider trading and junk bond scandals.

For this commentator, 'financial manipulation is as old as capitalism itself, if not older. The response today seems to be driven more by doubt and insecurity, than by the accounting shenanigans themselves' (Malone, 2002). There is a tendency to react to cases of improper behaviour in a crisis-like fashion.

Similarly, many of the issues raised by Enronitis are not new. Take the auditing issue. Michael Power, a leading authority on auditing, discussed (in the mid-1990s) what he called auditing and 'the dialectic of failure'. 'When companies collapse, for whatever reason, and have previously received a "clean" opinion from the auditors, public reaction focuses first on those auditors and the possibility of their failure', he notes. Failure spurs further attempts to improve auditing and provokes institutional change. 'The history of auditing reads, like the history of regulation more generally, as a history of failure' (Power, 1997, pp. 25–27).

In other words, there have been numerous examples in the past where companies have suffered fraud, or have collapsed financially, and people have asked: Where the hell were the auditors?

Enron in particular raises issues about the way companies rely on financial engineering practices, and how firms 'grow' today. This will be explored in Chapter 8. Many of these issues were not properly discussed during the bull market of the 1990s when there was considerable hype about the US economy and so-called 'new economy' companies. They are still neglected today, especially as discussions of 'greed' and regulation come to the fore.

From regulation to self-regulation

The aim of this chapter is to introduce the main theme of Part One, namely self-regulation. Today, there is a new dynamic for regulation. There is an ill-defined idea that all sorts of individual, professional and institutional behaviour is getting out of hand, and in need of restraint. Governments have been quick to redefine themselves as 'moral crusaders' in a world highly sensitive to unethical behaviour. Regulation seems to have taken on a logic of its own, divorced from serious considerations of whether it is needed or not.

At the same time, however, executives of corporations are keen to take the initiative to regulate their own behaviour and the behaviour of employees. Managers and corporations are far more worried about appearing unethical, abusive, reckless or irresponsible. They have reacted defensively to the new 'culture of suspicion'. The average executive now lives in a world of self-imposed ethical regulations – a world of ethical codes of conduct, ethics committees, ethics officers, ethical audits and ethical education programmes. A process of self-regulation has intensified in the last decade or so. Behaviour inside corporations, and relationships with stakeholders, are now subject to burgeoning rules and guidelines. The business world has developed its own vehicle for self-regulation, something called 'corporate governance', with its codes of best practice. In the name of accountability, responsibility and transparency, corporations have institutionalized a bewildering array of codes of conduct, ethical regulations, internal controls, risk management procedures, board reforms, new committees, new types of board position, audits and reporting obligations, and sustainable development and corporate social responsibility regulations.

The problem with this huge increase in regulation is not that it somehow impedes a mythical free market from operating properly but rather that the combination of government regulation – and self-regulation – operating in tandem, entrenches an irrational cautiousness and restraint. It is institutionalizing risk aversion. Just like in the world of science, where scientists are now counselled to adopt the 'precautionary principle' – do not experiment unless the outcome is safe and poses no risks – businesses have adopted similar principles.

Notes

1. In 1988 the Bank for International Settlements (BIS), based in Basel in Switzerland, established a special accord requiring banks to set aside capital to cover credit risk. See the Basel Committee on Banking Supervision (1988). Since then it has been added to in all sorts of ways. Also see Ben-Ami (2001, pp. 84–86) for a specific discussion and also an excellent critique of over-regulation and risk aversion in the financial sector.
2. The MEP Jens-Peter Bonde estimates that the number of EU legal acts in force rose from 1947 in 1973 to 23 027 in 1996 (see Brown, 2001).
3. Press release, 'Bonior says oil companies to blame for high gas prices', 21 June 2000.
4. Press release, 'FTC issues report on Midwest gasoline price investigation', 30 March 2001.
5. Correspondence with an in-house lawyer of a global oil company.
6. In July 2001 the Company Law Review Steering Group in the United Kingdom produced a report after a three-year enquiry. It made recommendations for a new company law, including the idea of a statutory statement of directors' duties requiring them to take 'due account' of relations with employees and other stakeholders (see Brown and Peel, 2001). Another example is Japan, where in the late 1990s the Japanese government began discussions to reform its commercial code which had been in place since 1899. The focus was to protect shareholders and make companies more accountable to them (see Harney, 2000).
7. See 'Challenges facing the Federal Trade Commission', Hearing before the subcommittee on commerce, trade and protection, of the Committee on Energy and Commerce, House of Representatives, October 2001.
8. Different interest groups even share very similar ideas about how corporations should use resources. The economic theories that they espouse are based on strikingly similar assumptions. Financial economists, who adopt the investors' perspective, argue that shareholders' capital should be treated as a *scarce resource*. That is, they have to take into account the efficiency in which they use capital. They should not treat shareholders' capital as free. Environmental economists and sustainable development advocates argue that 'natural capital' and 'social capital' should be treated as a scarce resource. Natural capital should not be treated as free, but should come at a cost for its use. Unfortunately, this is an agenda motivated by a strong sense of caution and restraint. In this new framework, nobody argues for more dynamic economic growth or greater technological innovation. The starting point is a greater sense of limits in the way that corporations can use resources.

9. The author has worked in a professional capacity for many of the global accounting and consulting firms.
10. See the white paper 'A new covenant with stakeholders: managing privacy as a competitive advantage', KPMG LLP (2001).
11. Correspondence with an e-privacy consultant.
12. Correspondence with an e-privacy researcher.
13. Taken from Lecture One, Spreading Suspicion, Reith Lectures 2002, A Question of Trust, presented by Onora O'Neill.
14. In the United States, legislation to protect whistleblowers began in the early 1980s with the Whistle-Blowers Protection Act passed by the state of Michigan in 1981 (see Vernon, 1998, p. 182). Recent films about the role of the whistleblower include *The Insider*, with actors Russell Crowe and Al Pacino.
15. Many of the facts and figures referred to in the following section are in the public domain and can be easily found on the Internet. Therefore this section will not reference every single event and fact used.
16. Jonathan Rugman, Channel Four Business Correspondent, Channel Four News (Britain), 30 June 2002.
17. Speech given to the Senate Banking Committee, 17 July 2002, as part of a twice-yearly report on monetary policy.
18. Interview with Paul Volcker, 'Restoring trust in corporate America', *Business Week*, 24 June 2002.

2

Self-Regulation: Entrenching Caution

Sometime in 2001 an in-house lawyer of a global telecommunications firm was invited to give a presentation at a technology conference. The conference was organized by one of the firm's software suppliers. Simple enough, one might think. The ethics department of the firm, however, was not so sure.

For a start, the supplier offered to pay for the in-house lawyer's flights and accommodation. For the ethics department, this provoked an ethical dilemma that would require lengthy deliberation. It was afraid that, by accepting the offer, the supplier might unreasonably expect some favour in return. They might expect more future business. The ethics department therefore insisted on a division of labour. Yes, the supplier could pay for the hotel costs, but they would pay for the flight.

But that was not all. The ethics department was also worried for several other reasons. It was worried about the in-house lawyer's presentation. It was worried that the firm could be misquoted in the American press after the speech was heard. As a result, it insisted on double-checking and vetting every single word of the presentation, to the frustration of the in-house lawyer. It was also worried that, by attending the conference, the firm might be seen to endorse one particular technology supplier. It feared this could upset all its other suppliers. This required further deliberation.

The cumulative affect of these anxieties and interventions was to delay the decision of accepting the conference invitation. Worse, at one stage it became doubtful whether the (highly frustrated) speaker would even be allowed to go. As one angry colleague commented, only slightly inaccurately perhaps, 'we can't go to the toilet around here without the ethics department getting involved'.[1]

This example is a microcosm of an irrational trend that has been gathering pace in recent years. The rise of ethics in business is a striking example of self-regulation. Ethics departments of corporations now vet and double-check various activities and proposals, because it is no exaggeration to say that corporations are paranoid about appearing unethical.

Ultimately, however, these new forms of self-regulation represent new forms of self-restraint. Companies start to become more risk-averse. What happens is that people are held back from conducting what would rationally be seen as normal and even enjoyable activities. Rather than leaving people to act autonomously, in the faith that in most situations people behave ethically, managers end up taking a paranoid view of human behaviour. Ethical disasters seem to loom large in the imagination, and managers fear to take chances.

Ethical considerations have risen up the corporate agenda. In the United States, all *Fortune* 500 companies have ethical codes of conduct, according to the Ethics Officer Association. In Britain, more than 60% of the top 500 companies have codes of conduct, the Institute of Business Ethics estimates. At the beginning of the 1990s, the figure was 18% (see Maitland, 1999).

Throughout the 1990s, corporations added to their ethics infrastructure. Many large corporations around the world added special ethics committees or ethics departments, and special ethics officers. They began to conduct ethical audits and send their executives on ethical training courses.

The process of self-regulation today is entirely new and historically unprecedented. Put simply, it involves more anxious and uncertain corporations relating to the new culture of suspicion outlined earlier. Through this process, managers feel that a whole new raft of rules and procedures are needed to prevent things from going wrong. Before long, managers begin to act not on strong beliefs and a confident outlook for the future, but on fears of what might go wrong.

Self-regulation is driven more by anxious corporations than by an anxious society, however. It is not just that corporations are reacting defensively to the culture of suspicion outlined in the previous chapter. Rather, they are coming to see self-regulation as a new way of relating to the world around them, in an age where they are not driven forward by the same belief systems as in the past.

If this seems a bit abstract, consider a few examples. It is very noticeable that in all the issues involving self-regulation today, only one side of the story seems to be put across.

Take the issue of excessive executive pay. Whether one agrees or disagrees with high levels of management pay, it is perhaps surprising that executives have not done much to refute claims they are greedy 'fat cats'. After all, who wants to be known as a 'fat cat' for the rest of their life? It is not a comfortable label.

One might expect some kind of fight back. Occasionally, it is heard that managers deserve high levels of pay because of their experience and work ethic. But this is very much the marginal view.

The reason there are few dynamic counter-arguments is that managers of corporations are *already* on the defensive. Many of the beliefs that might have equipped them to go on the offensive have broken down. For instance, it is easy to forget that even in the recent past, the capitalist world believed strongly in the concept of self-interest. Profit was the reward for risk-taking. The first and only responsibility of business to society was to make a profit.

It was fine to make lots of money within the bounds of the law. That was capitalism. You either liked it or lumped it. Remember the strident and aggressive slogan, 'get back to Russia'? It seems highly obscure today, but it is easy to forget that, not so long ago, this was what ideologues of capitalism used to say to people who opposed the workings of capitalism. Go and join the communists.

In the past, those running society were not so defensive about the workings of capitalism. They had certain strong beliefs that gave them a reference point for assessing other viewpoints. Today, many of the beliefs that the business world used to share have broken down.

Today's new self-regulation is a product of anxious and defensive institutions, lacking traditional beliefs, interacting with a society that is more anxious and defensive. This can be seen across the board, not just in business. Take another example.

There is considerable anxiety about the so-called risks and uncertainties of new technologies, such as genetically modified organisms, and how experimentation should proceed with these new technologies. Scientists are increasingly taking on board demands to regulate their own behaviour and regulate experimentation. They are adopting the 'precautionary principle', a new concept that embodies the belief that experimentation should only take place if the outcome can be guaranteed as safe beforehand. This effectively makes science impossible.

Why do scientists not protest more about this ridiculous concept? Certainly, some prominent scientists have come out strongly against the precautionary principle. But it is interesting why the wider scientific community has not put up more of a protest. The reason is that scientists used to have very strong beliefs in the values of reason, discovery, experimentation and notions of trial and error. In recent years, these beliefs have broken down. Because they lack the self-belief of the past, current generations of scientists are tempted to 'listen to society'. The trouble is that society is now far more fearful about behaviour and the future. Listening to society is a recipe for yet more irrational self-regulation. According to one commentator, 'by pandering to demands for more caution and self-limitation', scientists run the danger of setting themselves 'against the very motive force of science – a desire to explore and experiment' (Durodie, 2002).

Self-regulation: a schematic overview

As its name suggests, self-regulation involves professions and institutions taking a lead to lay down new guidelines on how they should behave. That is not to say that governments are not involved in the process. Self-regulation can be the product of a negotiation between states and institutions. Governments can threaten legislation unless institutions 'get their act together' and 'set an example' to regulate themselves.

Also, self-regulation can be imposed with existing law in mind. If institutions do get into a scrape with the law for any reason, they hope voluntary regulation demonstrates a degree of responsibility, which could perhaps lessen a penalty.

The process also works the other way around. In the area of sustainable development and corporate social responsibility, explored below, the business world has tended to lead the way. Governments have followed afterwards with various new guidelines, although often believing that voluntary regulation in the private sector is the way forward, as opposed to new formal law-making.

The 1990s was a time when boards of corporations everywhere devised new frameworks for managing corporations. These frameworks draw on the discussions taking place since the early 1990s: discussions of ethics, corporate governance, risk management, managing for shareholder value and, more recently, sustainable development and corporate social responsibility.

In the last decade, considerable intellectual effort by managers and consultants has gone into making connections between all of these ideas and practices. As a result they all overlap in various ways. Risk management is a key part of corporate governance. Socially responsible behaviour is now viewed as a key part of managing for shareholder value. The latest corporate governance reports in countries such as South Africa now incorporate all the latest thinking in the area of sustainable development and corporate social responsibility. By being socially responsible, companies believe they are managing risk better.

All of these frameworks involve a plethora of new self-regulatory initiatives. The initiatives capture the defensive way corporations now relate to the world around them. This book cannot possibly cover the whole history of each self-regulatory initiative in great detail – nor should it. The rest of this chapter will examine some of the initiatives taking place under ethics, corporate governance and sustainable development. The following chapter is devoted to risk management, which goes into more depth, while the final chapter in Part One examines the concept of managing for shareholder value.

The rise of ethics

The rise of ethics illustrates the way that the business world has become far more defensive in its relationships with the world. Over time, the rise of ethics has corresponded to a situation where managers have responded to change in a far more jittery and anxious way. Rather than refute the claim that their professional behaviour, and the behaviour of corporations, has become more unethical, managers have imposed more and more ethical regulation on themselves.

In an excellent book, *The Appearance of Impropriety*, two academics, Peter Morgan and Glenn Reynolds, discuss the rise of what they call the 'ethics establishment' in the United States. They note that, after the Nixon Watergate scandal in the early 1970s, public figures and institutions were worried about appearing unethical. Institutions, professions, and individuals started to worry about and regulate their own behaviour because they were worried about the 'appearance of impropriety'. For Morgan and Reynolds, it was the

Watergate reform legislation that 'institutionalized appearance ethics and brought it to the forefront of public debate'. (See Morgan and Reynolds, 1997. The facts that follow are taken from their book.)

Nixon resigned in August 1974. Soon after the whole affair, there was an explosion of articles on judicial ethics, and in 1978, The Ethics in Government Act was established, creating the Office of Government Ethics, and the first federal ethics programme.

The Act was accompanied by all sorts of new legislation. Laws emerged requiring financial disclosure obligations on executive-branch members, new rights for the public to access information, federal privacy laws, laws requiring presidents to notify congress of US covert actions, and official protection for whistleblowers, just to mention a few areas.

But the reaction to the Watergate affair was much wider. A whole range of institutions and professions outside of politics appeared to be on the defensive. The American Bar Association required accredited law schools to teach at least one ethics course. The American Medical Association revised its ethics code. The Board of the American Society of Newspaper Editors created a new statement of principles.

The business world was not slow to react. Business ethics centres, codes, courses and conferences sprang up. From 1976 to 1980, over 2000 business ethics articles were published in the United States.

This was the beginning of the obsession with ethics in the business world. But it was not until the late 1980s that ethics really became institutionalized. The reaction to the insider trading scandals of the late 1980s, according to Morgan and Reynolds, saw an even bigger surge of interest in ethics.

In the United States of the early 1990s, corporations reacted to the issuance of the Federal Sentencing Guidelines and ethics was further institutionalized. These guidelines introduced more severe penalties for corporate crimes. But they allowed for leniency if corporations already had in place a system to try to detect and prevent such violations. Corporations believed that more ethical regulation would demonstrate responsibility and help them to avoid harsh penalties.

The 1990s saw the rise of special ethics officers and ethics departments within corporations. By the mid-1990s, a third of US firms had an ethics officer, and one in five had an ethics department, in addition to the ethical codes of conduct. At the same time, business ethics had become a multi-billion-dollar consulting industry.

In the 1990s, the obsession with appearing ethical became *generalized* throughout society. Ethics has become a form of self-regulation. Because people are worried about appearing unethical, they restrain their behaviour in various ways. Everyone is continually invited to abide by ethical codes of conduct, whether they are 'ethical' or not. So, university professors are denied tenure because rumours of romantic links create the 'appearance of impropriety'. Donations to schools are refused because they may give the 'appearance of impropriety'. Corporations, for their part, now refuse to take part in all sorts of activities unless the ethical ramifications can be established.

Corporate governance

Corporate governance is one of the major new vehicles for self-regulation in the global business community. It includes a broad discussion in government, industry, academia and the professions about how companies should be run. For some academics, the issue of corporate governance is bound up with a broader debate about the relative merits of types of capitalism – in particular Anglo-Saxon capitalism and German and Japanese capitalism. A main issue is whether managers should prioritize shareholders or other stakeholders, such as employees, when running corporations.

Governance also involves a practical reform process, involving specific 'codes' of best practice – guidelines and principles for companies to follow – that have been laid down by special committees. In the year 2000, after a decade of reform, 23 countries around the world had introduced corporate governance guidelines and codes of best practice. These codes are often enforced through the national stock exchanges of countries, in the listing rules that public companies must abide by.

The self-regulatory initiatives under the corporate governance banner typically include protecting shareholder rights, reforming boards and re-examining the duties and responsibilities of directors, encouraging non-executive directors to monitor the board, the issue of excessive executive pay and linking management pay to firm performance, auditing, financial reporting systems, internal controls and risk management procedures. Recent corporate governance reports incorporate the latest thinking in the area of sustainable development and social responsibility.

More broadly, corporate governance reform includes many other measures to ensure accountability between managers and shareholders. So, for instance, in the Asian governance debates, families that run public companies but own majority stakes in them, the largest portion of the company's shares, are viewed as encouraging a conflict of interest between themselves and shareholders. They should not own majority stakes because that could encourage 'cronyism'.

Elsewhere, managers can pledge to give shareholders more information, perhaps non-financial information, so ostensibly the latter can make better investment decisions. Managers can be encouraged to own stock options, so that they have an incentive to increase the market value of the company and the share price, although this is an idea that has come under fire since Enronitis, and is being subjected to re-regulation.

Corporate governance covers shareholder rights. But it is also about managing in the best 'economic' interests of shareholders, to borrow the jargon. Here, companies have to think more deeply about how they can manage finance, growth, investment and strategy in the best interests of shareholders. This has become known as 'managing for shareholder value' – which, to add jargon onto more jargon, has been called 'the new ideology of corporate governance' by some – to be explored in Chapter 4.

The reform process of corporate governance has developed slightly differently around the world. In the United States, corporate governance has evolved more closely in relation to shareholder rights and shareholder activism than elsewhere.[2] In Asia, by contrast, corporate governance sprang up in relation to the issue of so-called 'crony capitalists' and the apparent widespread business corruption in Asia, which became more of an issue in the aftermath of the Asian financial crisis of 1997–98.

The whole project of corporate governance reform involves a variety of domestic and international institutions. The OECD for one is fully involved, and has published its own guidelines for corporations to observe. Then, there are specialist institutions that promote shareholder interests.[3]

What is corporate governance really about? Many of the issues at stake are not historically new. Issues such as what to do about fraud, the rights of shareholders, auditing practices, the duties of directors, and so on, go back a long way. The debate over whether firms should be run in the interests of shareholders or other social groups, namely employees, sounds contemporary, but has been trundling on for decades. It took place in the 1930s, and at various points in the post-war period (see Kaufman et al., 1995).

However, according to one study, 'corporate governance' was not a term in use before 1980. And, it was not until the 1990s that governance was so heavily discussed, and on a global level.[4] Corporate governance is arguably new because it represents an attempt to create voluntary rules, principles and guidelines on how directors and companies should behave, in an age where business is more anxious about its own behaviour, and more defensive in its relations with the world.

An underlying assumption of corporate governance is that manager and shareholder interests are more divergent than ever before. There is little faith in allowing directors to proceed in a self-interested fashion, without new voluntary regulation and various checks and balances. A telling phrase occasionally used in the corporate governance discussion is 'the entrepreneur gone wrong'. Here, there are heightened worries that allowing directors to act in a self-interested fashion, unchecked, can lead to fraud and gross opportunism. Robert Maxwell-type disasters loom large in the imagination. The underlying assumption of corporate governance is that managers cannot really be trusted to act without all sorts of guidelines to protect shareholders and enforce accountability to them.

So, for instance, the idea of letting boards set their own levels of pay, or nominate directors, without a set of new independent committees, is seen as far too risky. This could invite corrupt behaviour. The idea of allowing one executive to hold both the chairman and chief executive posts, a major governance debate, is seen as equally risky. Such a position might concentrate too much power in one person, which might lead to an abuse of that power and an abuse of trust, and the emergence of 'autocratic bullies' and 'empire builders'.

At the same time, there is little trust in allowing other directors on the board to carry on their duties and responsibilities without extensive new guidelines. The fear is that boards will simply 'rubber stamp' decisions. Here, new mechanisms are needed too, so that board members do not become lazy or complacent. They need to hold chief executives to account. Also, in such a world there is a perception that non-executives should play a more important role in monitoring boards.[5]

Additionally, it is believed that managers need to be more aware of business risks, to provide assurances that they are running a company properly. Under new corporate governance regimes, corporations have put in place various 'internal controls', which require that decisions throughout the business are verified and authorized, and people's behaviour audited, in order that directors can manage risk better.

Corporate governance reform began as a response to isolated cases of fraud and misdemeanour. In these cases it was important that justice was served. But somehow, there was little confidence in letting the rest of industry escape greater self-regulation. Even though initial governance committees and reports found little evidence that impropriety was generalized across industry, they still found it necessary to propose greater voluntary regulation.

Throughout the 1990s self-regulation under corporate governance reform seemed to take on a logic of its own. So, it began in relation to fraud. Over the 1990s, however, it broadened significantly. Corporate governance today has become an ongoing process of reform, a broad vehicle to adopt voluntary regulation in response to new anxieties as they unfold. Over the 1990s, the governance debate incorporated further issues, such as responsibility to stakeholders (e.g. employees), and went further into detail with risk management.

Corporate governance reform is not something that people get very excited about. Even those taking part in the debates often find them tedious, and wish they were discussing more dynamic areas, such as technology. Just repeating the term corporate governance more than a few times in one day can make lips seize up with sudden dryness. It is hard to feel passionate about self-regulation, after all.[6]

On other issues, and in private, many executives feel that, for instance, non-executives get in the way of running a business. Also, new codes of corporate governance, which now come along at regular intervals, are often interpreted with weary resignation.[7] But corporate governance reform has proceeded because of the more general dynamic behind self-regulation. Defensive managers and corporations now relate to a more anxious society.

Britain: an example of change

In Britain, initiatives under the corporate governance umbrella began in the early 1990s. The business world, including the accountancy profession and the London Stock Exchange, was worried about public perceptions in the wake of particular scandals and frauds. The Cadbury Committee, chaired by the industrialist Sir Adrian Cadbury, chairman of the Cadbury confectionary empire, was set up in May 1991 to consider 'the financial aspects of corporate governance'. A final report was published the following year.[8]

The Committee was – at least partly – a response to the collapse of Polly Peck in 1990. Polly Peck was a major FTSE-100 conglomerate run by the Turkish-Cypriot entrepreneur Asil Nadir. In the 1980s it was a darling of the stock market. But in October 1991 it collapsed, with debts of £522m, and Nadir was accused of fraud.

As the Committee got going in 1991, other scandals and frauds flared up. Regulators seized the operations of Bank of Credit and Commerce International (BCCI) in July 1991 after it was found to be involved in fraud, money laundering and various international crimes. And in December 1991, there was the discovery that £480m had disappeared from Maxwell Group Pension Funds.

Cadbury and the Committee members looked at safeguards to protect investors against fraud. One obvious area was bolstering the integrity of financial reports, accounts and audit statements. Cadbury also looked at the issue of 'internal controls' – forms of internal checking that might allow senior managers to detect possible wrongdoing. The area of board reform was also placed on the table. One question was: Why did board members fail to keep an eye on the actions of their superiors in the cases of fraud?

What was interesting about the early 1990s was that, although of course there were genuine cases of corporate crime that needed to be investigated, a more generalized moralistic attitude was forming toward directors and boards. First of all, a new worry developed that many chief executives could be intimidating 'autocrats'. The worry was that they could bully their sheep-like board members, the other directors of the company, into submission. What the Polly Peck, BCCI and Maxwell incidents seemed to have in common, for observers, was that too much power was concentrated at the top with charismatic corporate leaders. The fear was that this could lead to an abuse of power.

At the same time, there was also a view that other board members had become far too complacent and lazy. They had, for far too long, been sitting back and not properly vetting business decisions. Rather than exercise proper care and responsibility, directors probably were more concerned about slipping off to the golf course, the view went. Why had they not spotted the frauds and wrongdoings?

Around this time, other concerns began to be raised. An idea developed that greedy executives were paying themselves too much. In the early 1990s, the issue of excessive management pay exploded onto the scene, in both the United Kingdom and United States. In the United States, for instance, a 1991 edition of *Forbes* led on the issue of executive pay, summing up the attitude, if rather basically – 'It doesn't make sense.' People began to talk about executive pay on US television shows. Elsewhere, books were written on the theme for the first time (see Ward, 1997).

Back in Britain, excessive executive pay also became an issue in the early to mid-1990s. Newspapers became critical of pay increases and management perks. Pension funds demanded to see a greater relationship between executive pay and company performance. Politicians also attempted to make political capital out of the issue.

In 1995, the chairman of British Gas, Cedric Brown, found himself at the centre of the 'Cedric the Pig' campaign. While company annual general meetings (AGMs) are not typically the most scintillating of affairs, at the May 1995 British Gas AGM, protestors angry about Brown's 75% pay rise turned up with a live pig in tow to make their point (see Jones and Pollitt, 2001).

The business world – in close discussion with government – felt they had to respond to the issue of executive pay. Sir Richard Greenbury, head of British retailer Marks & Spencer, headed a second corporate governance committee. The Greenbury Report urged companies to disclose how they awarded executive pay, and to establish remuneration committees staffed by non-executive directors. These committees, it was felt, should make an effort to link pay rises to company performance. Here, the self-interests of directors should be balanced with the wider interests of other groups, namely shareholders.[9]

The Hampel Committee, the third major corporate governance initiative, was set up in November 1995, chaired by the Chairman of ICI, Sir Ronald Hampel, to review the Cadbury Code, how it was being implemented within companies, and the Greenbury recommendations. It issued a final report in January 1998. The London Stock Exchange then combined the Cadbury, Greenbury and Hampel codes in a Combined Code published in June 1998.

The Hampel report captures a shift in thinking about governance that took place in the mid-1990s. It suggested that the definition of corporate governance be expanded, to mean 'business prosperity', not just 'account-ability'. Hampel noted that it approached corporate governance

> from a somewhat different perspective. Both the Cadbury and Greenbury reports were responses to things which were perceived to have gone wrong – corporate failures in the first case, unjustified compensation packages in the second. Understandably, both concentrated largely on the prevention of abuse. We are equally concerned with the positive contribution which good corporate governance can make.[10]

This is an interesting shift for several reasons. Hampel's task was to ensure that the previous codes were being implemented. He was trying to sell a project of reform. Hampel was concerned that managers were taking a 'box ticking' approach to regulation. He wanted them to think in terms of 'principles' of governance.

He acknowledged there was a danger in laying down rigid rules and guidelines. Companies needed flexibility in complying with them. Arguably, Hampel represented an attempt to package reform in a positive manner. Hampel was essentially saying that, if directors run a company in a responsible manner, with the right board structures, responsible attitude to management pay, proper appreciation of shareholder rights, internal controls and audits in place, and so on, then this could lead to positive benefits. Voluntary regulation helps companies avoid fraud. But at the same time, went the message, it helps to further business prosperity.

This expresses a broader idea about self-regulation today. Self-regulation is posed as an *opportunity* for business. For example, an idea has developed in recent times that sound corporate governance leads to all sorts of business benefits. Why? One belief is that investors will trust companies more. As a result, this trust might enable companies to borrow capital at a cheaper price.

Although he did not articulate it as such, Hampel was opening the door for yet more self-regulation. By broadening the definition of corporate governance, the whole area of self-regulation was broadened. So, for example, Hampel talked about responsibilities to stakeholders. Previously, corporate governance concerned itself with accountability to shareholders. Since Hampel, it is interesting that new areas of voluntary regulation have sprung up precisely in this area, most notably through concerns about sustainable development and corporate social responsibility, explored next.

Also, after Hampel it was felt that a fourth report was needed, the Turnbull Report. The Turnbull Committee, chaired by Nigel Turnbull, Chief Financial Officer of Rank Group, was set up by the Institute of Chartered Accountants in England and Wales (ICAEW) and reported back in September 1999. Its mandate was to look at the notion of internal control in the former codes, and to elaborate on how companies should set up risk management systems.

Looking at some of the most recent corporate governance reports around the world, it is interesting to note how broad corporate governance has become. For example, the second King report, overseen by the Institute of Directors in Southern Africa, was launched in March 2002. It was the follow-up to the first King report published in 1994.[11] The report expands the domain of regulation in the traditional corporate governance areas. It suggests that boards should disclose a 'board charter' in the annual report. This charter should disclose the board's responsibilities, including its strategic plans, monitoring of operational performance and management, policies on risk management, communication and director selection.

But the final King report talks about 'integrated sustainability reporting'. In doing so it incorporates the latest jargon and thinking in the area of sustainable development and corporate social responsibility, explored next. Here, companies are encouraged to report on their ethical, social, environmental, and health and safety policies and practices.

The attempt to re-pose self-regulation as an 'opportunity' is a central feature of all self-regulation today. Of course, individuals do not tend to say outright that self-regulation is an opportunity. Rather, what they say is that demonstrating accountability, transparency and responsibility – perhaps by having risk management processes in place, special board committees that vet decisions, internal audit procedures, and so on – can lead to business advantages.

This situation arises when mistrust between institutions and the world becomes naturalized and no longer subject to debate. Essentially, professions and institutions take for granted that there is constant suspicion of their behaviour – by shareholders, consumers, employees and society in general. Over time, rather than feeling there is anything they can do about it, they have taken a more euphemistic view of the situation. It is almost as if they have said, 'Look, we are stuck with the fact that society distrusts us, we are stuck with all this regulation, we better make the most out of it. In fact, why don't we see it as a new opportunity?' Once this occurs, however, then everything can be subjected to more rules and guidelines without much question. In fact, caution and restraint are re-posed as positive virtues, although not fully consciously.

When one major area of corporate governance reform is examined today, that of board reform, it is quite astounding how board behaviour, and the interpersonal relationships of directors, is subject to an unprecedented amount of new regulation and guidance. The attempt to lay down codes of behaviour for boards is now an ongoing process. For instance, this becomes clear when looking at the way that consultants have taken the re-regulation process onto whole new levels, feeding vampire-like on the original governance codes and discussions. Every aspect of the working of a board is subject to rules and guidance and forms of standardization.

What do consultants look at? First, there is the vital question of the 'right' board size. But then, one has to think about the appropriate 'stakeholder representation' and appropriate age limits on membership. Then, there is the whole issue of encouraging directors on the board to speak up and hold the CEO or Chairman to account. Does the board have an appropriate level of involvement with CEO succession? Do they have the right processes in place to assess the CEO? Does the CEO have a mission or vision that is understood by all board members? Does the CEO spend an appropriate amount of time discussing the long-range vision of the company? Have they put in place the appropriate structures and processes to evaluate company strategies and objectives?[12]

Through these measures, there is an attempt to over-formalize behaviour because of an anxiety about letting people get on with the job. For instance, some of these proposals may be sensible – such as discussing the long-range vision of the company. But why the constant reminder that business leaders 'must' carry them out? Since the 1950s, the concept of strategic thinking has been a key management theme. The nuances of long-range planning have been discussed extensively for decades.

When Cadbury first began to investigate companies in the early 1990s, it is significant that he reported back that, on the whole, British corporations were well run. The Cadbury report pointed out that: 'the basic system of corporate governance in Britain is sound'. Again, in the conclusion, it argued that: 'the great majority of companies are both competently run and audited under the present system of corporate governance'. However, it added in the same sentence that: 'it is widely accepted that standards within the corporate sector have to be raised'. Again, the 'machinery is in place', but what is needed is 'the will to improve its effectiveness'.[13]

So, according to the report, 'the great majority of companies' are well run, with integrity. But they need greater regulation. This illustrates a classic example of all regulation today, and one of the major paradoxes with it. What happens in the aftermath of a series of scandals, and media attention, is that a special Committee is set up to investigate corporate governance.

Almost invariably, however, what the investigation finds is that the original breach of conduct is not something that is typically observable, or likely to be repeated, across industry. In other words, the Committee discovers the highly unsurprising finding that not every director behaves like the disgraced Robert Maxwell. But this does not temper the urge to create more regulation.

In the United States and elsewhere, the reaction to Enronitis has encouraged further self-regulation across industry, in the area of ethics and corporate governance, even though a very small number of US companies were actually involved in genuine misdemeanours. All corporations, whether or not they are well governed or have existing self-regulation in place, have felt it necessary to review their behaviour and adopt further rules and guidelines. Here, companies have felt they must 'get their own house in order', to 'set an example' and 'restore trust'.

One commentary on the process of post-Enron reform in the United States notes that 'the magnitude of do-it-yourself moves by business may be close to being unique, historically'. In other words, the reaction to Enron and others has probably provoked more self-regulation than ever before.

According to one political scientist, Mark Blyth, 'I can't think of a single incident where there was this amount of housecleaning internally.' Economist Murray Weidenbaum also notes that 'there is a very significant amount of automatic self-regulation' in the wake of Enronitis (see Francis, 2002). Companies are now, yet again, re-examining, overhauling and considerably adding to their policies on ethics, risk management, financial disclosure, accounting, auditing, board structures, and so on.

To summarize: self-regulation under corporate governance has come about because managers, on the defensive, now relate to a world that is more suspicious of their behaviour. In particular, it captures the way that relationships between managers and shareholders have come under strain. There is little faith in allowing managers to act in a self-interested fashion without various committees, checks and balances, codes, board reforms, and so on. There is little faith in allowing companies to be run without elaborate new controls, where employee decisions have to be verified and authorized, to be on the safe side, and new risk management processes.

Sustainable development: a new vehicle for self-regulation

Corporate governance discussions first took proper shape in the early 1990s. Not long after, however, the business world was embracing yet another jargon-intensive vehicle for more self-regulation – the area of sustainable development, or sustainability, and corporate social responsibility, or CSR.

The new sustainability and CSR obsession can be seen as a kind of evolutionary step on from corporate governance. In the governance discussions, managers have reacted defensively to a culture of suspicion, and accept that their own behaviour, and that of employees, needs to be more heavily regulated. Ostensibly, this is to protect shareholders. In the sustainability and CSR discussion, managers have accepted a society-wide idea that corporate behaviour is more unsustainable and irresponsible, and needs restraining and regulating in various new ways. If corporate governance involves the adoption of self-regulation to 'restore trust' in the manager–shareholder relationship, then CSR is an attempt to 'restore trust' in relationships with stakeholders – employees, suppliers, local communities and wider 'society'.

In this context, sustainability and CSR is the latest vehicle for voluntary regulation. At the same time, it is no exaggeration to say that sustainable development and CSR has become a kind of new mission for corporate managers. It has become central to their worldview and how they relate to the world around them.

Notions of sustainable development began in relation to concerns about environmental damage. The most common definition of sustainable development is the one offered by the Brundtland Commission of the United Nations in 1987 as 'meeting the needs of the present without compromising the ability of future generations to meet their own needs'. Sustainable development captures the idea that economic growth is increasingly unsustainable, given the supposed strain on natural resources. That is, without taming growth in the here and now, future generations will be left an impoverished natural world.

Today things have moved on. For a start, economic growth is said to be having a destructive impact on 'society' as well as the environment, causing poverty and greater inequality, among other things. But more to the point here, the notion of 'sustainability' for business is broader still. For one head of CSR at a global mobile network operator, for instance, 'sustainability is about ensuring we have a future – tomorrow, next week and in years to come'.[14] This is a much more generalized concept. Here, being sustainable is about continuity, responsibility, ethics. It brings in all aspects of running the business – from managing the finances, to protecting the brand, to looking after employees and operating in the local community.

A whole new language has emerged around sustainability and CSR. Corporations worry about leaving a destructive or negative 'footprint' on the natural world and society. They are more anxious about degrading 'natural capital' and 'social capital' – which are said to be scarce resources that cannot easily be replenished.

At the same time, sustainability and CSR allows firms to redefine, and extend, charitable ventures. Corporations see themselves as helping, or facilitating, employees to participate in society in various charitable ventures. That could mean helping the homeless in a local community, or it could mean setting up charitable ventures in the developing world.

Corporate managers often do not see the issue of sustainability and CSR in terms of self-regulation. Rather, they believe that CSR offers a number of business benefits. CSR is viewed as a 'key business differentiator'. That is, it can help to distinguish firms in the marketplace. It can offer 'competitive advantage' to firms that take it seriously. It is often said that it can help firms attract better employees and talent, since recruits will want to work for a company that takes social responsibilities seriously.

By being responsible at all times, companies also hope to protect their brands. It is often said that brand perceptions take a long time to build up, but can be destroyed overnight. Similarly, CSR is seen as a key way to manage risk, a theme explored extensively in the next chapter.

To make themselves more sustainable and responsible, corporations around the world have installed new management systems and frameworks. Typically, their objective is to reduce their so-called negative impact on the environment and society, ensure they have a so-called positive impact, and thus improve their behaviour across the board. That could mean anything from reducing carbon emissions to ensuring that employees are not stressed out in the workplace.

So, corporations devise principles and policies of what they want to achieve. Typically, they develop key performance indicators around them, and strive to achieve continuous improvement in various sorts of behaviour. They may use a variety of mechanisms, such as focus groups and audits, to get feedback from stakeholders on how to become more responsible. Finally, in the name of accountability and transparency, corporations report to stakeholders on their progress, issuing bulky reports.

One management system already extensively used is the 'triple bottom line'. This term was coined in 1994 by the environmental consultant John Elkington, founder of the London consultancy and think-tank SustainAbility. The bottom line usually refers to a financial result. But the triple bottom line proposes that companies should go beyond financial accounting and reporting, and proactively measure and manage their positive and negative impact on the environment and society.

To set up CSR frameworks, corporations typically conduct research to find out what other companies, and consumers, think about CSR. In one benchmarking study, for instance, one corporation discovered that 'best practice' organizations in this area tend to publish ethical codes of conduct, have recognized environmental systems and standards, publish CSR reports and have active community programmes.[15]

In the words of one leading consultant, 'more and more companies are approaching sustainable development as an overarching framework for assessing and planning their activities'.[16] Sustainability and CSR is *the* new mission for corporations in the new millennium. It is no exaggeration to say that everything is being reinterpreted from the new perspective of sustainability and CSR.

For example, in 2001 a leading human resources consultant reported that, rather suddenly, sustainability had become the biggest 'mega-trend' in the area of human resources. How come? Well, corporations are said to be unsustainable if they do not pay attention to issues such as workplace diversity, culture, employee development and communication. But also, the whole issue of the work–life balance is viewed as a key sustainability and triple bottom line issue. The starting point for discussion is that workplaces are stressing out workers and causing illness. Companies that encourage cultures where stress is epidemic are not contributing to the sustainable development of human capital, in the jargon. They are fostering unsustainable workplaces.[17]

A key part of the sustainability and CSR framework is 'dialogue' with stakeholders. To be responsible is to be responsive to the needs of stakeholders as they arise. The concept of stakeholder relations is becoming fully integrated into corporate policy, and strategic thinking and action.

According to a stakeholder relations manager of a European biotechnology firm, 'interaction with stakeholders is a vital part of our strategy to build a triple bottom line company'. For her, that means liasing, dialogue and partnerships with them on a regular basis.

This particular biotech firm faced opposition from groups opposed to genetic technology, because they use genetically modified organisms (GMOs) in their health products. They decided to 'establish a strategy to create dialogue with these stakeholders'.

That means that today, 'at least once a year, we invite these NGOs to visit us in the company. They come to see the labs, the plants, and key people within the company. We get their feedback, which proves very useful for us. It enables us to look into a crystal ball, and anticipate the issues that may come up in two to three years' time.'

The firm 'does not always agree with NGOs. The important point is not to agree though, but to respect each other's viewpoints. A good starting point for discussion is to see that there is a dilemma. This dilemma is not easily solved.' This dilemma involves different attitudes to biotechnology.

The firm has regular meetings with NGOs.

> When NGOs and business sit down for the first time, we don't always use the same language. We learn to accept and trust each other, despite differences in viewpoints. It is very important to say at the beginning of these meetings that the end point is not to gain a consensus. The point is not to agree at the end. It is the process of dialogue that counts.

According to this particular manager, sustainable development is 'very much a synergy approach. It is about minimizing risk, and optimizing opportunities. It helps us to minimize the adverse risks that affect our license to operate. A saying we have inside this company is, "you have to earn your license to operate".'

At the same time the firm sees sustainable development as an opportunity. 'There is a huge opportunity to attract young people to work for us. Surveys show that young people want to work for companies that have strong values and a vision of the future.'[18]

There are several interesting themes here. First, the point is not to agree or disagree when engaging with stakeholders. Rather, the *process* of dialogue becomes the important thing. Second, and related, stakeholder relations thinking, and sustainable development, is a new form of managing risk for companies. But third, it is seen very much as some kind of new opportunity. This notion of 'listening to stakeholders', and 'listening to society', is explored more below.

A further point here is that sustainable development and CSR also involve a whole range of institutions demanding greater accountability from corporations. These institutions, which now range from governments to environmental groups to institutional investors, demand that corporations do not behave in an unsustainable, irresponsible fashion, and want to see ongoing 'continuous improvement' in their behaviour.

The investment community has got into 'socially responsible investing' (SRI) in a big way. Here, institutional investors buy the shares of companies that are seen to be doing active good in society.[19]

Also, the media and other institutions have created special 'indexes' which rank companies according to their sustainable and responsible practices, to help investors choose between them. Hence, the FTSE, jointly owned by the *Financial Times* and London Stock Exchange, launched FTSE4Good in July 2001. In this index, tobacco companies, weapons firms and the nuclear power industry are screened out from the beginning, because they are deemed to be socially irresponsible. The American publisher of the *Wall Street Journal*, before that, launched the Dow Jones Sustainability Index. Companies that want to be included in such indexes have to demonstrate they behave in the right way. According to one company, complying with the Dow Jones Sustainability Index involves answering 87 questions, and takes one person three weeks to collect the information.[20]

Other initiatives abound. The Global Reporting Initiative was set up in 1997 by the US-based Coalition for Environmentally Responsible Economies (CEREs). It is being seen as a new global standard that can bring together the various competing standards for environmental and social reporting.

Regulators, who have been playing catch up in this area, have now started to get themselves in gear. In 2000, Kim Howells was appointed Britain's first minister for corporate social responsibility. Howells has preferred to encourage voluntary regulation in the private sector, rather than push for a statutory approach. More law, it is feared, might lead to a 'box-ticking' approach.[21]

European governments have been busy. The Danish government, for instance, has demanded that companies report on a wide range of social and environmental issues. These include wage disparities, ethnic representation, carbon dioxide emissions and policies on child labour. The European Commission issued a new report on corporate social responsibility in 2002.

It is important again to realize that sustainable development is now seen as a source of competitive advantage for companies, on a number of levels. The British social commentator, Will Hutton, for instance has suggested that companies that do not take social responsibility seriously will not even be allowed to list on stock exchanges. Referring to Shell, Hutton (2000) commented that:

> Shell's statement of five stakeholder constituencies to which it accepts responsibility, and its attempts to set benchmarks by which its performance is measured, are not an idiosyncratic initiative from a company seeking PR mileage. This is the future, and will one day be the precondition for a stock exchange listing.

It is believed that companies that already have sustainable and responsible credentials trade at a higher premium on the stock exchange. According to some analysts, the higher valuations BP–Amoco has enjoyed in recent years compared with other oil companies, can at least partly be put down to the fact it takes CSR very seriously. Investors believe that companies with CSR policies, frameworks and initiatives are more likely to manage risk better and protect their reputation and brand.

Corporations also expect new industries, markets and products to be created out of the sustainable development concept. Firms are very conscious of the way that new environmental regulations created all sorts of new markets in the area of eco-efficiency, such as waste management, or environmentally friendly technologies and materials.[22]

If society starts to take seriously the notion that it should cut back on its consumption, under the concept of sustainable development, that will inevitably lead to new types of industry, new markets and new products. Feasibly, everything could be affected, from agriculture, transportation, energy and housing, to electronics, IT and the media. Many corporations are already thinking what this future might look like.

A new agenda of irrational self-regulation and restraint

The concept that corporations should make themselves more sustainable and responsible, seems, on the surface, almost admirable. But there are major problems with this new agenda. Ideas of sustainability and responsibility play on the common-sense, but wrong, assumption that corporate behaviour is more damaging and irresponsible than in the past. Here, there is an assumption that corporations are wrecking the environment, being uncaring in the local community, stressing out employees in the workplace and ruining their work–life balances.

In the sustainability and CSR discussion, corporate managers are reacting defensively to very one-sided perceptions that have arisen in the 'culture of suspicion' that Chapter 1 explored. Once taken on board, these assumptions then lead to an irrational culture of caution and restraint in behaviour.

For example, US telecommunications firm AT&T claim that their telework programme for employees scores well from the perspective of the triple bottom line, one of the major management systems to be used in conjunction with sustainability and CSR.[23]

On the economic axis, AT&T reckons that telework has allowed it to get rid of 'unnecessary office space and overhead costs' and boost worker productivity. On the environment axis, they argue that when employees work from home, they use their car less, which cuts down on carbon emissions released into the atmosphere. On the social axis, they suggest that telework leads to a better work–life balance for staff, because they have more choice over where they can work. For AT&T, this is the notion of sustainability in action. The company is growing a particular part of its business – its telework division – but supposedly is using capital more efficiently, reducing its environmental impact, and not adding to worker stress and depleting 'human capital'.

This is an illuminating example. What is disturbing about it is the way that self-restraint, on a number of levels, is reinterpreted as a *positive* thing. For a start, AT&T does not have to build new offices. But also, not using the car, and being stuck at home glued to the telephone, is magically reinterpreted as a great example of sustainability.

This is the logic of sustainability and CSR. The underlying assumption is that corporations are causing damage to environmental and social systems. From this perspective, it is positive to exercise self-restraint. Being stuck at home, and not using the car, can be quickly dressed up as some kind of virtue.

This kind of caution and restraint – self-regulation – is irrational because corporations are not the unsustainable and irresponsible institutions they are made out to be. Before arguing why this is the case, it is worth looking more closely at some other areas of sustainability and CSR. As mentioned above, the CSR agenda involves defensive corporations listening to an increasingly suspicious and fearful society. In this new context, however, it is actually very damaging for corporations to 'listen to stakeholders'. The starting point is not acting to achieve a positive, ambitious goal, but minimizing damage in particular ways. Corporations are worried about losing their reputation, appearing unethical, and want to manage risk. So-called 'stakeholders', for their part, want corporations to minimize damage and exercise caution and restraint.

How 'listening to society' can be irrational

There are a number of problems with the concept of 'listening to society'. First of all, more often than not it means listening to stakeholder groups that are not properly elected and cannot be said to represent 'society' in any meaningful sense. As the biotechnology example above illustrated, NGOs are now being fully incorporated into the corporate machinery. These groups can be influential, and play a part in the process of voluntary regulation. Yet their leaders have not been elected, and their viewpoints not subjected to democratic debate and scrutiny.

Second, the notion of listening to society has a highly reactionary element to it, because 'society' can often be highly reactionary. It is not elitist or anti-democratic to realize that, without proper debate on issues such as the environment or new technologies such as GMOs, it is impossible to get two sides of the story. Fears and anxieties about risk can dominate the discussion. Reason and scientific evidence can fly out of the window.

When corporations say they want to 'listen to society', this hardly takes place in a proper democratic forum. Often, it means listening to groups that have few qualms about using scaremonger tactics and emotion in trying to convince an audience. Corporations that then self-regulate simply institutionalize these fears and irrational notions.

An example of this process involved the energy firm Shell, and its Brent Spar incident, in 1995. In June that year, Shell made a U-turn over its decision to dump the oil storage platform, Brent Spar, into the sea. Between 1991 and 1994 the company had commissioned 30 scientific studies on the different environmental impacts of disposing of Brent Spar. All of them had concluded that a deep-sea disposal, as opposed to a land disposal, would be the best option. Substances from the platform would not likely enter the food chain, would not cause environmental harm and would be less damaging to human safety.

In February 1995 the decision to dump Brent Spar into the sea was announced. By April, however, the British environmental activist group Greenpeace had clambered onto the platform and occupied it, and were busy launching a public relations campaign to block its sinking. In a series of events that have since become a classic case study for students of crisis management, Greenpeace were removed from the platform but had encouraged the public to boycott Shell's service stations.

In Germany, some went a bit further. There, some 50 stations were damaged, including two that were firebombed and another riddled with bullets from gunmen. At that point, politicians started to get involved. The German Chancellor Helmut Kohl began to put pressure on British politicians, and Shell, to cancel the sinking. Shell duly backed down over its original plans.

The Greenpeace campaign – as they themselves fully admit – was based on misinformation. Greenpeace appealed to irrational fears. They suggested that the platform was a 'toxic time-bomb', and placed adverts that suggested that, 'if you let Shell have its way, it'll soon be the only Shell left in the North Sea'. Rather unfortunately for them, Greenpeace also overestimated the amount of oil on board the Brent Spar. They said it contained up to 5500 tonnes of oil. In fact, it only contained around 100 tonnes (see Neal and Davies, 1998, pp. 23–24).

The Brent Spar event was a triumph of irrationalism over rational problem-solving. In the circumstances, there was a very strong case for deep-sea disposal. Each case has to be debated on its merits. But here, Shell had to go through a scientific process to debate the different options.

It sought expert, independent scientific advice, and 30 studies were conducted prior to 1995, including an Impact Hypothesis document, and a Best Practicable Environment Option document produced by independent assessors. The scientific studies concluded that its impact on the deep-sea environment would be extremely minimal and not harmful at all. The risk to humans would be very slight. Alternatives would be more risky to human life, and more costly to the company. Shell had to submit these documents to the British Department of Trade and Industry, where government scientists scrutinized them.

A former director of Friends of the Earth UK, David Gee, who supported Greenpeace in their endeavours, summed up the Brent Spar affair well soon afterwards. He suggested that: 'the incident has established the moral principle of "not dumping at sea" over the narrower technical "best practicable environment option"' In other words, scientific evidence had given way to a moralistic approach (see Neal and Davies, 1998 p. 25).

But at the same time, fear had also won the day. Greenpeace had appealed to anxieties about environmental destruction and risk. They had played the 'trump card of uncertainty'. They had little evidence that the dumping of Brent Spar would cause damage, but played on fears of what *could* happen if it was dumped.

Lord Melchett, UK director of Greenpeace, played a key role in that campaign. Four years later he was found in a field in the British countryside, destroying genetically modified corn that was deliberately being grown as a trial crop for experimentation purposes, and was arrested.

Greenpeace have long opposed even the *attempt* to experiment with genetically modified organisms. They have long advocated the use of the 'precautionary principle'. This is a principle that reverses the scientific 'trial and error' with the notion of 'trial without error'. In other words, it counsels that scientists should not experiment unless they can know in advance all potential hazards: the precautionary principle quickly makes genuine scientific experimentation impossible.

Shell could have concluded that the Brent Spar affair represented a new and irrational trend in British society. It could have reasoned that rational problem-solving had been defeated by fear and anxiety.

In private, its executives may well have done. Certainly, at the time, a whole range of social commentators had strongly made that point. Shell could have gone on the offensive. It could have lobbied politicians to its cause. It could have tried to win the war of propaganda by proclaiming the importance of scientific principles and reason.

But Shell was on the defensive. Shell did not just back down from dumping Brent Spar into the sea. In response to the incident, the company has gone much, much further. It is the defensiveness of Shell that has led it to try to extensively re-regulate its own behaviour.

Feeling defensive, Shell felt it had to somehow make amends, and clean up its act, even though it had not done anything wrong. It felt it had to become far more ethical, environmentally sensitive, emotionally aware and socially responsible. It felt it had to get in touch with the sensitivities of people – even if these sensitivities were unfortunately informed more by prejudice than reason.

Since 1995 Shell has poured huge energy and resources into a whole range of initiatives, based around stakeholder relations, sustainable development and the triple bottom line. The Brent Spar incident was not the sole reason for conducting these initiatives, but there is no doubt it had a profound impact on the company.

In 2002, a Shell manager working in the area of sustainable development who had since come into the company, reflected on the Brent Spar incident to the author. Should Shell have upheld the principles of science in this case? Should it have argued that it was in the right?

> Well, you have to ask the question, 'what is right?'. We believe that what is right is according to society. The way to establish the answer of what is right is through a dialogue. Just relying on the scientific results does not cut it. At the end of the day, the feeling of the public was, Shell should not do that, they should not dump the Brent Spar. It is the same thing when you dump your ashtray out of your car. People do not like it. Greenpeace had spoken for public opinion. Shell had not sufficiently done that.[24]

From the perspective of public relations, one can have sympathy for these views. They are understandable in their own terms. But there is a huge problem with them. One cannot assume that society is always right. Society is frequently wrong. That is not a patronizing view. It simply recognizes that, in the absence of a proper public debate, and where special interest groups such as Greenpeace use scare mongering tactics to win over public opinion, reason and democracy quickly fly out of the window. What emerges is a distortion of the truth. And, any regulation or self-regulation that follows on this basis is also likely to have a distorting effect. The danger is that institutions unnecessarily pursue an agenda of caution and restraint across the board in their behaviour.

Sustainable development – does it make sense?

So far, the second half of this chapter has argued that sustainability and CSR is really a new form of self-regulation. Corporate managers are reacting defensively to the notion that corporate behaviour is more unsustainable, irresponsible – and more destructive to common interests. They are far more worried about the so-called negative impact of corporations on the natural world and society, and want to listen to stakeholders in an attempt to show responsibility. This encourages an irrational caution and restraint. Managers begin to act not on strong beliefs and a confident outlook for the future, but on fears of what may go wrong.

How much sense does the new agenda really make? Does it reflect an underlying need to be more sustainable and responsible? If corporations were behaving in an unsustainable and irresponsible fashion, wrecking the environment, rampaging in the local community, and producing degraded workplaces for employees, then this new bout of self-regulation might make sense. However, it is not difficult to see that this type of behaviour is not taking place.

This final section takes a broader perspective on the concept of 'sustainable development'. An overarching idea that informs this new self-regulation is that economic growth and industrialization more generally has become unsustainable. Companies need to contribute to a more sustainable future by being responsible in various ways.

Yet the sustainable development outlook captures an extremely narrow and one-sided view of economic growth and industrialization. It inflates and exaggerates the destructive dimension of these processes. It then argues that, because economic growth is having a destructive impact, growth needs to be tamed in various ways. Individuals and organizations need to exercise caution and restraint.

The following will argue that self-regulation is irrational because economic growth is not unsustainable as is commonly thought. A more balanced perspective is to realize that economic growth and industrialization have brought enormous benefits to humanity. At the same time, society has dealt pretty well with the destructive side of this process – which shows that growth is not unsustainable in the way that is conceived.

Sustainability – a distorted worldview

Sustainable development has taken on the status of an official social objective. Governments and corporations everywhere have signed up to it.

In the abstract, it is certainly true that being 'unsustainable' does not make sense. If, through the process of industrialization, humanity used up all its natural resources, from oil to fish stocks, degraded the soil, the sea, freshwater and the air; then there would be something very wrong indeed. If, through growth and industrialization, people became poorer and poorer, and their life expectancy plummeted, then it might be time to ask some serious questions. If, over time, corporations became less and less responsible – making unsafe, damaging products, and fostering unsafe working environments – then there would be a problem. Future generations would not be left much of an earth or a society.

Yet absolutely no evidence suggests this is happening. There is something very wrong and misguided about the sustainable development concept. In particular, it does not seem to capture the real relationships between economic growth, industrialization and the impact on the natural world and society. It seems to *inflate and exaggerate* the destructive aspect of growth and industrialization. Also, *fears* of what might happen if society continues on its present course are used to argue against growth, and for caution and restraint, in the here and now.

Throughout history, industrialization and economic growth – the process of using resources to produce things, the process of consumption, the use of technology to do things more efficiently, the expansion of the division of labour, the creation of wealth, and so on – have led to huge human benefits. Society has created a better world than the previous one.

In particular, individuals are no longer at the mercy of natural forces that were beyond their control. In the past, if an individual contracted a disease as basic as influenza by today's standards, the relative un-sophistication of society meant they had little chance of survival. Similarly, the production of food was at the mercy of weather conditions and natural plagues. Also, the meaning of individual freedom was limited in a society where humanity organized itself very primitively, and had not taken control over natural forces.

The net outcome of industrialization has been hugely positive. Because society has managed to organize better, and gain more control over natural forces, individuals live longer and have better qualities of life. That means more and better food and better shelter. It also means having all the goods that embody technological progress. It also means more freedom. Given the choice, most people today would not want to go back to pre-industrial times.

It would be wrong to pretend though that the process of industrialization has been trouble free. In various forms, problems have been thrown up that society has had to deal with. One of these problems, the destructive impact on the environment caused by industrialization, has actually been dealt with very well. Many problems have actually been *reversed*, as the environment has been cleaned up in various ways.

Of course, there is a common belief that, as industrial development and economic growth have progressed, society has sat back and let terrible things happen to the environment. However, in reality nothing could be farther from the truth. Human beings have tended to respond imaginatively to new problems as they have arisen.

For example, fears have been expressed in the past that humanity would run out of resources. They were proved wrong. Also, none of the facts supports the idea that through industrialization, the soil, the sea, freshwater and the air have become more degraded. In developed nations, evidence suggests that where the industrialization process has had a destructive impact, society has dealt with it very well.

An excellent contribution to this debate comes from Bjørn Lomborg, the author of *The Skeptical Environmentalist: Measuring the Real State of the World*. Lomborg became a sceptic when he realized that environmentalists' claims about the state of the world bear little relation to reality (see Lomborg, 2001).

Lomborg has been one of the few writers to actually look at statistics and take a historical approach to examining problems. Lomborg's book is based on an exhaustive examination of official statistics to examine the state of the environment. His main message is that things are getting better, not worse, when it comes to the state of the natural world.

Lomborg shows that many of the environmental problems that we think have got worse have actually got better. Take air pollution. 'We often assume that air pollution is a modern phenomenon, and that it has got worse and worse in recent times.' However, he says, 'the air of the Western world has not been as clean as it is now for a long time'.

In the early days of industrialization, air pollution was appalling in a city like London from 1700 to 1900, largely because of the burning of coal. Even in the 1950s, smog was bad, killing 4000 Londoners in one week in December 1952. But today it has dropped back to the levels seen in the Middle Ages. Elsewhere, official statistics show that emissions such as particles, sulphur dioxide, lead, ozone, nitrogen oxides and carbon monoxide have all fallen, and in dramatic fashion.

Air pollution obviously is just one issue. Yet it reflects the more general trend. Lomborg argues persuasively that we are not overexploiting renewable resources, such as food, water and forests. He writes, 'many have a strong feeling that the forests are simply disappearing'. But when it comes to the idea of rapid deforestation, 'there are no grounds for making such claims. Globally, the overall area covered by forest has not changed much since 1950,' he writes. Again, he uses official statistics; in the forest example using UN statistics. Nor are there serious problems with non-renewable resources, such as energy and raw materials.

A more balanced view of economic growth

A more realistic perspective on economic growth would be to say that, on balance, it has benefited human beings, and society needs more of it. Along this road, of course, there have been problems, accidents and, occasionally, damage done to the environment. Yes, companies have dumped chemicals into rivers. Society has experienced horrible industrial accidents, such as Chernobyl.

But these are not a good argument against economic growth. If the whole process of industrialization and economic growth had somehow led to a degraded society and natural world, then it might be time to say, enough is enough. But on the whole, we have benefited hugely from economic growth. Moreover, humanity has proved adept at mitigating destructive impacts. Many problems of industrialization have been tamed.

Past fears that economic growth and industrialization would degrade the natural world, leaving humanity in a terrible fix, have always been proved wrong. Previous predictions that natural resources would run out, for instance, have been proved hopelessly inaccurate. For environmentalists, this has always been hard to swallow. In other words, growth *has* been sustainable. The economy has grown, and people have consumed more, but natural resources have not been used up, and the natural world has not been overly impoverished.

Fears of resource depletion go back a long way, as Lomborg points out. In the nineteenth century, the economist Stanley Jevons predicted that the Industrial Revolution would suddenly end because of a coal shortage. But he forgot to take into account the fact that coal would be used more effectively, new coal reserves would be found, and new energy sources would be found, such as oil. The US Bureau of Mines believed with confidence that oil would run out in 10 years' time – in 1914. The Department of the Interior was a little more optimistic – they gave oil 13 years – back in 1939 (see Lomborg, 2001).

The 1970s saw the rise of the modern day doomsday scenario. In 1972, the book *Limits to Growth*, commissioned by the international think-tank Club of Rome, warned that in the coming century, population growth would overwhelm the world's supplies of land and minerals and the capacity of the atmosphere to absorb pollutants. Growth would be unsustainable. But it was hopelessly wrong. It failed to recognize the reality of technological progress and new discoveries. Even before 2000 was reached, it became evident that the estimates were looking in very poor shape indeed. People had discovered new petroleum and gas reservoirs, and had found more ways to extract more petroleum from known reservoirs. Substitute materials had been found, and methods of extraction had improved, among other things.

The issue of global warming

This section will briefly look at the issue of global warming. One argument today is that economies need to be sustainable and cut back on consumption and growth, and companies need to be more 'responsible', because of the risks of global warming – the possibility of horrible disasters that society will not be able to cope with, such as rising sea levels and freak weather conditions.

Global warming refers to the warming of the earth and the climate, measured by the temperature of land, sea and air. Since about 1910, global temperature has been on an upward curve. This increase in temperature is linked to the greenhouse effect, an increase in greenhouse gases that trap heat and keep the earth warm. It is likely that economic activity is making a contribution to the heating: it is not just a natural cycle. For example, extra carbon dioxide, one of the main greenhouse gases, has been thrown up into the atmosphere by the combustion of oil, coal and gas (see Lomborg, 1998).

There is genuine uncertainty about global warming: over the contribution particular gases make, over future temperature rises, and therefore over the consequences to society. A reflection is the fact that the Intergovernmental Panel on Climate Change (IPCC), which produces reports for governments to set policy, commissioned a number of independent studies to predict future scenarios, and they showed that global temperatures could rise by anything between 1.4 °C and 5.8 °C, depending on the data and computer model (IPCC, 2001).

Global warming is an attractive issue for environmentalists precisely because genuine uncertainty surrounds it. As a result, the 'better to be safe than sorry' card can be played with full gusto. In many other areas of debate, environmentalist arguments and forecasts have not turned out to be very accurate when measured against the facts and reality. Society has not run out of resources as predicted, and the natural world is not in a dire state as suggested. Nobody as yet knows what will happen with global warming, however. So there is more scope to play more on society's fears of what might happen. In an age where society is far less tolerant of risk and uncertainty, this is a powerful issue for encouraging 'the precautionary principle' on a grand scale.

Global warming may cause problems that humanity will have to confront and proactively manage. Or, it may not. There is no automatic reason to believe that it will cause problems that humanity cannot deal with.

However, the strength of risk aversion in society today makes it almost natural to assume that self-restraint and self-regulation are the best courses of action. The fear is that an uncontrollable monster, global warming, has been let out of the bottle. We envision a world where houses are suddenly under the sea and people are being blown about by horrible hurricanes. These scenarios are daft anyway, because they paint a future where humanity has not anticipated such problems, and is suddenly caught off guard. It is easy to forget that a defining characteristic of humanity is its ability to progress through greater control of natural forces. In reality, there are choices in how society can deal with potential problems, and it is irrational to automatically advocate a path of self-restraint, just to be on the safe side.

Environmentalism is more often than not based on a *moral* argument, often independent of reality, reason, facts and science. The argument against industrialization and economic growth has often been a moral one. 'Look at what we have done to the earth', has been the message. 'How disgusting of us.' Unfortunately, this crusading moralism quickly eclipses any balanced consideration of the benefits of economic growth, or what human beings really have done to the planet.

There are striking parallels between environmentalism and a religious worldview – the kind of worldview that was common before industrialization. Religions typically stress that human beings should be humble before God and worship God as the creator of mankind. They establish moral codes for people to live by, if they want to avoid being punished by God in the afterlife.

In the environmental worldview, the natural world becomes a kind of God that human beings must worship. Environmental catastrophe, such as the dreaded global warming, is almost a punishment that human beings deserve for being wicked. Human beings have to be humble before nature. And, people have to abide by all sorts of moral codes. If they want to be good, and avert environmental catastrophe, they have to cut back on their consumption.

These kinds of parallel are often explicit. For instance, in the influential book *Natural Capitalism*, the authors favourably quote the conservationist Wendell Berry:

> ...we must learn to acknowledge that the creation is full of mystery; we will never clearly understand it. We must abandon arrogance and stand in awe. We must recover the sense of the majesty of the creation, and the ability to be worshipful in its presence. For it is only on the condition of humility and reverence before the world that our species will be able to remain in it (see Hawken et al., 2000).

Of course, not everyone sympathetic to environmentalism has such strong feelings about the natural world. But the moralizing impulse of environmentalism has had a very influential impact on society. There is now a widespread perception, shared by broad sections of society, that human beings have been very destructive to the natural world, and are wrong to 'meddle with nature'. Increasingly, there are calls from many quarters that individuals should cut back on consumption, perhaps using their car less, or renouncing a so-called obsession with material things. Organizations at the same time need to show much greater responsibility in their actions and be more sustainable. The issue of global warming is interpreted through a pre-existing tendency to see human behaviour as arrogant and destructive. Again, this makes it difficult to gain a more balanced appraisal of the situation.

As Lomborg points out, there is a price to be paid for panicking and allocating resources on the basis of anxiety. By underestimating society's capacity to deal with future problems, and by worrying about risk and what might happen, resources are diverted away from human welfare in the here and now. Lomborg persuasively argues that rather than rush out to spend at least US $150bn a year on implementing the Kyoto agreement on global warming, on the basis of anxiety about the future, around half that money could be spent on providing all the Third World with the basics of education, clean water, health and sanitation. At the same time, there are several areas of the global warming issue that need further discussion and analysis before any firm conclusions can be made about the dangers and the need for corrective action. Scientists need to apply themselves to resolving some of the areas of uncertainty that surround the global warming issue.

Today, we seem to be in a situation aptly summed up by Murray Bookchin, another environmentalist who was disgusted by the myths perpetuated by fellow environmentalists. He wrote that: 'In a very real sense, we seem to be afraid of ourselves, of our uniquely human attributes (Bookchin, 1995, p. 1).

Conclusion: the dangers of self-regulation

Self-regulation is a new dynamic in the business world. Yet it proceeds on an irrational basis. The ill-defined, but powerfully felt notion that management and corporate behaviour is more unethical, irresponsible and reckless than in the past is a one-sided perception of reality. Managers, however, have reacted defensively to such notions.

The outcome is that managers wrap their own behaviour, and that of employees, in new red tape. Worried about what might go wrong, there is a process of trying to avoid risk in all sorts of situations.

The next chapter takes another new self-regulation and examines it in more detail. According to Hutter and Power (2001), '...corporate risk management is a form of self-regulation, although senior management would not articulate it in such terms'.

Risk management has been a key area of corporate governance reform. But it is also a discipline in its own right. The next chapter examines how managers have internalized a society-wide intolerance of risk and uncertainty by setting in motion a huge range of self-regulatory initiatives under the banner of risk management.

The problem with the enormous rise of risk management is that it entrenches a new intolerance of risk and uncertainty. So, before being allowed to take action, employees need authorization under new risk controls. Rather than take chances, managers feel they must filter every decision through elaborate risk assessment schemes. Companies now seek to hedge risks that in the past would have been accepted as business risks. Managers are now far more obsessed with the discipline of crisis management. Rather than just get on with it and take risk, and act on strong positive beliefs, more and more action is predicated on the fear of what might go wrong.

Notes

1. Correspondence with in-house lawyer, European telecommunications firm.
2. For example, in the mid-1980s, groups were first formed to represent institutional shareholders' interests. Leading shareholder rights activists Robert Monks and Jesse Unruh established the Council of Institutional Investors in 1985. Organizations were also established which advised shareholders on how to vote. In 1986, Monks established the organization Institutional Shareholder Services.
3. For example, Pensions Investment Research Consultants (PIRC) is the leading British institution that monitors corporate governance for pension funds, major institutional investors in the stock market. PIRC defines corporate governance as having three major strands: protecting rights; minimizing risk; and enhancing value. See their website www.pirc.co.uk
4. The study referred to is Corporate Governance: History, Practice and Future, Chartered Institute of Management Accountants, 2000.
5. Any executive can now find themselves being accused of being an 'autocrat'. An interesting example was an interview with Sir Richard Greenbury after he had stepped down as Chief Executive Officer and Chairman of the British retailer Marks & Spencer, by the British journalist John Humphrys on British radio. Humphrys put it to Greenbury that 'people say you had too much power for too long, you were too autocratic...you exercised too much power and should have delegated more...you were both chief executive and chairman...' Greenbury responded by saying 'I would strenuously deny I was autocratic...I was extremely demanding...tough but fair...I had strong views, when I couldn't persuade people of my views I would back down.' Quotes from the Radio 4 programme, On The Ropes. 'Former chairman of Marks & Spencer, Sir Richard Greenbury, talks to John Humphrys about his life and career', BBC Radio 4, 9.30 pm, 22 August 2000.
6. Correspondence with lawyers who specialize in corporate governance issues.
7. Correspondence with company executives.
8. See Report of the Committee on the Financial Aspects of Corporate Governance, December 1992.
9. See the report, Director's Remuneration: Report of a Study Group Chaired by Sir Richard Greenbury (July 1995).

10. See Committee on Corporate Governance: Final Report (Hampel Committee) January 1998.
11. See the website www.iodsa.co.za
12. These examples were taken from Conger et al. (2001, p. 107).
13. See Report of the Committee on the Financial Aspects of Corporate Governance, 1 December 1992.
14. Correspondence with head of CSR, global mobile network operator.
15. Correspondence with head of CSR, global mobile network operator.
16. Correspondence with a leading ethical and social accountability consultant.
17. See interview with Owain Franks, Chairman of the PricewaterhouseCoopers Human Resources Consulting Practice in the United Kingdom and Europe, www.pwc.co.uk
18. Correspondence with a stakeholder relations manager, European biotechnology firm.
19. According to the Social Investment Forum, an American NGO, SRI in America passed US $2 trillion in 1999 – one in eight dollars under management. See 'Ethical investment: warm and fuzzy', *The Economist*, 14 July 2001.
20. Correspondence with European telecommunications company.
21. See 'Report due on corporate social responsibility', *Financial Times*, 6 March 2001.
22. Correspondence with sustainable development managers of major corporations.
23. See AT&T's 1998 Employee Health and Safety report.
24. Correspondence with manager of sustainable development, Shell.

3

The Rise of Risk Management

In an episode of the popular US TV medical drama *ER*, a woman falls out a hospital window by accident. The immediate response by a member of staff, perhaps fearing litigation or a public relations disaster, is 'call the risk manager!'.

Call the risk manager indeed. At the beginning of the 1990s, risk management was an important, but essentially peripheral, business activity. Risk managers mainly worked in insurance and finance departments, to protect companies from particular risks they could face.[1] By the end of the decade, however, something unusual had happened. Some time around the mid-1990s, executives of global corporations everywhere started to worry much more about 'the risks that kept them awake at night'.[2]

Executives began to worry much more about risk exposures and worst-case scenarios. Some firms appointed Chief Risk Officers (CROs) for the first time, to sit on the board and act as permanent risk management consultants for the chief executive. Internal risk managers suddenly found their services in great demand by executives who had previously not shown great interest in risk management. Firms began to set in motion a huge range of initiatives under the banner of risk management. By the end of the decade, corporations had institutionalized elaborate frameworks for managing risk, under the heading of 'enterprise-wide risk management'.

At the same time, a mini-industry in risk management blossomed. New markets sprung up in the most specialist areas, such as risk modelling software. Corporations used this software to simulate every conceivable risk scenario they could face. The rise of the risk management consultant was a striking trend. The professional services industry began to breed a new army of risk management consultants. Such consultants began to focus on every possible risk that could impact a company.

Weird and wonderful new financial and insurance markets emerged in order that corporations could hedge risk. Reinsurance and insurance firms started to investigate how they could insure risks that companies previously accepted as part of doing business, such as failed R&D projects. Lawyers suddenly came out of the woodwork. They made bold claims that they were the authentic risk managers all along, with hundreds of years of experience.

Risk management became big business, and a bandwagon that everyone wanted to jump on – in a relatively short space of time. Risk managers themselves – some bewildered by and sceptical of all the new attention – joked that, since everyone had now become a risk manager, they were struggling to define what their own jobs were.[3]

It is significant that the rise of risk management is a difficult trend to explain. For some, its rise in profile has something to do with the 'new economy' and the so-called speed of change. For others, companies are under increased pressure from shareholders, who are demanding less volatility and more stability in financial results over time. This trend is forcing companies to manage risk. For others, corporations face increased 'reputational risk' because of more active stakeholder groups. Also, the rise of a global media is blamed, where managers are managing in a kind of 'global goldfish bowl'. In this context, corporations have to watch what they say and how they act. For others still, globalization, increased competition and new technology are key. De-regulation is often seen as important, yet so is regulation.

Of course, one could argue that all these developments are important. But in fact, they are all misleading. There is a tendency to explain behaviour with reference to external 'drivers of change' such as the so-called pace of change. But the real explanation lies closer to home. Managers now share a society-wide perception that life is more risky, uncertain and unpredictable. Like society, they feel more exposed to risk. But at the same time, they feel they must show responsibility for managing risk, because they are on the defensive about appearing to be reckless and irresponsible.

In recent years, individuals in society have become far more worried about what might go wrong in life, and are more prone to act on these fears. Some sociologists have been at the forefront in documenting this trend.

For instance, leading sociologist Frank Furedi has argued persuasively that we live in a *Culture of Fear*. Individuals in society have a more developed 'risk consciousness'. That is, they tend to be more aware of dangers, hazards and the possibility that things could go wrong. This is not a psychological affliction, but a development that stems from social trends, such as the breakdown of older political traditions that gave people a sense of confidence in the future. Writing in the 1990s, Furedi noted that

> the past decade has seen a veritable explosion of new dangers. Life is portrayed as increasingly violent. Children are depicted as more and more out of control. The food we eat, the water we drink, and the materials we use for everything from buildings to cellular phones, have come under scrutiny.

He also writes that

> reactions to such routine dangers pale into insignificance in relation to the big threats, which are said to put humanity's survival into question...Our imagination continually works towards the worst possible interpretations of events. Expectations of some far-reaching catastrophe are regularly rehearsed in relation to a variety of risks.

Examples include scares about lethal diseases, such as Ebola, to AIDs and Mad Cow disease, to environmental catastrophes such as global warming (see Furedi, 1997, pp. 20–21).

The 1990s was a period when the business world internalized this society-wide fixation with risk, crisis and catastrophe. What was very odd about the 1990s was that, rather suddenly, managers became much more anxious about the worst thing that might happen to their company. They felt more exposed to risk. They became more preoccupied with risks such as total loss of reputation. Executives began to worry about the 'risks that kept them awake at night'.

For example, one of the peculiar things to emerge in the business world has been a fixation with corporate collapse and crisis. This is a recent trend. Business catastrophes are now pored over and analysed to death in a way that they were not in the past. Consultants now specialize in knowing everything there is to know about crises, such as oil spills, health scares, banking failures, failed marketing promotions, product recalls and litigation payouts. A whole new spate of books on crisis management has appeared in recent times. Other consultants spend considerable energy on examining the impact of catastrophes on share prices, and to their surprise find their reports in great demand.[4] For a whole variety of consultants, catastrophes are often used as morality tales in poor management and the pitfalls of not managing risk. Here, managers are cautioned of the dangers of 'falling asleep at the wheel'.

The first point about the rise of risk management then is that managers are reacting to a society-wide obsession with risk and crisis. They have internalized a society-wide tendency to worry about the downside of human action. The second more important point is that managers of large corporations are already on the defensive in their relations with the world, as we have seen in earlier chapters. They are already worried about appearing to be reckless, unethical, irresponsible and so on. So, managers could challenge the new obsession with risk as irrational. They could refuse to worry too much about risk management. As explored below, corporations have actually got far *better* at managing risk than in the past – and not because of initiatives in the last 10 years. However, managers have tended to gravitate towards risk management because they are afraid of appearing irresponsible. They are worried that, if they are not seen to manage risk, they will be deemed reckless.

Many modern risk management consultants do not question whether society and institutions indeed face more risk than in the past, or whether those institutions are failing to manage risk. They have a material interest in perpetuating the risk management obsession. They rarely point out that perceptions of risk frequently can be out of kilter with the statistical probability of risk. Many consultants tend to reinforce the society-wide idea that there is greater 'risk' out there for business.

A typical commentary of this nature is the book *World of Risk*, by Mark Daniell, managing director of the consulting firm Bain & Co in Asia. For Daniell,

> we are now living in a world of rising risk and increasing volatility. Everywhere, we seem to encounter increasing and intensifying risk. Business risk. Economic risk. Environmental risk. Political conflict and risk of military engagement. Risk of unforeseen harm from criminals and disease. Risks to the retentions of our unique cultures and to the spiritual foundations of our lives. We even run the risk of unpredicted new catastrophes as complex new systems interact, such as distributed computer networks, the Internet, and modern capital systems (Daniell, 2000, pp. 3–4.)

In these one-sided perceptions of reality, 'risk' is elevated to the status of a kind of supernatural force dictating what humans can and cannot do.

In reality, though, human beings tend to reduce risk over time because they increase their knowledge of their surroundings and enhance their ability to control the future. Of course, people and institutions face risk. Life is not risk-free. But what is new about today is a subjective *perception* that life is more risky.

Consultants often employ the idea that risk management is an opportunity, or confusingly, that 'risk' is an opportunity for companies. Are they saying that companies should pump more resources into radical innovation, or make bold investments in conditions of uncertainty? Not quite. They are not advocating bold risk-taking.

Rather, consultants cannot market risk management by going into the boardroom and asking managers to avoid risk. That is not feasible, because of the nature of dynamic change in the world. Companies have to take risks and embrace uncertainty in order to progress – although Part Two will show how this has been severely compromised, as companies approach markets far more conservatively, through the obsession with customer loyalty, brands, incremental innovation and safe forms of growth through mergers and acquisitions.

Consultants suggest that if companies manage risk – if they protect themselves against loss of reputation and brand dilution, ensure greater stability in financial results and avoid surprises, make sure customers do not desert them, make sure their IT systems do not crash, avoid fraud, and so on – this provides an 'opportunity' for them. It might help them protect their brand. Or, it might enhance shareholder perceptions of them. Or, it might help them create trust among consumers.

A plethora of new initiatives

The rise of risk management, then, has little to do with the ubiquitous 'globalization' or new technology. Risk management has become elevated because society is more worried about the downside of risk, and managers are more worried about appearing to be reckless and irresponsible in running a corporation. Managers feel that, if a mistake were to happen, they would be unable to put their side of the story. Better to be safe than sorry.

Senior managers therefore have new demands today – demands for information and assurances about risk. As a result, corporations have overseen an unprecedented number of initiatives under the risk management umbrella.

Beginning in the early 1990s, corporations everywhere implemented risk controls, attempted to audit risk exposures on a regular basis, and interviewed people in key positions on their attitudes to risk. They tried to 'embed' risk management into company culture so all employees could be conscious of where mistakes can happen. They encouraged employees to read hefty documents on their policies toward risk and risk management. They set up 'risk working groups', and 'risk task forces', special panels to review risk. They appointed CROs for the first time. They set up new information flows and lines of reporting from board level to business unit. They attempted to turn risk management departments into internal risk consulting units for the whole company.

Companies attempted to quantify their 'risk appetite', i.e. how willing they are to take risk, and their 'risk tolerance', i.e. how much money they have in the bank to tolerate losses. They spent more time estimating the 'maximum possible loss' their business could face.

Risk managers have spent more energy 'converting the worst fears of the business' into financial terms so that they can be assigned a priority for risk evaluation and control. Again, all this activity is new to the last 10 years or so. It did not exist before. Going into the new millennium, major corporations had implemented 'enterprise-wide' risk management frameworks.[5]

The rise of crisis management, a kind of elder sister to the risk management concept, also captures well the defensiveness of managers today. In recent years, practitioners have put forward the notion that, in managing a crisis, managers have to consider that 'perceptions are reality'. What does this mean?

In a crisis, such as a health scare, there is often considerable confusion about the source of a problem or risk, and who is to blame. The new view today is that it does not matter whether corporations are in the right or the wrong. Managers should just come out and start apologizing left right and centre, to 'restore trust'.

If the public 'feels' that a corporation might be to blame for, say, a strange and mysterious illness, then this feeling, or perception, is what matters, not the root cause. 'Perceptions are reality.' To safeguard the reputation of the corporation, managers should start apologizing, and begin to 'build links' with the community. 'Successful crisis management', according to one expert, 'is about being seen by stakeholders to take the appropriate action and heard to say the appropriate words' (see Larkin, 2001).

A whole new *etiquette* of managing a crisis has emerged. Like in the world of ethics, the key is to be seen to be doing the right thing. When something goes wrong, companies are increasingly exhorted to admit they were responsible, independent of the truth. For example, US drinks corporation Coca-Cola initially denied it was responsible for contamination of its drink in Belgium in 1999. It came under fire for not admitting it was responsible, despite little evidence. It was seen as 'arrogant'. On the other hand, those companies that do claim responsibility immediately, and enact an elaborate crisis management plan, receive great kudos.

The rise of risk management is a very contradictory development. During the 1990s, corporate risk managers began to investigate how they should put in place new frameworks. What they tended to find through these investigations, however, was that risk was *already being well managed* within the corporation. That is, employees, in different departments, were aware of potential hazards and uncertainties, and were mindful of them. Through the daily routine of their jobs, and over time, they had accumulated knowledge of the type of things that could go wrong.[6]

Nor has industry as a whole faced greater exposure to risk over the same period as risk management has been elevated. Risk managers do not report an increase in total risk exposure for their company. What tends to happen in the course of business is that particular risk exposures increase, while others decrease.

For instance, according to the risk manager of a chemicals company, the move the company made from base chemicals into fine chemicals increased the risk of liability. For the first time, the company's products were entering the human body. But at the same time, the company had moved into fine chemicals precisely because the base chemical industry was considered too cyclical and volatile, in terms of its economics of prices and supply and demand. So, other types of risk were being reduced at the same time. The company was not facing an overall increased exposure to risk. The hope was that if the company could get on top of the liability issue, it would reduce its risk.[7]

There are of course many *particular* areas where risk exposure has increased, either in particular industries, or in particular business areas. Litigation is an example, especially for particular industries – the US tobacco industry comes to mind. With the rise of e-business, companies have to be wary about, say, the risks posed by hacking. But industry overall does not face increased exposure to risk. Yet risk management somehow continues to escalate in importance.

The issue of reputation risk

It is interesting that, in recent times, corporations have reported that 'loss of reputation' is the greatest risk facing their organization. Observers have noted that corporations pay far more attention to risks to 'intangible' assets, such as reputation and brand. In the recent past, corporations might have reported that physical risks such as fire were their biggest problem.

The new focus on reputation and intangible risk reflects a few trends. First, it reflects that corporations, as they have increased their risk management skills, and their wealth, can cope pretty well with even the most severe tangible risks, such as fire. Corporations have learnt to control and reduce many risks. Also, multinational corporations are on the whole very cash rich. With several billions of spare cash sitting in the bank, there are not many hazards that can actually cause them much damage.

More substantially, the new concern about reputation captures the peculiar new relationship between corporations and the world today. Corporate managers sense there is more mistrust of big business. One might say that the overall reputation of big business is at an all-time low. But managers feel there is little they can do about it. This is why, in the reputation discussion, the dominant theme is that once a company suffers a loss of reputation, there is little they can do to recover.

The new obsession with reputation expresses a sense of powerlessness among corporations in their relationship with the world. There is a sense that if a crisis did occur, managers would stand little chance in putting their side of the story, even though a corporation may be falsely accused. Of course, crisis management, as mentioned earlier, is in vogue, and there is no shortage of advice from consultants on how firms should cope. Yet the dominant theme here, again, is that 'perceptions are reality'. In other words, there is little point in appealing to reason. Companies need to accept that society is right.

A sense of powerlessness has not always been in evidence. In the 1970s, *Fortune* magazine ran an article on the US oil company Mobil, and how it dealt with various social debates about the oil industry back then. It noted the 'aggressiveness and consistency with which it speaks out in defense of its interests, the interests of the oil industry, and what it perceives to be the national interest'.

Mobil, the article noted, had been in a variety of rows, 'complaining loudly about inaccuracies and distortions on TV news shows', among other things. The chairman and CEO, Rawleigh Warner, Jr, was quoted as saying that 'people know that if they take a swipe at us, we will fight back' (see *Fortune*, September 1976).

Whether or not one agrees with this strategy, it certainly provides an interesting contrast with today's mood. This kind of combative language seems a throwback to another era. Corporations today have very little appetite to 'fight back'. Today, managers aim to 'listen to society' at all times and establish 'dialogue' with stakeholders. Rather than fighting back, managers would probably prefer to go on an ethical training course. In the oil business, rather than fighting back, corporations have already re-branded themselves with new environmentally sensitive logos, and invite NGOs to their board meetings.

In the past, not every firm was like Mobil. But the point is that corporate managers did not feel so vulnerable in their relationship with the world around them. They felt they could express their self-interest, put their side of the story, and go on the offensive. Today, corporations are far more defensive. If a corporate reputation were to come under siege, they feel less able to put across their side of the story.

Risk management in the abstract

It is worth looking more deeply at risk management, first from a technical point of view, and then from a historical perspective, to back up some of the points made above.

From a technical point of view, risk management usually is understood as a process. It involves well-defined stages, such as identifying, assessing, controlling and transferring or hedging risks.

To take a simplified and fictitious example: a firm in the chemicals industry might assess the risk of a fire. It may conclude, going on its history, and that of the industry, that a fire might occur once every 30 years. It could try to control the risk by training staff to deal with materials. It may put in place measures to control a fire should one break out, such as water sprinklers, and make sure the fire brigade is immediately contacted. Finally, it may feel uncomfortable in paying for the damage a fire could create, and may want to insure the risk through an insurance policy. Or, it may work out that it is cheaper to retain the risk by self-insuring, taking the chance that it would pay for the fire, but saving money on insurance.[8]

Overall, the rationale of traditional risk management is to assess how and why a company experiences losses, with a view to minimizing those losses. These losses could take place in a variety of areas within a corporation, and the above process can be applied to all sorts of working activities.

Risk management draws on a number of useful distinctions and tools. An important distinction is between passive and speculative risks. The practice of risk management has traditionally involved dealing with those non-strategic risks that do not have potential for upside – *passive* risks, or hazards. Such risks include a fire burning down a building, or breach of a regulation leading to a fine. Passive risks are not central to running a business. They do not fall into the area of strategic decision-making. Firms are not going to advance in their marketplace by controlling these kinds of risk.

Speculative risks, by contrast, involve those risks that have both potential for upside and downside. Often called business risks, or entrepreneurial risks, these are the risks that companies take when competing in markets. A classic example is a new product launch. A new product can either be a runaway success, or consumers can vote with their wallets and refuse to buy, meaning that an upfront investment in product development and marketing could be wasted.

Another typically employed distinction is between high frequency, low severity risks, and low frequency, high severity risks. The former refer to losses that occur on a regular basis, but are manageable and do not cripple firms financially. Such risks can be controlled, because they are subject to a pattern. The latter refer to unexpected catastrophes, which cannot easily be anticipated, and tend to cause much more damage to firms. An earthquake could be an example, or, for a drug firm, a drug that causes an unexpected fatal illness and puts the firm out of business.

So, risk management in the technical sense can be a very useful tool for assessing, controlling and hedging risk. It has made sense for corporations to employ specialist risk managers to do this.

The problem today is, first, a heightened sensitivity to, and exaggeration of, risk exposure. Managers share a society-wide perception that there is more risk and uncertainty out there, and that they need to take greater precautions. They feel that organizations are more exposed to risk. At the same time, managers are far more worried about appearing to be irresponsible. From this situation, risk management has been hugely elevated in importance, and given a status that it does not really deserve. Rather than accept a degree of risk and uncertainty, companies have gone overboard with the risk management concept. Rather than being a useful tool, it starts to become an unnecessary self-regulation. Through the elevation and institutionalization of risk management procedures, companies end up becoming far too cautious.

Corporate risk management – a brief history

It is important to realize that companies have always faced all sorts of hazards and commercial uncertainties in the past. Many were far greater than those faced today. But firms did not feel the need to elevate risk management into a major, generalized management tool. It was only in the 1990s that risk became such an area of anxiety, and risk management gained such an inflated importance.

One of the earliest references to the term risk management was in 1956 in the United States. Russell Gallagher, the manager of a corporate insurance department, wrote an article in the *Harvard Business Review* (Gallagher, 1956). He wrote that 'in the postwar battle for tighter cost control, many managements have been making greater efforts to cut down the effects of accidents or damage to the company's physical assets'.

Gallagher suggested that risk management might become more of a discipline within the corporation, perhaps under the control of a full-time risk manager. It should become a more scientific, coordinated process. He put forward ideas for analysing risks, averting them, insuring them, and suggested that risk managers have more access to information to do the job, from executive travel plans, to production budgets and sales figures.

Various discussions of risk sprung up in the 1950s, but they tended to be highly mathematical in nature. Often, probability theory was applied to try to predict how businesses would fare in volatile markets. It was not until the early 1970s that risk management started to gain a wider purchase in business, particularly in the United States.

Managers began to react to the more volatile economic climate. In the early 1970s, the Bretton Woods agreement – the system where the exchange rates of currencies were pegged to each other – collapsed, and rates began to fluctuate. The oil crisis of 1973, where oil prices shot up, led to further volatility in the economic environment. Managers then started to look more closely at the practice of risk assessment. Risk rating and risk assessment consulting services emerged, mostly concentrating on 'country risk' – how economic volatility in overseas countries could affect western corporations (see Ting, 1988).

The term risk management gained more currency in the 1970s. The first educational qualifications in risk management were provided in 1973 in the United States. The US Professional Insurance Buyers Association changed its name to the Risk and Insurance Management Society (RIMS) in 1975 (see Vaughan, 1997).

Non-financial corporations began to buy financial derivatives in the early 1970s. These were financial risk management tools that allowed them to hedge adverse variables, such as currency movements. The emergence of the modern corporate treasury department in the 1970s was motivated in part by the greater need to hedge exposure to volatile financial markets (see Harris-Jones and Bergin, 1998, p. 11).

However, non-financial corporations did not develop risk management departments, or institutionalize risk management practices, as a response to these developments. A study of non-financial corporations in 1973 found that fewer than 25% claimed to have established an in-house risk assessment capability, and only around 10% of respondents used outside risk consultants. Another survey in 1975 found that 'few multinational corporations have developed systematic approaches for determining the political fortunes of their overseas markets'. Banks, by contrast, were more advanced. Chase Manhattan set up a 'country risk committee' in the United States in 1975, for example (Ting, 1988).

In fact, in the 1970s, risk management was not really a term in common use. For advice on risk issues, executives would consult widely with a number of different constituencies, including public officials, diplomats and academics. Nevertheless, even this was done on an *ad hoc* basis. For non-financial corporations, the move to formalize risk management practices and manage risk in a centralized, systematic way had to wait until two decades later.

More intensive risk management practices – if they were called that – tended to be confined to particular industries, such as energy, nuclear power and transport, or particular projects, such as oil exploration or space travel. In these areas the need for extra management supervision stemmed from the operational complexities and safety requirements particular to those institutions and projects.

In the 1980s, attention turned to the issue of political risk. A main catalyst was the overthrow of the Shah in Iran in 1979. In the process, multinationals lost an estimated US $1bn in corporate assets through the Iranian revolution. According to some reports, around 75% of all multinational corporations lost nearly all their Iran-based assets. At that point, some began to argue that multinationals should establish in-house political risk divisions. But the rise of risk management was still a decade away.

By the end of the 1980s, and the fall of the Berlin Wall, it was looking as if many longstanding political conflicts around the world were winding down. Commentators at the time noted that many corporations were closing their political risk departments. As a practice and a discipline that could have wider business application, risk management was far from being institutionalized in very large corporations (see Raddock, 1986, and Ting, 1988).

Even the establishment of risk management departments toward the end of the 1980s had more to do with applying internal cost-cutting principles to insurance departments. Firms wanted to lower their insurance premiums. They could do that by demonstrating greater responsibility for managing risk.[9]

For example, in the United States, a global electronics company changed the insurance department's name to risk management in 1988. The new objective was to minimize resources to the area of insurance management, to cut back on staff, and to outsource insurance affairs to third parties.

A French IT and telecoms firm set up a formal risk management department in 1990, merging its environmental protection and loss control functions. The main rationale was to cut costs and further self-insure, the definition of which is to cut back on insurance purchase and establish an internal provision for loss.

A large European drugs firm established a formal risk management department in 1991. The main rationale was to improve the efficiency of the firm's insurance buying, improve relationships with insurance brokers, understand risk on a global basis, and bring down the cost of insurance purchase.[10]

Change in the 1990s

What began to happen in the early to mid-1990s was qualitatively different, however. During the 1990s, corporations set in motion a huge number of initiatives in the area of risk management, for reasons mentioned earlier in the chapter. For the first time, firms were developing enterprise-wide frameworks for dealing with risk and uncertainty. Also, risk management was becoming a regulatory and compliance issue for the first time through the corporate governance codes.

Take a few examples. In the mid-to-late 1990s, at a British pharmaceutical firm members of the board were asked to think of a major risk that worried them. They were then charged with championing the reduction of that particular risk, and asked to report back on their progress. These risks included treasury exposure, product design and recall, patent infringement, supply chain, fraud and political risk.

The company also looked into setting up a 'risk review' panel. The panel would be made up of peers, consultants, and others with an interest in risk management. The major aim was to examine ways to embed risk management through the organization. Here, risk evaluation procedures would have to be embedded in all key business decisions. This so-called 'top down, bottom up' approach would mean that senior management would be responsible initially for setting the agenda in risk management, and then line managers and ordinary members of staff would report back on potential hazards facing the company.[11]

In 1994 Marks & Spencer, the UK retailer, set up a new audit committee to audit all aspects of company operations on a regular basis. This covered interviewing the treasury director on a regular basis to ask him about his handling of derivatives, and regular interviews with the insurance manager to discover how insurance was being bought and how risk was being managed in the organization.[12]

It is striking that corporations everywhere during the mid-1990s were conducting very similar initiatives in the area of risk management. A leading European car manufacturer established a 'risk task force' to 'quantify those risks large enough to trouble the company'. A global US diversified consumer products company set up a 'risk working group' in 1996 to pool together their risk management disciplines in areas such as insurance, currency risk, credit risk, the risk of fluctuations in the company pension fund, and the impact of earnings volatility on the balance sheet.[13]

Risk management departments themselves began to change to address the new needs of senior management. The whole area of insurance became less important. Risk management departments in the United States, the United Kingdom and Europe were developing into internal risk consulting practices.

In 1998, the department of a prominent European telecommunications company changed its name from Group Risk and Insurance to Risk and Insurance Solutions, and issued a revised mission statement to raise its profile. The department began to promote itself as a 'centre of excellence' throughout the company and create a more risk-aware culture. Individual project managers were encouraged to call on the centre for risk mitigation procedures. At the same time, the department began to coordinate itself better with the human resources, health and safety, security, internal audit, environmental and legal departments.[14]

The attempt to insure speculative risk

A new trend is that managers, and the insurance industry, want to insure the downside of speculative risks. Previously, these risks were accepted as part of doing business. Such risks include R&D failure in the drug industry, and the chance that a film could flop at the box office. Other areas include damage to reputation and brand, intellectual property infringement and technological obsolescence.

A recent survey interviewed 30 organizations in the financial and business services sector to examine changing forms of commercial insurance. Over two-thirds of respondents acknowledged that corporations were demanding insurance cover for the possibility that new products could fail. This was particularly high in the pharmaceutical industry, but other industries mentioned included heavy industry, transportation, movies, consumer electronics, toys, space, oil, energy and telecommunications. With regard to the drug industry, one respondent suggested that 'the biggest risk is that a firm invests massively in R&D but a competitor beats them to market with a similar product' (Denton Wilde Sapte, 2000).

Elsewhere, insurance professionals have racked their brains to discover whether 'damage to reputation' can be insured against. In one study, an insurance broker considered whether it could link insurance cover to negative headlines in the media. If a company received, say, ten negative headlines in a particular incident, the broker debated whether the insurance company could pay out a certain amount of money.[15] Also, it has not been unusual for insurance brokers to receive the most bizarre corporate requests for insurance. One insurance broker that the author talked to received a telephone call from a major global corporation. The request? Can you insure 'loss of monopoly position?'.[16]

Speculative risks cannot be transferred in their entirety to the insurance markets. (The insurance broker turned down the above request.) That would actually negate the principle of the market economy. Sure, companies would never make any losses, because those losses would be constantly insured. That may sound a good idea, but to insure those losses, the insurer would demand a very high premium. Insurance companies usually work on the principle of the 'law of large numbers', or the 'socialization of risk'. They collect lots of premiums from many entities to cover the probability that at least a few of them will make claims over and above the individual premiums they pay.

Individual speculative risks, however, such as product launch failure, cannot be spread easily in this way. As a result, an insurance firm would charge a great deal of money to cover itself for the risk. In turn, that would be very expensive for the company trying to transfer the risk. It would also mean that the company would be denying itself the upside potential of any risk it might take, because any financial success would be offset by such a high insurance premium. It may receive US $1bn dollars in revenues from a new product, say, but end up paying out US $2bn in insurance premiums.

Some members of the insurance community have experimented with the idea of 'earnings insurance', a policy that would cover the total earnings volatility of a corporation – effectively insuring the bottom line. Ultimately, such requests take the risk management concept too far, and generally are considered too silly by members of the corporate and insurance community. They get rejected as executives and managers remind themselves that some risk-taking is necessary and not everything can be hedged away. But the fact that things have gone this far is indicative of the wider obsession with the downside of risk (see Denton Wilde Sapte, 2000).

Weird and wonderful hedging markets have sprung up in recent years, closely connected to the new risk management obsession. One of the stranger hedging markets to develop is that of weather derivatives, a market Enron was heavily involved in building up. A survey conducted in 2001 reported that 3264 weather derivative contracts had been entered into since the first contract was signed in 1997.[17]

Weather derivative contracts act as a form of insurance to cover the risk that unexpected weather conditions, such as unexpected temperatures, rainfall, wind or snow, disrupt business conditions. Some firms have discovered that there is a correlation between unexpected weather and their revenues.

The major buyers have been energy companies, which lose out, say, if winters are warmer than expected. Many other firms have now bought weather derivatives, including those in agriculture, beer and soft drinks, car wash, commercial real estate, film studios, golf course operations, snow removal and theme parks.[18]

For example, in 2001 The Rock Garden restaurant in Covent Garden, London, bought a weather derivative to protect it against the risk that bad weather in the spring would put customers off from eating there. If a certain number of days between March and June fall below a certain temperature, the restaurant would receive pay-outs from an insurance company.

A few years before, the wine bar chain Corney & Barrow, based in the City of London, entered into a similar agreement. In 2002, it was reported that Heineken, the Dutch brewing company, was seeking to hedge its exposure to rainy Saturdays, on the basis that bad weather on that day upset its sales.[19]

Elsewhere, the world of risk management meets the arcane world of financial engineering, as companies work out elaborate new ways to hedge risk and avoid volatility. Here, every kind of risk possibility has been mapped out, it seems. For instance, companies can try to fix the price of raising capital in the future, if something unexpected were to happen. One such deal involved the French tyre maker Michelin. It signed a contract whereby it would be allowed to access capital at a certain price if gross domestic product (GDP) fell in the countries in which it was operating. Such a fall in GDP, it was anticipated, would affect its financial position because of a slowdown in the economy.

Many other kinds of risk transfer deals now take place. For example, making a movie involves risks. There are no guarantees that films will score at the box office. So some studios have struck deals with investors and insurers to transfer the risk of the film not turning out to be a success, to investors and insurers.

In a recent example, the insurer American Re Capital Markets struck a deal with Steven Spielberg's Dreamworks studio to raise US $450m to be spread over 10 years. The deal guarantees that films' production costs in the studio will be met. Instead of the studio worrying about whether the film will be a success at the box office, it knows it will get cash over time from investors (who, for their part, are making an investment in a bond). In this way, the insurers and investors take the risk that films made will be a success. This technique cannot guarantee the success of films, of course. It cannot get people into the cinema. It just means that investors and insurers take the risk of failure. Investors are dependent on the revenues of movies at the box office for getting their money back and interest payments.

In 1998, Destination Films raised US $100m on this basis to make 10 films. However, two films were never released, and the others were flops at the box office. They only raised $65m, and $300,000 in video rentals. Destination Films filed for bankruptcy in 2001 and the insurance companies had to pay the investors what they were owed.[20]

Conclusion

The rise of risk management cannot be explained with reference to the 'usual suspects' – globalization, the new economy, increased competition, more active stakeholders, and so on. The rise of risk management again illustrates the characteristics of today's self-regulation. More anxious corporations now relate to a more anxious society. Managers share a society-wide perception that there is more risk and uncertainty out there. However, they are also on the defensive, and are worried about appearing to be irresponsible. As a result, risk management has become hugely elevated in recent times.

The rise of risk management is a contradictory development. In reality, corporations manage risk pretty well. But senior managers are on the defensive. Worried about making mistakes, they have institutionalized a whole range of new risk management initiatives and frameworks. In the process, however, a cautious approach to risk has become institutionalized. Rather than accept a rational level of risk and uncertainty, managers feel they need assurances all the time in the course of the business and in their decision-making.

The next chapter examines what happens when a more regulated approach impacts finance and the allocation of resources. In recent years, relationships between managers of companies, and the owners, the shareholders, have become far more strained. Levels of trust are at an all-time low. The result has been the re-regulation of this relationship and finance and investment.

Managers are now obliged to manage in the economic interests of shareholders – managing for shareholder value. The frameworks that managers have now put in place under this banner are really a new form of financial self-regulation. As a result, the whole area of investment and growth is now subject to far more self-restraint than in the past. This is the area where self-regulation is leading to the more insidious caution and restraint.

Notes

1. Much of this chapter is based on primary research. This includes 14 in-depth interviews with risk managers of major multinational corporations on the history of risk management over the 1990s, written up in Pickford (2001). It also includes personal correspondence with the risk management industry when the author was editor of *Risk Financier* magazine (EMAP), the magazine devoted to the convergence of the insurance and financial markets, from 1997 to 2000. In addition, the author has carried out several pieces of research in the risk management area for a range of institutions, which involved further correspondence with risk managers and the financial and insurance industry. The author has also written numerous articles on risk management for the trade press.
2. This is a phrase that gained common parlance in the mid-1990s.
3. Correspondence with risk managers.
4. Correspondence with a risk management consultant.
5. See Hunt (2001b) for a written summary on these initiatives.
6. Correspondence with corporate risk managers.
7. Correspondence with risk manager of Dutch chemicals corporation.
8. There is a whole literature on the technical aspects of risk management. See, for example, Vaughan (1997).
9. Correspondence with corporate risk managers.
10. Correspondence with risk managers at a US electronics company, a French IT and telecoms company and a European drugs firm.
11. Correspondence with risk manager, British pharmaceuticals firm.
12. Correspondence with risk manager, Marks & Spencer.
13. Correspondence with risk manager, European car manufacturer, and a US diversified consumer products company.
14. Correspondence with risk manager, European telecommunications firm.
15. Correspondence with risk management consultant.
16. Correspondence with insurance broker.
17. See Press Release, 'The Weather Risk Management Association Releases Results of Industry-Wide Survey', June 29, 2001, www.artemis.bm and also see www.wrma.org

18. See *Risk Financier* magazine, December 1998, p. 1.
19. See details of such deals on www.artemis.bm, a portal devoted to the Alternative Risk Transfer (ART) market.
20. For details of these two deals, see the paper, 'Extending the Boundaries of Securitisation', Professor Rae Weston (2001), available on the Internet.

4

Managing for Shareholder Value: The New Financial Risk Aversion

Relationships between managers and shareholders have come under considerable strain in recent times. Both groups seem more intolerant of risk and uncertainty. Managers, as the previous chapter argued, are more anxious about risk issues. Investors, for their part, seem to want more assurances about the risks and uncertainties of their investments. A call has gone out that corporations disclose more information about risk, for instance, and elsewhere, in the name of accountability, shareholders want increasing assurances that quarterly financial targets will be met. In many cases where shareholders resort to litigation, they seem unable to accept that there are never solid guarantees with investment. While institutional shareholders want to see a rising share price, to increase the value of their investment, like every group in society, they are more preoccupied with issues of risk.

A sign that management–shareholder relations are more strained is the phenomenon of chief executive officer (CEO) churn, widely researched and discussed. As many have noted, the average tenure of the CEO is plummeting fast. Although mergers and acquisitions are an important cause, boards are more likely to react to business performance problems by offering up the CEO as some kind of sacrificial lamb to shareholders, in an attempt to win back their favour. In the early 1990s in the United States, some kind of watershed seemed to be passed when an unprecedented string of CEO sackings took place in *Fortune* 500 companies, including General Motors, Compaq and IBM.[1]

In this climate, over the last decade or so financial management, and there-fore strategy, investment and growth, have become subject to new informal rules and guidelines, collectively known as 'managing for shareholder value'. US consultants Stern Stewart suggest that

> today's CEOs know that if they fail in a big way, whether from malfeasance, misfeasance or nonfeasance, they're out... Hence all the corporate trumpeting of shareholder value initiatives. As any reader of annual reports knows, the mantra of 'managing for shareholder value' has become a sine qua non of corporate political correctness (Ehrbar, 1998, p. 15).

Stern Stewart use the phrase 'political correctness'. 'Management correct-ness' may be a better substitute. What became noticeable about the 1990s was the way that, under the banner of managing for shareholder value, growth it-self became subject to a kind of strict 'management correctness'.

Relatively suddenly, a new orthodoxy swept the business world. Managers told themselves they must manage in the best economic interests of share-holders. They must concentrate on so-called 'core competences' and not di-versify into areas in which they have no knowledge or expertise. They must only invest above the cost of capital, a hurdle rate that embodies share-holder expectations of risk and return. They must only grow if it is 'capital efficient' to do so. They must focus on generating cash and avoid tying up capital in the core business. They must not divert 'free cash flow', another term for surplus capital, back into 'unnecessary' or 'inefficient' productive investment. Rather, far better to return the cash to shareholders, who can invest it themselves in financial assets where returns may be more certain. Managers should not be 'empire builders' – supposed egotists who pursue growth in an irresponsible, reckless way without regard to questions of capi-tal efficiency. Relatively suddenly, finance growth and strategy has become subject to more informal guidelines. It has become a more self-regulated sphere.

Shareholders want greater accountability over the 'efficiency' in which capital is allocated. But elsewhere, mistrust between managers and sharehold-ers, and the general discomfort for risk and uncertainty that has infiltrated both groups, expresses itself in other forms of accountability initiatives.

Shareholders and the analyst community in the 1990s began to demand guarantees that managers could accurately forecast quarterly earnings, or profits. Managers, for their part, became newly obsessed with hitting targets. They were worried that failure to hit targets would be interpreted as a form of poor management. They also had the knowledge that the stock market does not like surprises, such as a missed financial target, and can often quickly dump the stock, leading to a plummeting stock price.

The problem with today's more regulated approach to investment is that managers have institutionalized a kind of business version of the precautionary principle. Here, managers are more reluctant to invest unless they can quantify the precise returns and risks. A major trend is that if they cannot guarantee returns, managers just return the cash to shareholders, who, in the theory, might be able to invest it elsewhere for a more guaranteed return. This is now known as a sound form of governance.

The vehicle for doing this is the share buyback, or share repurchase. Companies buy back their own shares from investors and reduce the amount in circulation, a reverse of the practice where they issue new shares to raise new cash. In the United States alone, around a trillion dollars was returned to shareholders in this way in the second half of the 1990s.[2] Elsewhere, share buybacks became popular in the United Kingdom and in Europe.

Corporations have always given a portion of profits back to shareholders in the form of dividends. But share buybacks are different. Handing back huge amounts of cash to shareholders is rationalized under new informal rules that, if companies are not sure about the returns they will receive by investing in projects, it is far better to return cash to shareholders, who might be able to invest it elsewhere for more guaranteed returns in financial assets.

In the jargon, this upholds the idea of 'capital efficiency', but really embodies the new intolerance for taking risk today. As the management writer Gary Hamel argued polemically, 'fresh out of ideas? No compelling investment opportunities? No problem! Take the cash being produced by today's business model and return it to shareholders' (Hamel, 2000, p. 40).

Elsewhere, managers have few qualms about stating their risk-averse motives for such action. For instance, Jack Welch, former chief executive of US firm General Electric, indicated that buying back stock is a safer way to create shareholder value, compared with taking a 'wild swing' on an acquisition or investing in new technology – in other words, a safer way than taking a risk (see Kennedy, 2000, p. 60).

The early attempts to try to regulate the manager–shareholder relationship were made in the 1980s in the United States. Then, financiers and financial economists bemoaned the 'agency' problem that they believed had arisen between managers and shareholders.

The issue of agency referred to a situation where shareholders could not control or discipline managers to act in their economic interests. In their view, managers were not using shareholders' funds (a strange concept itself, to be explored later) in an efficient way, that is, a way that could earn a high return. Financiers attempted to address this through financial innovation. An example was the leveraged buy-out (LBO).

LBOs took place when financiers bought firms in order to shake them up and boost their market value. They bought up the shares of firms and encouraged managers to become owners by buying shares too. They would take more control to restructure companies, sometimes but not always engaging in asset stripping activity, in an effort to increase market value.

Debt was used to buy shares, and for the first time was conceived in terms of an outside discipline on managers to be more efficient with resources, because they were forced to pay back high interest repayments. Financiers, such as the firm Kohlberg Kravis Roberts (KKR), were of course motivated by the prospect of high returns. But they saw themselves as liberating shareholders by exercising far more control over management behaviour to act in shareholder interests. (See Baker and Smith (1998) for a good overview on KKR).

The LBO did not become a typical vehicle to exercise control and regulate managers in the interests of shareholders, however. Its use in the United States peaked in the late 1980s. In fact, it was only typically used in mature industries that were struggling to grow, rather than more dynamic hi-tech industries.

During the 1990s, however, managers in the United States and Britain, and increasingly elsewhere, began to pay far more attention to the economic interests of shareholders. They established new management frameworks based on the concept of managing for shareholder value. The result has been a more rule-bound, self-regulated approach to corporate finance, investment and growth.

This idea of financial self-regulation may initially seem odd, given the image of the 1990s. For example, how can this be a period of regulation, caution and restraint, when stock markets and economies appeared to be booming? Chapter 8, Fear of Growth, will return to some of the issues in more depth. The point here is that the 1990s were not all they were cracked up to be. It is important to make a distinction between activity in the financial economy – investment in financial assets such as shares and their circulation, and the activities of financial institutions such as investment banks – and activity in the real economy, the production and consumption of goods and services. Certainly, the 1990s experienced high levels of liquidity in the financial economy, soaring bull markets and furious financial activity. But the performance in the real economy was not that impressive. Investment in real assets has been poor, and a more regulated approach to corporate finance plays an important part. After all, the 1990s was the time when organic growth – growth through genuine real investment – went out of fashion. Of course, there have been pockets of real growth and dynamism in the economy in recent times, such as in IT and telecommunications. But even here, notions of genuine growth have to be carefully separated from the financially-engineered 'lite' type of growth. A company such as WorldCom, it is now realized, was not as dynamic as first thought. By growing through acquisitions, and boosting its share price, it might have acquired the appearance of dynamism, but the reality was something different.

Perceptions and critics of managing for shareholder value

The notion of managing for shareholder value has had its critics. Many believe that managers should run corporations in the interests of other stakeholders, such as employees, or focus more on the customers rather than shareholders. Often, there is a perception that managing for shareholder interests leads firms to focus one-sidedly on downsizing and cost-cutting. Workers are the main victims in this scenario.

Since the collapse of the 1990s bull markets, and the string of US business scandals, more criticism has come forward. Not only is managing for shareholder value built on a flawed concept – the concept of rational and efficient markets, critics allege – it has led to a system of perverse incentives and distorted the whole capitalist system.

As one commentator put it, 'the boom and bust in the stock market, the rise and fall of the technology companies, the massive sums wasted during the telecoms boom and the ensuing corporate scandals have all followed more or less directly from the indiscriminate pursuit of shareholder value' (Chancellor, 2002).

Stock options have received special criticism. The idea behind stock options was supposedly that managers would manage in the interests of shareholders, because for the first time their own pay would be linked, or aligned, to use the jargon, with rises in the company's stock price. When stock prices rose, the shareholders benefited but managers could sell the options and benefit personally as well.

Through the system of stock options, it was hoped, executives would have an incentive to manage in the best interests of shareholders. Stock options were therefore seen as a part of managing for shareholder value.

However, in recent years it has been fashionable to allege that stock options have encouraged managers to manipulate company profit figures. In this story, managers have encouraged the stock market to believe firms were in better shape than they actually were, to bid up the stock price. Thus managers would receive high pay and bonuses through the stock option system. Shareholders suffered from distorted valuations that fooled them into investing even more. When the market lost confidence in these high valuations, shareholders saw billions wiped off the value of their investments. Among those critical of this alleged behaviour has been Alan Greenspan, Chairman of the US Federal Reserve, in a speech given in Spring 2002. Or as one put it, 'the alliance between shareholders and managers has faltered on the greed of the latter' (Chancellor, 2002).

Of course, many executives did pocket a great deal of money through the stock option system. But stock options are only one aspect of the concept of managing for shareholder value. They have received a lot of focus because they appear to confirm more general perceptions that executives are greedy and conniving. The real trend in the business world is not that a tiny minority of people have become very rich, or are any more or less greedy than in the past. What is genuinely new about the last decade is the willingness of corporations to subject financial and investment behaviour to greater self-regulation, caution and restraint. This has a macro expression, explored in Chapter 8. When the 1990s is taken as a whole, America's economic performance was the worst on record since the 1930s, in terms of average annual increases in real GDP, which measures total government and business investment, and consumer spending, in the economy.

Managing for shareholder value – a new financial self-regulation

To understand why managing for shareholder value is a new financial self-regulation, we have to backtrack several steps.

The history of the shareholder value concept is bound up with two, inter-related developments: the history of a set of ideas, developed in the academic field of financial economics; and the emergence of new ideas of accountability and transparency in the late 1970s and 1980s, which were taken far more seriously in the 1990s.

In practice these two areas have considerably blurred. Financial economics embodies a desire for regulation within it. For example, in the 1970s, financial economists themselves turned their attention to agency theory, the fact that managers were not subject to discipline and regulation in the way they wanted them to be.

The influence of financial economics

Financial economics is a relatively new branch of economics that properly emerged in the 1950s. Its subject of study is the stock market. It addresses issues such as the value and price of securities and the decision-making process of investors. Whereas classical economists dealt with much broader questions of 'value', such as the value of physical commodities in market economies, financial economists deal with the narrower question of the valuation of companies, and the value and price of shares traded on stock markets.

An important area of financial economics relates to corporate finance: how financial managers make investment and financing decisions. In this area, the dominant issue under consideration is how corporations can manage their finances, and overall strategies, so that they appreciate the economic interests of shareholders. The economic interest of the shareholder is the increased value of their investment. Managers should aim to grow the valuation of their company and increase the values of their shares as traded on the stock market.

In the 1950s, academics working in the field of financial economics started to explore how corporate investment and financing decisions could affect the valuation of shares. For example, in 1951, the US academic Joel Dean in the book *Capital Budgeting* recommended that firms make investment decisions by looking to the capital markets for an appropriate hurdle rate (a rate of return that companies hope to achieve when making an investment). That is, they should take shareholder interests into account when thinking about rates of return. In 1958, two academics, Franco Modigliani and Merton Miller, published a paper called 'The cost of capital, corporation finance, and the theory of investment'. They argued that the market value of a firm as traded on the stock market is not affected by the way a firm finances itself, its particular mix of debt and equity, or the capital structure.[3]

Financial economics took a new direction in the late 1970s and early 1980s. What began to happen was that the field of financial economics started to assimilate a society-wide desire for more regulation.

The 1970s was the era when many of the regulations and self-regulations in place today began in embryo form. The business ethics movement began then, ostensibly as a reaction to the Watergate scandal, as described earlier. Early notions of corporate governance were developing, even though the term was not in use. Risk management began to take off, although in muted form. Institutions such as the OECD insisted that companies adopt new codes of conduct for the first time.

Ralph Nader, who for some regulation experts is the single most influential person in the history of regulation, wrote a book called *Taming the Giant Corporation*, published in 1976. Nader put forward the types of regulation that have become commonplace today. Nader talked the language of board reforms, respecting shareholder rights, responsibilities to stakeholders, the need for corporate disclosure, such as 'social impact disclosure' in areas such as pollution and employment discrimination. It would take 20 years, however, for society – and the business world – to come around to the idea that 'taming the giant corporation' would be a highly desirable objective.[4]

In the 1970s, the relationships between managers and investors began to come under strain. Managers began to be suspected of corrupt and unethical behaviour. The slowdown in the economy did not help matters. It became common to believe that managers played a big part in leading the United States down the wrong economic path, for instance. A more generalized desire for regulation began to impact the discipline of financial economics.

During that time, financial economists in the United States, in particular Harvard academic Michael Jensen, founder of the *Journal of Financial Economics* in 1973, started to put forward some of the key ideas that would later influence the way companies would be run during the 1990s. Along with William Meckling, another financial economist, Jensen wrote a paper in 1976 called 'Theory of the firm: managerial behaviour, agency costs and ownership structure' (Jensen and Meckling, 1976).

Jensen and Meckling's concern was with something called agency theory, which involved examining potential conflicts of interests in the contractual relationships between managers and investors. They argued that every time managers did not manage in the interests of shareholders, the latter would effectively be out of pocket. They would incur an agency cost, because they would have to spend time and money to try to discipline managers to manage in their interests.

Jensen and Meckling were not the first to theorize the area of conflicts of interests between managers and shareholders. Many of the discussions had taken place in the 1930s. In 1932, the lawyer Adolph Berle and the economist Gardiner Means wrote a seminal book, *The Modern Corporation and Private Property* (Berle and Means, 1999).

The book looked at the historical separation of ownership and control that had widened since the nineteenth century. In the nineteenth century, the owners of a business also tended to be those who controlled, or managed, it. With the rise of the modern corporation, however, a new division of labour opened up between those who owned the corporation and helped supply the original capital, the shareholders, and a new management class who controlled the corporation. Through this process, shareholders were at the mercy of management decision-making. There was a danger that managers could swindle shareholders and prevent them realizing a return on their investment.

Throughout the period after the Second World War, there was always an awareness that managers could behave in this way. But it was tempered at the same time by a belief that, on the whole, managers tended to behave ethically and could be trusted. It was important to punish wrongdoers, but not necessarily impose new regulation on everyone.

This view started to change in the 1970s. A new sensitivity to ethical behaviour was beginning to develop. But also, the slowdown in the economy led many to raise questions about the nature of the post-war boom, and how managers allocated capital.

For financial economists, fears were expressed that managers had, throughout the post-war period, been highly inefficient with the use of capital. An idea developed that managers were continually investing in projects with low rates of return, especially in industries perceived to be mature and low growth, such as oil. They were also needlessly diversifying into areas with low rates of return. For example, the conglomerate form of business began to be attacked.

This was an interesting take on the situation. For instance, the postwar boom was a highly successful period of economic growth in the history of humankind, in terms of its ability to raise the living standards for a greater percentage of the population in Western nations. However, financial economists took a more moralistic, and narrow, view of the situation. From their narrow perspective of the shareholders' interests, something had gone wrong. Managers needed more discipline and regulation, although often not spelled out in those terms, to act in the interests of shareholders.

The concern was that shareholders could do little to influence management behaviour. Jensen was one of the first to suggest that the way that firms financed themselves could act as a kind of discipline on managers who had become uninterested in the interests of creditors and shareholders. Getting into debt was a good thing, from this point of view, because it focused managers on the interests of outside providers of capital.

By having to pay regular interest repayments, managers, the hope was, would pay more attention to running a tighter financial ship. This was the first time that finance became viewed in a regulatory framework. Getting into debt was conceived as a way of disciplining managers and getting them to take on board the interests of outside financiers.

The corporate governance writer Margaret Blair has summarised this situation well. She writes that:

> Critics of large, widely traded companies have often argued that managers are too free to build empires with fancy office buildings and corporate jets or to buy out other companies that they do not know how to run well. The process of having to seek new funding every time they want to make such investments should help to keep this tendency in check. In other words, debt can be a means by which investors exercise some control over corporate decision making, because each time a company wants to spend money on major new investments, investors have an opportunity to evaluate what the company is doing and decide whether to invest more money in the company (Blair, 1995, p. 35).

Financial economists also debated how managers could use surplus cash and how they should invest. Jensen talked about the problem of 'free cash flow' (Jensen, 1986). He summarized some of these ideas in a series of roundtable discussions in 1997, held by the consulting firm Stern Stewart, a leading proponent of the idea of managing for shareholder value.

> You have an organization generating lots of cash, more than managers can possibly invest in positive net present value projects. In that kind of environment, we have a serious problem in the capital markets, a serious organizational

problem: how do we motivate managers and organizations to get rid of the cash, to pay it back to investors? By the late 70s and 80s, it reached the point where companies could destroy as much as one half of their value by failing to pay out their free cash flow and instead reinvesting in low return projects or diversifying acquisitions (Chew, 1998, p. 130).

Jensen and others put forward the view that managers should give back spare cash to investors so the latter can invest it elsewhere to get a higher return. In recent years, as mentioned above, corporations have returned huge amounts of money – individually sometimes up to US $10bn – to shareholders, in the form of buying back their own shares. Today, this is frequently called a responsible form of corporate governance. But it was never always thus. Even in the 1980s, a view prevailed that the share buy back was an *inefficient* use of capital.

As one commentary noted, 'In the past, repaying cash to shareholders might be seen as an indication that management are unable to identify suitable investments . . . the practice was for any surplus cash to be used to diversify into non-core businesses or to enter into riskier transactions within the core business.' In the 1990s, 'it is more likely to be seen as a positive decision to return cash to investors and will become regarded as good corporate governance'.[5]

At one time, it was assumed that productive reinvestment was a good thing because it led, among other things, to growth and new productive assets. Today, rather bizarrely, it is reinvestment in productive capacity that is more likely to be viewed as wasteful, inefficient and irresponsible! Ambitious investment is often likely to be seen as a sign of unethical and wanton 'empire building' on the part of managers. It is interesting that notions of managing for shareholder value embody the notion that over-investment is far more of a problem than under-investment.

On a number of other fronts, the wisdom of growth in the post-war period was being challenged. During this period, companies had felt free to diversify into related or unrelated business areas. The new gospel, however, would be focus on 'core competences': managers should not diversify into those areas where they do not have expertise.

For instance, the Boston Matrix was a framework put forward by the Boston Consulting Group (BCG) during the 1960s. It advocated the idea that a single business could have different business units earning different rates of return, and that these units could subsidize each other.

In an article written in 1970, called 'The product portfolio', Bruce Hendersen of the BCG wrote that:

> to be successful, a company should have a portfolio of products with different growth rates and different market shares. The portfolio composition is a function of the balance between cash flows. High-growth products require cash inputs to grow. Low growth products should generate excess cash. Both kinds are needed simultaneously (see Stern and Stalk, 1998, p. 35).

Today, this idea is akin to sacrilege in the business world. Shareholders, it is said, do not like diversification in this way. For a start, they can diversify themselves, by investing in different shares in a portfolio. But also, the idea of having different rates of return under one roof, in one company, goes against the idea of capital efficiency. It is considered better that the money earning a low return is redeployed elsewhere. And, if firms should diversify, they should adopt the Jack Welch approach: only acquire businesses that are number one or two in their market.[6]

Today, then, there is an idea that it is better for shareholders to invest surplus funds in financial assets where growth opportunities are greatest for them, than for that same capital to be invested in productive assets and activity where the eventual returns for shareholders may not be as great. Shareholder interests, not company interests, should dictate the direction of funds. This is a central tenet of managing in the economic interests of shareholders.

The attack on the conglomerate is a regular cornerstone of recent thinking in financial economics. Conglomerates grew during the 1950s, especially in the United States. A trendsetter was the Litton company, founded in 1953 by the entrepreneur Tex Thornton. With US $3m in sales in 1953, it managed to become a US $100m company in four years, through an acquisition-buying spree using company stock. Litton initially bought small high-tech electronic firms. But eventually it diversified into shipyards, frozen foods and microwave ovens. In the United States, other conglomerates grew, such as ITT and Gulf & Western. ITT began to diversify in the 1960s, after existing as a telecommunications firms. By the mid-1970s it had acquired some 300 companies, from insurance to hotels to auto parts (see Ward, 1997, pp. 54–55).

Of course, the conglomerates represented a lazy form of growth. The idea was to pursue sales and profits growth by buying up unrelated businesses, rather than bold investment in productive and innovative activity. Today, however, it is not just that the conglomerate is out of fashion. It is not just that diversification is out of fashion. More substantially, organic growth is out of fashion. Investment is out of fashion.

Again, it is revealing that advocates of managing for shareholder value consistently see over-investment as far more of a problem than under-investment. This is because the theory prioritizes capital efficiency over investment. It attempts to formalize and provide certainty to the returns that shareholders receive, and the kind of growth that companies pursue. This means that firms are encouraged to return cash to shareholders rather than invest in projects where they cannot guarantee certain returns for shareholders. Overall, it represents a more self-constrained and regulated approach to investment and growth.

Managing for shareholder frameworks – the example of economic value added

In the late 1980s, and more into the 1990s, the ideas developed through financial economics were translated into practical management frameworks for the first time. The most popular one to date has been economic value added (EVA) developed by the New York consultants Stern Stewart. Executives of many companies, including Coca-Cola and Monsanto in the United States, and Siemens of Germany, now explicitly use this framework as their guide to managing the company and allocating resources. Many other companies use variations on the framework, and virtually all major corporations today in the United States and Britain use some framework which is based on shareholder value principles.

Stern Stewart ground their ideas explicitly in those developed in financial economics over the past 50 years. Their main concern is encouraging managers to manage in the best economic interests of shareholders.

What these frameworks represent is a more regulated approach to managing a corporation. They embody the idea that managers have been inefficient with resources in the past, and have pursued irresponsible forms of growth. They try to encourage managers to think about notions of 'capital efficiency' rather than growth. That is, managers should think about profitability and returns on investment at all times. The trouble is, in the process this rules out risk-taking investment where it is hard to predict returns beforehand.

Instead of a relaxed approach to risk-taking and uncertainty, there is a frenzied attempt to formalize things that cannot easily be formalized.

According to Stern Stewart, there are four major ways of creating shareholder value: cut costs; invest above the cost of capital (explored below); withdraw capital from operations where returns are not generating the cost of capital; and engage in financial engineering (in the jargon, adjusting the capital structure between debt and equity) (see Ehrbar, 1998, pp. 134–135).

So, shareholder value has also encouraged an obsessive and interminable focus on cost-cutting. As one of the world's leading experts in corporate finance has noted, 'the markets usually roar with approval' when companies announce cost-cutting measures. For instance, when US firm Eastman Kodak announced in 1997 that it was laying off 10 000 people, saving an annual US $400m in payroll, there was a flurry to buy its shares. Its market capitalization rose by US $2bn within a few days. Cost-cutting is often justified on the basis of generating cash flow and capital efficiency. Rather than tying up capital in the business, which may not be earning a return, it is better to create more liquidity and divert capital to areas of higher return.[7]

The idea that companies should only invest above the cost of capital is at the core of frameworks such as EVA. It is important to understand, because it embodies the greater discomfort both managers and shareholders have for risk and uncertainty today. It is an attempt to try to formalize the returns shareholders might receive.

The cost of capital is the expectation that outside investors have for a return on their investment. This expectation, in the theory, should be used as a hurdle rate influencing the types of project companies invest in.[8] For instance, an investor may be able to get a 12% return by investing in a financial asset, such as a share. If that same investor sees that a corporation is investing in a project where the returns may be 11%, and they hold the shares of that corporation in their portfolio, they may argue for the corporation to give them the money so they can invest in the share with the 12% return.

When shareholders examine their portfolio of investment in shares, they have different expectations about the levels of return they will get on investments, in the form of the capital appreciation of the share price, for a given level of risk. One way they can judge companies is through a relative measure of the returns each company gives, relative to the risks posed to the certainty of getting a return. A bank (bank A) that offers a 15% return for the foreseeable future but is relatively low risk is more attractive than a bank

(bank B) that offers a 15% return but has risk tied up in its business – perhaps because it has entered a high risk emerging market.

If a firm wants to manage for shareholder value, it needs to understand the shareholders' risk–return requirements. If bank A suddenly made an investment of US $100m which increased its risk above bank B, but could still only offer a 15% return on its share price, it would be said, in the jargon, to be investing below the cost of capital. In this scenario, it would be deemed to destroy shareholder value. Why? Because the shareholder is better placed than the company itself to get the same return, relative to a better risk profile. The company should give the US $100m back to the shareholder, so that the shareholder could invest in the shares of bank B.

In this sense, managing for shareholder value is about appreciating the economic interests of shareholders. This might sound like commonsense, but there is a problem: nobody can predict what return they will get in the future. If a company is taking genuine risk, then predicting a return on an investment is very difficult.

When a corporation takes shareholder value seriously, it has to consider that it should return cash to shareholders if shareholders can get a more guaranteed, and immediate return. But this is essentially a safety first approach – and not necessarily the best option for the shareholder. If the company took the risk, and it paid off, it could achieve a return of double shareholders' expectations.

The more regulated and risk-averse nature of managing for shareholder value is exposed when even advocates freely admit the difficulties of applying the theory in large parts of the economy, particularly in the dynamic, hi-tech industries.

Managing for shareholder value relies on being able to calculate whether investments will return particular levels of profit, at particular levels of risk. But in industries such as drugs, aerospace, oil and IT, managers are confronted with long timescales for investments, where hefty capital investments have to be made, and where the precise risks and returns are hard to calculate. Here, even advocates of shareholder value admit that it becomes too restrictive.[9]

The treatment of long-term, risky investment tends to be a subject that advocates of shareholder value are not keen to talk about. Typically, one finds a short note at the back of shareholder value books. This note attempts to find some way to try to square the circle between the necessity of taking risk and accepting uncertainty, and the more regulated approach that shareholder value theories take.

Take the following example. Stern Stewart, the proponents of the EVA framework, argue that EVA encourages managers to 'propose investments with distant payoffs'. But then they add the rider, 'but only when they believe (and don't just hope) that the investment will return more than the cost of capital' (see Ehrbar, 1998, p. 170). But there is one small problem: risk-taking always requires 'hope', because of the degree of uncertainty. This is not a bad thing, but a necessary part of growth and innovation. With genuine risk-taking, there are no guarantees.

All these developments reflect a deeper problem. Rather than feeling relaxed about taking risk and dealing with uncertainty, there is an attempt to over-formalize and regulate everything through elaborate new rules and frameworks. Instead of feeling confident about what could go right, action is predicated more on the fear of what could go wrong. The new rules and guidelines under the notion of managing for shareholder value have entrenched a new risk aversion at the level of investment. Essentially, the equivalent of the precautionary principle is being applied in the world of business.

It would be far better to have a situation where there is acceptance that mistakes can be made. But it is not difficult to see why this situation, in today's climate, cannot come about. Managers are on the defensive, and more distrusted by shareholders. In this climate, an act of risk-taking can quickly be reinterpreted as an act of greed, waste or inefficiency.

The attempt to formalize risk and uncertainty is not just leading to irrational behaviour in the whole sphere of investment. It can also be seen elsewhere, in the obsession with holding managers to account for financial results.

The accountability obsession

In recent years, an obsessive and paranoid atmosphere has been created through the fixation with setting particular quarterly financial targets, trying to meet them, and then reporting them to the financial markets.

The analyst and investment community has become obsessed with the notion of accountability in meeting financial targets. Analysts are looking for ever more specific estimates of how companies will perform in the future. Investors, for their part, are increasingly prone to dump the stock of companies that only slightly miss those targets. Companies respond, in what is known as a game of 'managing expectations'.

The attempt to create accountability in the management–shareholder relationship, and create all sorts of new rules and regulations, has back-fired. An irrational pattern of behaviour has emerged. If companies announce 'worse-than-expected' profits, and stock prices fall violently in response, there are calls among the financial community for chief executives to 'reassure' investors or even resign. In this game, which has become ritualized, chief executives are exhorted to get on the phone to talk to investors. Here, all the talk is of 'restoring confidence', and 'calming' nervous investors. The chief executive who does not take part in this game, probably because he/she has decided it is a ridiculous and stupid charade, is seen as highly irresponsible and uncaring.

There have been numerous examples of this ritual, especially in the more volatile technology sectors. In September 1998, French telecom firm Alcatel's stock was roughly halved in value, from US $41bn to US $21bn. By all accounts, the market had over-reacted. For a start, Alcatel had an-nounced record net income of FFr 62bn. However, it had missed its forecast results by a few percentage points. In a more jittery market, missing a fore-cast, even if relatively slight, tends to be blown out of all proportion.

The chief executive of Alcatel, Serge Tchuruk, was forced on the defen-sive. He said, 'Let's put things in perspective. What Alcatel announced last week is record net income for a French company . . . .' When asked if the stock market reaction was excessive, he replied, 'yes, absolutely'. Facing the in-evitable hysterical calls for his resignation, Tchuruk said it was 'out of the question'.[10]

Many analysts and investors have believed the volatility in the stock market to be excessively jittery and unnecessary in recent years. They are often the most sceptical of stock market patterns of behaviour, because they are the ones caught up in it.

In January 2001, Adobe Systems suffered a plunge in its share price. The company had suggested that its expectations for revenue results pos-sibly could be slightly lower than forecast. When, in a CNN Talking Stocks session, John Carey of Pioneer Investments was asked whether it was an over-reaction, he suggested: 'I think it was. And that's very typical of what hap-pens when a company disappoints investors by a few pennies. Markets can sell off like that. But I wouldn't worry too much about this particular company. It's very good long term.'[11]

In a very significant development, the all-too familiar vehicle of the share buyback is now resorted to when stock prices suddenly plunge, and managers are on the defensive. Companies try to reassure investors by handing them huge sums of money – buying back their own shares. In other words, companies are now allocating resources on the basis of 'reassuring' nervous investors and trying to 'restore confidence'. This is something that the board of Alcatel proposed in the aftermath of its stock market fall, mentioned above.

Another example came in February 2000, when Carnival, the US cruise operator, suffered a severe share price fall. The reason? Apparently, the CFO had made a so-called 'public relations blunder' – the modern-day equivalent of religious sacrilege – by suggesting at a leisure conference that orders were lagging expectations. Investors reacted to the news by selling off the stock and the price was bid down. Straight after, the company pledged to return US $1bn in buying back the stock and returning cash to investors. Why? 'To steady its battered share price and reaffirm confidence in its business', according to one commentary (see Alison Smith, 2000).

If shareholders are unconvinced, there is always litigation. Shareholders themselves have become far more intolerant of risk and uncertainty. They respond by litigation and class action lawsuits. In many cases of litigation, shareholders do not seem to accept the classic law of the market, namely that share prices can go down as well as up.

The whole focus on meeting expectations, forecasts and targets, has, as many admit, become an irrational game. In recent years in the United States especially, it had led to an obsessive focus on numbers. Some managers have found the situation too irrational, and have come out and tried to challenge this state of affairs.

For instance, in 2000, Barry Diller, the Chairman of US Networks, suggested that the process of managing expectations of investors 'has little to do with running a business and the numbers can become distractingly and dangerously detached from fundamentals'.[12]

Again, for some executives, this process has gone too far. It is impossible to predict the future and make the accurate assessments of risk and uncertainty that analysts and investors now demand. The obsessive focus on accountability asks the impossible, namely that financial targets will always be met and on time. Some executives now simply refuse to get involved in this game. For instance, the chief executive of Gillette, James Kilts, deliberately blanked analysts in a meeting in June 2001 when he was asked for yet more specific estimates of how Gillette would perform.[13]

As analysts realize, this game does not particularly benefit either managers or investors. Managers get trapped in a cycle of short-term thinking. It also ends up backfiring on the financial community. Investors like to see transparency in profits. They want to know that healthy profits reflect healthy companies.

However, when the chips are down, and companies worry about missing targets, it can become convenient suddenly to try to boost cash flow before a target is announced. For example, a firm might suddenly sell off a business unit to hit a financial target. But shareholders end up suffering because they are not given a true picture of the company's financial health.

The more jittery relationship between companies and investors reinforces a need to constantly reassure investors about risk. For instance, CFOs are now encouraged to have constant 'dialogue' with banks and shareholders in order to reassure them about risk and uncertainty.

Elsewhere, there is now a constant fixation with the issue of information. Investors, it is said, always need more, and new forms of information about companies to make better decisions. Again, however, this really represents a more regulated approach in a situation where shareholders are not prepared to accept that mistakes can be made, and both sides are more intolerant of risk and uncertainty.

To take just one example, a whole raft of proposals have been put forward in the area of 'risk reporting'. Here, companies are exhorted to provide yet more information about risk to investors, even though they have been doing it already in several areas. Shareholders want greater knowledge about the prospect for gains and the prospect for losses. Such thinking was recently put forward in the United Kingdom by the Institute of Chartered Accountants of England and Wales in a report revealingly titled: 'No Surprises: The Case for Better Risk Reporting'. However, not all executives were convinced by the argument that they should try to communicate every conceivable risk that they face in commercial operations, and elsewhere, to shareholders. As one managing director of a financial services firm put it: 'The idea that a subject as complex as business risk can be included as a statement in the annual report and accounts, when our whole business is about risk management, is absurd.'

Others were rightly concerned that risk reporting would add to the burgeoning re-regulation and self-regulation of business that has taken place in recent years. As one chief executive of a property firm put it:

> You will find enclosed a copy of our company's report and accounts and will note that there are 21 pages of Chairman's statement and financial and operating reviews, 3 pages on corporate governance, 2 on environmental policy, 3 on director's reports, 6 for the remuneration committee report, 2 on reports on directors' responsibilities, auditor's reports, corporate governance and internal control, 2 on accounting policies and 17 pages of statutory report and accounts. In total the book covers 76 pages. Surely this is enough without adding more unnecessary statements.[14]

Managing in shareholders' interests – a weak idea

So far, this chapter has examined the way that growth and investment has become more regulated through the ideas of managing in the interests of shareholders. But there is another issue. Why should shareholder interests be paramount in the first place? The case for putting shareholders first is surprisingly weak. This can be considered from two perspectives: the economic and the legal.

One of the glaring contradictions with the theory of managing for shareholder value is that, economically, it is not difficult to show that, objectively, shareholders hardly contribute anything to economic growth. From the perspective of the wider economy, shareholders always have played a very passive role, and always will.

It is well known that the bulk of reinvestment in the economy comes from retained earnings, the profits that firms make in the course of their operations. Of course, shareholders provide funds to corporations when the latter issue shares in an initial public offering. But thereafter, profits are generated through operations and the selling of goods in the product market. As firms generate profits in this way, and reinvest, shareholders cease to play an economic role. This fact has been well observed by a range of commentators. Doug Henwood, author of *Wall Street*, notes that in the United States, '...the stock market contributes virtually nothing to the financing of outside investment', that is, the investment or capital expenditure (Capex) of corporations. Adding an extra historical dimension, he notes that

> between 1901 and 1996, net flotations of new stock amounted to just 4% of nonfinancial corporations' capex. That average is inflated by the experience of

the early years of the century, when corporations were going public in large number; new stock offerings were equal to 11% of real investment from 1901 through 1929. Given the wave of takeovers and buybacks in recent years, far more stock has been retired than issued; net new stock offerings were −11% of capex between 1980 and 1996, making the stock market, surreally, a negative source of funds (Henwood, 1997, p. 72).

Elsewhere, between 1970 and 1994, in the United Kingdom stock offerings were −4.6% of investment, in Germany 0.1% and in Japan 3.5%. Again, in these countries the vast bulk of investment comes from the profits generated through operations and the process of selling goods and services in the real economy (see Corbett and Jenkinson, 1997). In other words, shareholders do not contribute to profit generation, production and reinvestment in the slightest. They are in fact, with the possible exception of the consumer, the most passive 'stakeholder' in the whole capitalist process.

The function of the stock market has far more to do with the needs of shareholders than those of corporations and the real economy. This is because of the peculiar nature of what equity represents as a financial security. When companies receive capital by issuing new shares, this capital is not like bank capital or credit. It does not have to be paid back. That is why it represents a significant innovation in the history of finance. Companies can raise capital by issuing shares, but they are not obliged to pay it back. Rather, the shareholder is forced to sell his or her shares to another investor to be reunited with the original sum of money. However, to make this situation work, markets are needed for the selling, and buying, of shares.

This is where stock markets come along. First, they provide markets so that investors can easily sell their shares. Second, since these shares are traded it is possible that they will rise in value, making the investment more attractive for the investor. Stock markets are 'mechanisms of liquidity' more than anything else.[15]

The claim that companies should be run in the interests of shareholders is a reassertion of the legal dimension of the corporation, and the property rights of the owners, the shareholders. However, the legal position of the shareholder is also extremely weak. This was eloquently spelled out as long as 70 years ago by Berle and Means in their classic book, *The Modern Corporation and Private Property*.

As Berle and Means first pointed out, ownership of company stock (shares) is a very strange form of private property indeed. Shareholders own shares, but they do not own the physical property, or even intangible assets, of a company. The 'quasi-public corporation', they noted, 'has destroyed the unity that we commonly call property'. And they add, 'Men are less likely to own the physical instruments of production. They are more likely to own pieces of paper, loosely known as stocks, bonds, and other securities, which have become more mobile through the machinery of the public markets' (Berle and Means, 1999, pp. 7–8).

In a preface to a later edition, Berle talks about the 'institution of passive property'. What shareholders actually 'own' is very passive. They have certain rights and expectations, such as voting rights and expectations of dividends, but on the whole their property is a strange form of property, and their rights are passive. The 'increased size and domination of the American corporation has automatically split the package of rights and privileges comprising the old conception of property', notes Berle.

The fact that shareholders have both a weak economic and legal position is bound up with the development of the corporation. A brief detour into history is needed here. In the nineteenth century, capital was required to fund industrial development, but states did not have the will, or resources, to provide it themselves. In the United States, for instance, individual states in the mid-nineteenth century were financially weak. The modern corporation was created, with the help of states, as a vehicle to pool capital from lots of different investors, so industrial development could be financed. It overcame the limitations of older forms of business organization, such as partnerships, which could not raise capital in the form of issuing new shares. At the same time, states wanted to retain control over these new economic entities. So, they ensured that they retained the right to regulate them, and that entrepreneurs would have to get permission from them to set them up in the first place.[16]

Corporations were given rights to issue shares to investors, to raise funds. These shares gave rights of ownership, but the concept of ownership did not mean much. It was always a weak form of ownership. The reason is that there is a contradiction between the socialization of capital and the way that capital remains in the form of private property. When companies issue shares, they effectively socialize capital. That is, capital is being pooled together from lots of individual investors. But shares remain in the form of individual, private property. The result? As more and more sums of capital are pooled together, the individual shareholder gets an ever-decreasing share, and becomes ever more powerless.

To gain power, shareholders have to become majority shareholders. But as companies needed more and more capital, and issued more and more shares, this became impossible for everyone except the hugely wealthy. Through this process the huge majority of shareholders were rendered powerless.

The concept of limited liability embodies the strange form of property ownership that is share ownership. Shareholders are supposed to be the owners, but if a firm collapses and is made bankrupt, then shareholders do not have the responsibility for paying other groups that have lost money, such as the creditors, the banks. They have limited liability inasmuch as they can only lose the value of their original investments. They do not have obligations to anyone else. So, because shareholders do not have full responsibilities, they do not have full rights.

In recent years a new twist has developed: the rise of institutional funds. The proportion of equity held by institutions in the United States increased from 6.1% in 1950 to 48% in 1997. Particular funds, such as mutual funds, have been especially fast growing (see Ben-Ami, 2001). This produces an even odder situation. The economic and legal position of the shareholder is still passive and weak, but shareholders now have greater institutional representation. That means shareholders have institutions that lobby corporations to act in their interests. But essentially they can only lobby to respect the limited rights shareholders have. Institutionally, shareholders are in a stronger position than in the past, but their rights still remain passive. There is only so much they can do. Therefore, even today, the most ardent shareholder activist acknowledges the limitations of the concept of shareholder rights, because the concept of limited liability still holds.[17]

From regulation to a timid approach to markets

It might be tempting to believe that self-regulation today is some kind of passing fad. Or, that it has little impact. Unfortunately, nothing could be farther from reality. Today there is a permanent new dynamic for self-regulation in business. Corporations have responded defensively to a social climate that demands caution and restraint in behaviour. As they have tried to prevent things from going wrong, and imposed all sorts of guidelines on their behaviour, corporations have become far more risk-averse. Rather than take chances, behaviour is subject to all kinds of new ethical vetting, double-checking, auditing, risk analysis and deliberation by committee. Investment not only has to be ethical, sustainable and socially responsible before it goes ahead, it has to meet new stringent financial criteria.

Part Two of this book explores the defensive way that managers approach commercial markets. Today, a peculiar view of the marketplace has emerged. Competition is always said to be increasing and intensifying; customer behaviour is said to be more unpredictable; technology is viewed as creating great discontinuity; and the pace of change is now assumed to be speeding up. While these views are highly one-sided, managers are more worried about being able to compete and survive, and have sought to protect themselves more against commercial risk and uncertainty. In the process, corporations have become far more cautious in the way they approach customers, innovate and grow.

Notes

1. See Ward (1997). In the United States, churn at the top has increased in recent years, in relation to issues such as the plummeting stock market and business scandals. But substantial change seemed to take place during the period from the 1980s to the 1990s. One study by Rakesh Khurana of MIT found that a chief executive was three times more likely to be sacked for the same performance problems in 1996 compared with 1985 (see the page CEO stats on www.ceogo.com). A study conducted by Booz Allen Hamilton suggested that the number of CEOs departing between 1995 and 2001 because of financial performance problems increased by 130%. According to a study by the Cranfield School of Management in the United Kingdom, only 7% of executives had survived over the last 10 years (see Skapinker, 2000).
2. Data from Thomson Financial Securities, quoted from 'Oil giants roll out those share-buyback barrels', *Financial Times*, 6 August 2000. The 1990s was the period of mega buy-back programmes. The biggest share buyback of the 1990s, according to research group Commscan, was Coca-Cola's US $9.99bn stock repurchase in October 1996. In 2000, US pharmaceutical group Merck planned the repurchase of US $10bn of common stock, the largest corporate share buyback ever up to then. Its announcement was made in the final hour of trading on Wall Street and helped boost the shares by 5%. From 1983 to 1999, the US oil company ExxonMobil returned US $26bn to shareholders. See Hill (2000).
3. For a good overview of developments in the post-war period, see Jensen and Smith (1984).
4. See Nader (1976). Nader was considered by Braithwaite and Drahos to be the most influential single person in the history of regulation (see Braithwaite and Drahos, 2000).
5. See the magazine *Corporate Finance*, p. 29, January 1995.
6. For their part, members of the BCG have not remained silent on this new situation. In 2000, Larry Shulman, joint head of strategy practice at the BCG, wrote a long opinion piece in the *Financial Times* called 'Freedom from Shareholder Tyranny', 25 July 2000. 'Pension funds have made clear that corporate managers should not regard diversification as an option. Diversification is an activity the institutional investor sees as central to its own role. If managers diversify, the investors' portfolio gets reshuffled uncontrollably' (Shulman, 2000). The problem, he wrote, was that corporations were piling up massive cash mountains but

felt restricted in how they could invest. His take on the situation was that such companies would eventually go private to pursue alternative investment strategies.

7. See Michael Copeland, 'Copeland on capital efficiency', a paper on the website www.monitor.com. A version also appeared in the *Harvard Business Review*, September–October 2000 issue.

8. See, for example, Johnson (1999, p. 29): '...the cost of capital is connected to the expectations of lenders and investors – the suppliers of capital. In turn, the expectations of suppliers of capital will drive the selection of long-term investment for the future.'

9. See, for example, Black et al. (1998, p. 166): 'There is certainly something very different about technology-intensive industries when it comes to SHV [shareholder value] analysis. The uncertainties and risks involved are very high ....' Also, on p. 170: 'Innovation is certainly at the centre of the high technology sector, both as the basis for competition and as the prime determinant of industry evolution. However, there is no comprehensive valuation approach specifically tailored toward technology companies. In its absence, capital markets usually utilize comparable company analysis, market multiples and in some cases discounted cash flow (DCF) to value technology companies. Each of these has serious flaws. Comparable company analysis and market multiples cannot be applied if the company under consideration is unique, as is often the case if novel technologies are involved. Cash flows are notoriously difficult to forecast for high growth technology companies ....'

10. Quoted from *Exchange Telecommunications Newsletter*, 25 September 1998.

11. Quoted from transcript, 'Talking Stocks', CNNfn, 31 January 2001.

12. See 'Just say no to Wall Street', Monitor Company and M.C Jensen, 23 January 2002. Extracts of this article were published in the *Wall Street Journal* and the *Financial Times*.

13. See 'Just say no to Wall Street', Monitor Company and M.C Jensen, 23 January 2002.

14. See 'No Surprises: The Case for Better Risk Reporting', The Institute of Chartered Accountants in England and Wales (1999).

15. This phrase was taken from Adolph Berle's 1967 preface to the revised edition of *The Modern Corporation and Private Property* (Berle and Means, 1999): '...stock markets are no longer places of investment as the word was used by classical economists. Save to a marginal degree, they no longer allocate capital. They are mechanisms for liquidity' (p. 18).

16. See Prechel (2000) and Roy (1997) for a discussion of the rise of the corporation in nineteenth-century America.

17. See Nell Minow in Chew (1998, p. 23) where she says '...my agenda as a shareholder is limited, which is one consequence of my limited liability'. Also, see the Hampel report, the third corporate governance report in Britain. It says that 'it is also important to recognize the limitations on shareholder action'. Shareholders are 'subject to constraints' and are 'not experienced business managers'.

PART TWO

A Timid Approach to Markets

5

Industry in Defensive Mode

In the summer of 1999 the *Los Angeles Times* published a scathing article on its front cover. Entitled, 'In Hollywood, more business than show', the article argued that the 'gamble and go-by-the-gut mentality that historically characterized studio executives has been fading fast'. Studio chiefs, it suggested, were now in the business of concocting 'endless risk-reducing schemes to finance films without threatening the balance sheet'. Perhaps most revealingly, executives themselves agreed that risk aversion had gone too far. Walt Disney Studios Chairman Joe Roth had this to say: 'I think the industry is in a highly defensive mode trying to couch every intuitive call with a defensive strategy to protect itself from losing too much money. It's less about the elation of taking a shot on a picture and having it work.'

Sony Pictures Chairman John Calley suggested that: 'There's more and more preoccupation with the downside...concern about risk-aversion. I prefer to think of it as an upside business, rather than a business that you have to be in to support the continuing value of your film library.'

Tom Pollock, former chairman of Universal Pictures, suggested even more strongly that: 'Owners have lost their belief in the movie business, and the mentality is not how much you can make, but how little can you lose.' Several other industry veterans concurred, believing executives to be 'defensively oriented'. (see Eller and Bates, 1999).

The movie business has always been characterized by a high degree of risk taking. An estimated 60% of all films released at the box office end up becoming 'turkeys'. Yet risk seems to have become a source of anxiety for studios and film-makers, rather than a source of excitement. 'The fun is gone', said Michael Fuchs, one time head of Warner Music, yet another executive to come out of the closet and bemoan the lack of risk taking in the industry. 'It's a risk averse, caretaker type of business now' (see Finke, 2002).

Risk aversion in the movie industry is not just a mental state. It has arguably reshaped the whole industry. The business of film-making today, as everyone recognizes, is about building a franchise. The idea is to nurture a brand around a film and its characters. Such a brand, it is hoped, will outlive the film itself and take on a life of its own. That way, the brand can be marketed even more through sequels, and licensing and merchandising. As one commentary put it, 'if the character is a hit, then marketing the next movie or video or theme park ride becomes much easier because the consumer knows what he or she is buying. It also becomes easier to sell the character in television shows or video games' (Rushe, 2002).

The franchising approach has come to the fore in the last few years. In 2001, half of the top 10 grossing films in the United States were sequels. Many proved successful. *Rush Hour 2* took US $226m at the box office; *The Mummy Returns* US $202m. *Jurassic Park 3*, *Hannibal* (the follow up to *Silence of the Lambs*) and *American Pie 2* each took more than US $100m.

When the Hollywood film release schedule for 2002 was announced, there were more sequels yet. As some commentators pointed out at the time, very little was actually new. The major studios promoted 13 sequels, including *Star Wars*, *James Bond*, *Star Trek*, *Terminator 3*, *Matrix 2*, *Men in Black 2*, *Harry Potter 2* and part two of *Lord of the Rings*.

The attempt by individual studios to build franchises around films is, as many recognize, a defensive response to competition. As one executive put it, 'the market is so difficult. There are five or six new films opening each week. It is a lot easier to get heard above the noise if people already know something about the movie.' According to Todd Cunningham, managing editor of the film-trade magazine *Variety*, there is an element of studios playing safe with sequels. 'It's a sure bet for them unless they mess up.' Rather than hitting the consumer with something new, fresh and unexpected, which may be risky, studios hope to hit them with something they already know about.[1]

The aim of building a franchise is therefore largely about avoiding risk. Studios hope to secure greater revenues on safer, more reliable ground. The aim of the franchise, like brand building, is to build up a loyal customer base in order to minimize the risks of new releases.

In recent years Hollywood has developed several other mechanisms to avoid risk. When they are produced, films are increasingly pushed through 'test screening' processes. Films are moulded to audience tastes. Test audiences are asked a series of questions about the film, such as: What did they think of the star? Would they recommend the film? This information is then used to fine-tune films before release. Increasingly, if audiences give the thumbs down to films at the test stage, then the actors and production crew are recalled and scenes are re-shot. Similarly, if audiences warm to the film first off, then studios go ahead and often double the advertising budget. They feel more confident they have a success on their hands.

An example of this process was the film My Best Friend's Wedding, starring Julia Roberts. The film, like most today, was shown to a special test audience before release. The audience gave the film good scores. The producers, however, were hoping for 'fabulous' ratings. The fabulous ratings were not forthcoming because the audience expressed doubts about the character played by Julia Roberts. For this particular audience, Roberts' character was too 'scheming' and morally ambivalent. Anxious about this information, the scriptwriter Ron Bass and director PJ Hogan met up again to write in new scenes to solve the problem. What they wanted to do was act on the test audience's concerns by giving Julia Roberts' character the chance of redemption in the film for previous bad behaviour. In this way, any worries about immoral behaviour would not be left hanging in the air.

A new scene was written in, where Roberts' character apologized to the character played by the actress Cameron Diaz. All in all, six new scenes were put into the film. The overall product had become more of a happy, feel-good type of film. The new version was shown again to a test audience, which gave it higher scores than the previous audience. Rather than take a lead at the level of innovation and creativity, to hit the audience with something fresh, increasingly Hollywood seems to be adopting a kind of 'listening to the customer' approach.[2]

The patterns of behaviour evolving in the movie industry are hardly unique. In fact, they are playing themselves out in every industry today. All corporations are far more uncomfortable with risk and uncertainty, and are on the defensive. As a consequence, they are devising new ways to minimize risk, by only creating products that consumers are already familiar with, testing products through focus groups before launch, and developing brands as 'comfort zones of safety'.

The pharmaceutical industry has always taken risk to develop drugs, tolerating a high degree of failure, and taking a long-term portfolio approach to product development. The cost of developing a single drug is around US $600m. Only around US $170m is spent on the compound used in the finished product. The remainder is spent on experimentation with compounds that eventually fail. All this experimentation is necessary to produce a final drug. There is no way around it.[3]

However, in recent times, drug companies have become more and more uncomfortable with risk and uncertainty. It is no exaggeration to say that the whole area of R&D has become an area of much greater anxiety. Of late, the industry has partaken in considerable soul-searching about the low productivity of drug development. In 2001, many major drugs companies did not manage to launch a single new drug. Whether this was a bad year, or a harbinger of things to come, is unclear. But the industry is said to be 'in crisis' nevertheless.

There is now a full discussion on whether drug companies should bother with R&D at all. The whole thing just seems too risky to stomach. In the last few years, drug companies have been thinking the unthinkable: whether they want to do any in-house drug discovery at all. They would rather get the whole messy affair off the balance sheet and become marketing companies. The head of research at the Anglo-American firm SmithKlineBeecham (SKB) even suggested in 2002 that SKB might spin-off its drug discovery business if results did not pick up.[4]

A report issued in late 2001 by the Boston University School of Public Health revealed some interesting trends. In the mid-1990s, US brand-name drug makers employed roughly equal numbers of people in R&D and marketing. But over the next five years, the gap between them soared in favour of marketing. While marketing employees rocketed from 55 348 to 87 810, R&D employees declined slightly from 49 409 to 48 527. Marketing was found to be the only job category that drug makers had expanded substantially.

The authors of the report were critical: 'Despite the industry's constant claims that it is committing ever more resources to R&D, its own employment data suggest the opposite.' In addition, 'these staffing patterns call into question the brand name drug makers' self-definition as "research-based" companies. Since they now employ nearly 40 000 more people in marketing than in research, they might more appropriately call themselves

"America's marketing-based pharmaceutical companies". Their priority today does not seem to be developing new treatments but defining and selling their brands.'5

The increased spending on marketing and brands in the drug industry in recent years is rationalized by the desire to relate more to 'the patient'. This is on the understanding that patients everywhere are now supposedly becoming choosier in the kinds of brand-name drugs that they want. Traditionally, brands, and the concept of brand building, have not been important in the industry. One reason is that the relationship with the consumer has been fairly indirect. Under normal circumstances, the consumer has not been given much of a choice over brand names of drugs. Typically, the doctor makes that choice when the patient asks for a prescription. Advertising, in addition, has been tightly regulated. The deregulation of advertising in recent years in the United States has made it viable for drug firms to advertise in certain media for the first time, and spend more on advertising.

But there is a more substantial reason for the relative historical unimportance of brands in the drug industry, compared with other industries. A drug succeeds or fails on its intrinsic properties. If a drug does not cure a disease, there is little way of dressing it up as attractive through branding. The battle for the consumer tends to be won or lost in the laboratory, not on the billboard. By contrast, a food or drinks company has more scope to attempt to transform a mediocre product into something special through the magical wand of the brand.

Yet today, brand building is becoming far more important in the pharmaceutical industry. For instance, in the past, drug companies did not really bother with elaborate marketing devices to build brand loyalty. Now, large pharmaceutical companies use the technique of 'consistency', a marketing device to attempt to get particular brand names to stick in the minds of consumers. They are also spending far more resources on packaging and design in the hope that consumers will remember their brand. So, companies have devised all sorts of new names and logos for drugs. They have also experimented with radical new colours for the drug itself.

Another conventional reason given for the elevation of branding and advertising in the drug industry involves patent expiration. In the next few years, record numbers of drugs will lose their patents. As a result, large pharmaceutical companies are expecting many copycat or generic drugs to flood the market. This will inevitably mean more competition. However, a case could be made that drug companies have known about this patent expiration for a long time – 20 years in some cases. This seems a convenient excuse for acting in a more defensive manner.

Also, these excuses are hardly new. The drug industry has always faced problems. An article in *Fortune* magazine in December 1976 reported that, 'for several years now, it has been fairly easy to make a case that the drug industry has come upon hard times'. Echoing exactly the same contemporary concerns, it suggested that a major reason was that 'patents have been running out on whole families of wonder drugs developed during the Fifties'. Drug companies are complaining now that patents are expiring, but they were doing the same nearly 30 years ago. In another parallel with today, the article noted that launches of new drugs had slowed in the mid-1970s, and this was causing anxiety. And in yet another strange parallel, it stated that the industry was hoping that biotechnology would come to the rescue – a hope still expressed today.[6]

If these problems are not new, and the industry seems to have coped before, what is new is the scale of the talk about 'crisis', and the seriousness in which firms are considering whether to bother with R&D – something they have never really considered before. Yet in many ways this reflects a serious lack of perspective. Another *Fortune* commentary, this time in 2001, suggested that:

> Pharmaceuticals stocks have shone for decades as growth stalwarts...today the argument for loading up on such stocks seems stronger than ever. Baby-boomers are ageing, for one thing, and older people buy more pills. Virtually every week newspapers carry headlines about breakthroughs in understanding and treating disease, and the exploding promise of biotech. The top companies have enormous reservoirs of scientific know-how and armies of effective salesman. Medicines are playing an ever larger role in health care, which in turn accounts for an ever-growing part of GDP (O'Reilly, 2001).

The key to understanding the behaviour of drug companies is that greater worries about the future are dictating how they behave today. There is no plausible objective reason why the industry should be in a 'crisis'. This defensive behaviour is driving them to 'get closer to customers' and compete more through branding, rather than redoubling their efforts to compete through new drugs and innovation. Already, as the *Financial Times* reported in 2002, this is aggravating employees who want to get on and do proper research. 'Big Pharma companies' increasing concentration on marketing rather than science is a common frustration for core research staff' (Jenkins, 2002).

Corporations have also resorted to mergers in order to try to protect themselves from further financial instability – even though most of the industry doubts whether mergers will solve any problems. Instead of redoubling efforts to do something new and exciting in the lab, executives seem to be more keen in throwing in the towel.

The problems of this new risk aversion are industry-wide. Over the course of the 1990s, a cry went out that the US aerospace industry has become far more risk-averse. This came to a head in 1999, when the industry standard magazine, *Aviation Week*, ran a series of bold and controversial articles that, among other things, accused industry of short-term thinking and risk aversion. It argued that the industry needed to restore a much-lost tolerance for risk-taking. Senior managers at Boeing, taking the articles seriously, issued an email to the company's 220 000 employees in response. They argued, among other things, that Boeing's investment of nearly US $2bn in R&D in the prior year demonstrated that it was not simply interested in the short term (see, for example, Scott, 1999).

The author of those articles, William Scott, is not entirely convinced. Regarding himself as a 'sputnik baby' because he grew up in the 1950s, he has been involved at various levels in the aerospace industry since the 1960s. Now a senior editor at *Aviation Week*, the industry for him has definitely become more risk averse in the last 15–20 years.

On both the government and civilian sides, the incentives to take risk are not there, he says. For example, in the past, if the troops needed a new technological system, people were given the proper money to innovate in a fairly free fashion.

> There was a willingness to experiment and try things out. People made things happen. The attitude on the whole was, get the technology out there, and follow it up with paperwork later. Today, that does not happen. People that take chances are more likely to slapped down as 'non-team players'. As a result, they quickly learn that the way to move up the bureaucracy is to take less risk. They learn that staying out of trouble is the best thing to do, and cover their back with paperwork.[7]

Scott adds that 'people used to be recruited by industry to take risks and radical jumps, especially at the corporate labs such as Lockheed's Skunk Works'. The Skunk Works played a pioneering role in developing America's jet fighters, surveillance aeroplanes and stealth fighters. 'Today, I hear complaints from new recruits that paperwork seems to have replaced risk taking and taking chances.'

Historically, a willingness to take risk has characterized the aerospace industry. According to one leading aerospace analyst, Pierre Chao, throughout history, companies have been willing to take on phenomenal technological risk. These have been what you could call the 'big hairy leaps', such as flying, supersonic flight and sending the first man to the moon.

> But in recent years, a lot of people would argue that the industry has become increasingly timid. Some would say a new mantra has developed, that of shareholder value. And companies such as the aircraft manufacturers are worried about short-term earnings. They are also looking for areas where they can grow but consume less capital at the same time. They are looking for 'capital efficient' growth. Often this means putting money into, say, customer services, where there is far less upfront capital investment needed than say, developing a radically new type of plane.[8]

What has changed in the aerospace industry? Certainly, the possibilities for radical technological leaps have not gone away. There are a whole host of technologies that need purposeful exploration, commitment and investment. In the space arena, there are all sorts of possibilities for radical propulsion technologies. But one thing is more certain: there does not seem to be a consensus around taking bold risks with resources in the way that existed in the past. A certain will seems to be lacking. When it comes to space, there seems to be a 'been-there-done-that' mentality.[9]

A similar thing could be said for the commercial side of the industry. It would be wrong to suggest that no progress has been made in the last five decades of flight. The cost of flying for the consumer has come down, meaning more people enjoy air travel. And, the aviation industry has managed to improve the safety record of flight.

But it is not difficult to see that radical change has been avoided. The airline industry has been notoriously conservative. The technologies for supersonic flight, and for drastically reducing flight times, have been around for some time. Even more incremental change has been avoided. Even now, long distance flights remain uncomfortable as people are crammed sardine-like into cabins. Over the years, designers in the industry, and outside the industry, have come up with numerous ideas for change. But to their frustration, aircraft manufacture is still not as passenger-centred as it could be.[10] But it is not at all beyond the stretch of the human imagination to change aeroplane designs – nor the economics of the industry – to allow more seating room for everyone. But often the industry has been very unwilling to take a more radical direction. As Bill Scott of *Aviation Week* says, 'the problem with incremental innovation is that things move along very slowly'.

Perceptions of risk

These industry examples help to introduce some of the main themes of Part Two of this book. Capitalism has always involved commercial risk-taking. In the trade-based economies of the past, individual merchants took risk in buying goods at a certain price, and selling goods at a higher price. If prices of commodities fluctuated in between, they could either gain or lose out.

In the economies of today, large corporations take risk in myriad ways, to pursue profits, innovate and fulfil human needs. Pharmaceutical firms gamble that drug development will result in marketable drugs. Movie studios bet that films will score at the box office. Telecom firms invest in new infrastructure for mobile networks to develop new markets.

Today, however, something has changed. In the last decade or so in the business world managers have come to see markets as far more risky, uncertain, unpredictable, volatile, turbulent, complex and chaotic than ever before. In this world, competition is always said to be 'increasing'. Customers are viewed as more fickle than ever before, and more likely to hop over to the competition. Everything is said to be changing at a faster rate than the past. The idea that the 'pace of change is speeding up' has just become a commonplace assumption. Technological change is viewed as creating 'discontinuities' which make it difficult to plan ahead in any kind of meaningful way.

Taking these views on board, managers have taken a much more protective, defensive approach to customers, markets, innovation and growth. A new obsession with building relationships of customer loyalty has sprung up. Here, managers explicitly tell themselves that retaining existing customers is less risky and expensive than winning new ones. Corporations are retreating from genuine innovation. And growth takes place through safe options such as mergers and acquisitions, rather than investment.

Yet the marketplace has not become the chaotic and complex place that managers and consultants make it out to be. Rather, they tend to see it as such, because of their unwillingness to strike out more ambitiously.

The myth of unpredictable markets

...if you step back, you will see that what is happening now is of an entirely new dimension. It's not just the increase in the rate of business change – we all know markets are moving faster. It's that the magnitude of the increase is making the future completely unpredictable. It's not just that customers know more and want more; we all know that the nature of our relationship with them is changing. It's that their needs and demands are no longer predictable. It's not just that competition has heated up – we all know the basic rules of competition have been rewritten by deregulation, the breakdown of industry boundaries, globalisation, and non-stop technological shifts. It's that we can no longer predict which rules will change next. We are experiencing what scholars call discontinuities, drastic changes that destroy companies, reinvent industries, and make skills obsolescent (Fradette and Michaud, 1998, p. 16).

These ideas are now so familiar in the business world as to have achieved the status of commonsense. Over the last decade, many people have come to the conclusion that the future is 'completely unpredictable'. The 'needs and demands' of customers are 'no longer predictable'. The 'rules of competition' have been rewritten. We are experiencing 'discontinuities', because of deregulation, globalization and technology.

Yet when examined it becomes clear that all these ideas are extremely odd. A number of trends are assumed to be leading to a greater powerlessness, such as globalization, or new technology. Yet this is hard to square with reality. It is a one-sided perception.

Take the Internet. Remember the idea in the late 1990s that the Internet would erode the power of large corporations? Here, the Internet would change everything, and nimble start-ups would run rings around the slow dinosaurs. Yet the reality was always that the largest corporations with the power and resources would benefit the most from the Internet. They have used the Internet to extend their control in various ways.

From a more balanced perspective, the whole history of technology in industry is really about extending control. Firms have been able to appropriate new technologies, from the typewriter in the late nineteenth century, to mainframe computers, to the Internet today, to become more efficient and extend control over their operations.

Taking a broader view still, this is the very purpose of technology in society. From the earliest technologies such as primitive knives and axes, to the invention of the compass, gunpowder and the printing press before industrialization, to the various new technologies in the nineteenth century, such as the telegraph, electricity and the internal combustion engine, humanity has always used technology to do things more efficiently, and gain control over nature and the environment. Technology is a human invention to extend human control.

Today, there is a strange view of technology. There is a tendency to view technology as leading to a loss of control. Of course, new technology can often be a pain. There are notorious challenges in implementing IT systems in the workplace. And when computer systems crash, one might feel that technology is not serving human beings very well. When an ATM machine swallows your debit card for no reason whatsoever, it puts a downer on the evening. But the reality is that those systems were designed with a broader purpose in mind, which they generally serve. They make things more efficient than before.

Again, take the idea of globalization. In the business world it is often assumed that globalization has led to a loss of control. With competition so global, it is said, nobody knows which firms will emerge from where. But something is not quite right about this idea. After all, it is large corporations that have internationalized their activities, benefiting from the opening up of world markets. In fact, corporations have benefited immensely from the internationalization of economic activity. For many multinational corporations, overseas profits provide an important supplement to domestic profits.

It is also interesting that during the last decade, sources of competition that posed a threat to US and European interests in the past, namely Japanese firms, have struggled, as the Japanese economy in general has stagnated. Yet this has been the very time when the Western business world has felt competition to be more intense.

One of the odder ideas to emerge in recent years is that the pace of change has speeded up and become more unpredictable. The first problem with this viewpoint is that it suffers from a kind of historical amnesia. There has always been dynamic change in capitalism. In fact, change in other periods of history was far more profound than change today.

A human being living through the period of industrialization would have been confronted with the emergence of the telegraph, the telephone, electricity, electric motors and machinery, photography, radio, motion pictures, the internal combustion engine, not to mention huge social change as people flocked from the countryside to the cities. The telegraph made it possible to send a message from New York to Chicago in five minutes, while before it took around 10 days.

In 1844, the Mayor of New York, Philip Hone, wrote:

> this world is going on too fast. Improvements, Politics, Reform, Religion – all fly. Railroads, steamers, packets, race against time and beat it hollow. Flying is dangerous. By and by we shall have balloons and pass over to Europe between sun and sun. Oh, for the good old days of heavy post-coaches and speed at the rate of six miles an hour! (quoted in Steiner and Steiner, 2000, p. 20).

A few years later, Karl Marx and Friedrich Engels wrote about the nature of capitalism in *The Communist Manifesto*:

> Constant revolutionising of production, uninterrupted disturbance of all social conditions, everlasting uncertainty and agitation distinguish the bourgeois epoch from earlier ones. All fixed, fast-frozen relations, with their train of ancient and venerable prejudices become antiquated before they can ossify. All that is solid melts into air, all that is holy is profaned... (Marx and Engels, 1967, p. 3).

The economist Joseph Schumpeter wrote on the theme of 'creative destruction' in industry in the 1940s:

> The opening up of new markets, foreign or domestic, and the organizational development from the craft shop and factory to such concerns as US Steel illustrate the same process of industrial mutation – if I may use that biological term – that incessantly revolutionalizes the economic structure from within, incessantly destroying the old one, incessantly creating a new one. This process of Creative Destruction is the essential fact about capitalism (Schumpeter, 1975).

Peter Drucker once characterized the economy as 'one of violent technological flux, rapid obsolescence, and great uncertainty...'. It sounds contemporary, but Drucker actually wrote it in 1959 (Drucker, 1959). Discussions of the rapidity of technological innovation and obsolescence were commonplace in the 1960s.

So, there is nothing new about rapid change. But second, what has changed in recent years is the dominant *perception* of change. In today's discussion of change, there is a heightened *anxiety* about change. In the past, change was often interpreted as disruptive, but also as exciting and thrilling. Today, change is more one-sidedly experienced as something to be anxious about. Change is out of control, it is suggested. We need to slow things down.

This is now a commonly heard sentiment. According to one writer,

> from the rapid invention of new technologies such as micro-robots and genetically modified food, to our soaring emissions of carbon dioxide in the earth's atmosphere, we seem to have our collective foot slammed down on the world's accelerator pedal. It is time to think creatively about how we can slow things down, how we can ease up a bit on that accelerator pedal.

For this writer, 'unless humanity acts to slow its technological momentum, catastrophes will do it for us'. For him, 'the complexity and speed of our social and technological systems are unlike anything we have seen before and these factors are now pushing against the upper limits of the human brain's abilities' (Homer-Dixon, 2001).

The idea that human beings create technologies to solve human problems disappears here from the equation. For example, one could easily argue that we need to speed up the development of genetically modified food so it can be used to help alleviate problems such as hunger in developing countries. In reality, change is often very slow, even at the level of science and technology. When are we going to see broadband Internet access for everyone? When is biotechnology finally going to become a success, after all these years of promise? Why hasn't more progress been made in space exploration?

It is not difficult to see that on many other levels we live in very conservative times. In culture, there often seems to be a recycling of the past, in movies, music and art, rather than genuine creativity. At the political level this is an era where, for the first time in modern history, any idea of genuine change has been completely taken off the agenda. In many areas, faster change is needed. The pace of change is far too slow.

It is not so much that change is faster than we can cope with. It is more that we have lost a framework of bold ideas and purpose in which to direct change. Previous generations experienced great change, but they had a framework of confidence in human ability to direct change. Today, because we lack this, change is experienced one-sidedly in an anxious fashion.

What is arguably new about today is an unwillingness to shape change and the future in a purposeful way. For example, in recent years, a new, Darwinist language of adaptation has permeated the world of business. Managers and consultants now tell themselves that they must 'change or die', or 'adapt or die'.

This is an interesting formulation of attitudes toward change. Change is something that happens to people, rather than a notion that people shape change. The notion of 'adaptation' is very different from a notion of leadership or being a pioneer. It is a reflection of timidity in the face of change: an unwillingness to take a lead. The notion of adapting is really a euphemistic word for 'surviving'. In a world of fast change, the only thing corporations can do is survive, it is assumed.

The attitude of only adapting, rather than pioneering, has grave consequences for innovation. None of the genuine innovation of the past would have been possible if individuals and institutions were trying to adapt to change all the time. Pioneers attempt to do something new that has not existed before, whereas adapting implies a kind of reconciliation with existing reality. There is a difference between shaping change and keeping up with change.

Getting closer to the customer

The next three chapters examine the way that managers, having taken on board ideas that the marketplace is far more risky than before, seek to avoid risk in all sorts of new ways. They orient firms more defensively to markets. The following chapter examines the new obsession with the customer in the business world. In a world that managers see as far more risky and unpredictable, 'getting close to the customer' has become a highly elevated objective. Managers now seek to create a comfort zone of safety around them by focusing obsessively on building customer relationships of loyalty. The new obsession with the customer is a major expression of how managers approach markets in a more timid fashion.

Notes

1. Quoted in 'Battle of the sequels, Part 1'. All facts and figures from the same article.
2. This process was described in *The Hollywood Machine, Battle of the Blockbusters*, a documentary screened on BBC2, 22 June 2002.
3. These figures were estimated by the US investment bank Lehman Brothers; see 'R&D: development time static', *Financial Times Life Sciences*, October 2000.

4. *Financial Times* Survey, Healthcare: Pharmaceuticals, 'Dearth of new drugs worries pharma sector', 30 April 2002.
5. Press release, 'Drug industry marketing staff soars while research staffing stagnates', Boston University School of Public Health, 6 December 2001.
6. See 'Future drugs that will be lifesavers for the industry too', *Fortune*, December 1976.
7. Correspondence with Bill Scott.
8. Correspondence with Pierre Chao, aerospace analyst for investment bank Credit Suisse First Boston, New York.
9. 'Aerospace, the veterans say, has lost the excitement and innovative spirit of the Cold War era. "There's no longer the camaraderie or inspirational leadership", says Richard Cook, a former industry executive' (see Nicoll, 1999).
10. 'Aircraft design has not changed fundamentally in decades', notes *The Economist*. See 'The way we fly now', 21 July 2001. Also see this article for a review of the book *Free Flight: From Airline Hell to a New Age of Travel* by James Fallows. This book discusses a radical solution for reform in the aviation industry, namely the greater use of smaller aircraft with new designs.

6

The New Obsession with the Customer

British product packaging design agency SiebertHead had decided that enough was enough. Risk aversion in the business world had gone too far. It made a public declaration in June 2002 that product innovation and design was suffering in the fast-moving consumer-goods industry, because of the anxieties of corporations. According to the agency, things had got so bad that the notion of triangular chocolate, embodied in the Toblerone product, and the idea of a Polo mint, first manufactured in 1948, would be considered too 'difficult and too risky' propositions in these cautious times (see Matthews, 2002).

'The innovation and inventiveness that used to go on just does not happen today', says Satkar Gidda, sales and marketing director of SiebertHead. 'People within corporations seem to be more scared of making a mistake.' What tends to happen, he says, 'is that people still have good ideas for new products and designs. But they get killed today in one of two ways. The first is that people high up in office say no straightaway. The second is that the concept gets researched to death with focus groups, and eventually dropped when the risks cannot be quantified.'

Gidda points to a revealing example that illustrates today's obsession with listening to the customer. A client wanted a design done for the packaging of a product. SiebertHead proposed a new design concept that was 'different to all the other designs out there and would make the product stand out on the shelf'. The client was reluctant to go through with the design. SiebertHead, confident about its design concept, argued that the concept should at least be market researched. Unusually, they took responsibility for the market research. The concept won out among consumers in the test.

Meanwhile, unbeknown to SiebertHead, the client had carried out two bouts of research on its own in secret. The product was a success in these tests too. But even then, the client took about a year to make a decision to accept the design.

'There was just so much deliberation', says Gidda. 'I can understand managers do not want to make mistakes. But you have to have confidence in what you are doing. Companies today tend to go for safe bets.' They launch line and brand extensions, he says, products that are not genuinely new but tweaks and updates on existing products. Clients never see themselves as risk-averse, says Gidda. They see themselves as being 'responsible'.[1]

This chapter looks at the way that increasingly risk-averse corporations try to get ever 'closer to customers'. Corporations now expend enormous energy on trying to create relationships of loyalty with customers. There is nothing wrong in having good relationships with customers, of course. But clearly, something new is happening today. More afraid of taking a leap into the unknown, corporations have become obsessed with customer loyalty as a way of creating more certainty in their business going forward. Today's obsession with the customer has a highly defensive motivation. The starting point is not the creation of new markets with original new products, but hanging onto existing customers, and wringing more business out of them.

This can now be seen on a number of new levels. Corporations want endless assurances that little will go wrong in launching a product. So, as the above example illustrated, companies do not feel comfortable unless they have researched products to death in focus groups. Corporations increasingly only feel comfortable with launching 'brand extensions' – products that consumers are already familiar with in some way because of existing brand familiarity. Enormous effort goes into developing relationships of customer loyalty. So, brand building has become hugely elevated in importance. Here, companies try to build connections and rapport between themselves and consumers, via the product, often through the medium of emotion, culture and lifestyle. At the same time, the whole area of customer service and customer satisfaction has become an area of much greater anxiety. Upsetting a customer today is akin to some kind of religious sacrilege. As corporations themselves admit, worshiping the customer has become a new kind of religion.

In this context the rather sudden rise of 'customer-babble' is a sign of something deeper. The traditional notion that 'the customer is always right' would seem basic in the extreme today. In the late 1990s, companies everywhere told themselves to 'delight' their customers at every conceivable point of interaction, or 'touch point'. That could mean creating a more delightful brand. Or, it could mean delighting customers through a superior customer service. The failure to delight was viewed as nothing less than a disaster.

Companies today declare that the 'the customer is king'. But even that seems a bit passé. As executives themselves proclaim, rather improbably, 'the customer is the head of the company!'. Companies exhort themselves to create the most 'memorable' experiences for their customers. They attempt to 'exceed customer expectations' at every possible opportunity. The rise of customer-babble is clearly silly on one level. Yet unfortunately, it expresses a deeper anxiety about losing customers. Corporations are going overboard in trying to cement deeper relationships with customers at every opportunity, because of a new defensiveness.

The problem with today's customer obsession is that it represents a highly conservative approach to markets, growth and innovation. Take innovation. It is arguable that the vast swathe of the genuine risk-taking, experimentation and innovation of the past has had little to do with 'listening to the customer' in any kind of narrow sense. This is borne out by the fact that genuine innovation often has the capacity to confuse people. From the first movies, to the radio and computer, genuine innovation often provoked initial confusion. If such innovation were tested in a focus group, a firm would probably conclude it would not work out because of puzzled consumers.

Similarly, when mobile phones were first launched, many people were adamant that they would never need one. Today, many of those same people would not feel comfortable stepping outside their house without their mobile phone. In fact, put more strongly: genuine innovation can never be a straightforward response to articulated customer needs. It would not be genuinely new.

There are many well-known examples of innovation that have not involved 'listening to the customer'. According to minivan creator Hal Sperlich, as reported in *Fortune* magazine, 'in 10 years of developing the minivan, we never once got a letter from a housewife asking us to invent one'. Similarly, the personal cassette player, or Walkman, was the inspiration of Sony founder Akio Morita, who once commented, 'The public does not know what is possible, but we do. So instead of doing a lot of market research, we refine our thinking on a product and its use and try to create a market for it . . .' (Morita, 1987).

The writers Keen and Mackintosh, authors of *The Freedom Economy*, make an interesting point in relation to this issue. There is a difference between innovation that merely adds convenience to people's lives, and innovation that contributes to greater freedom. They use this distinction to explain why in recent times certain innovations have failed in the market while others have lasted the distance.

For instance, the concept of home banking has received 20 years of investment. While it has added features and some level of convenience, it has not made that much difference to people's lives in terms of increasing their freedom. People can pay their bills online, or pull up their account balance. But then, just as easily, they can ring up their bank over the phone.

By contrast, the long-term success of the Automated Teller Machine (ATM), or cash point machine, was more inevitable, according to the authors. Like many genuine innovations, it was not an instant success. In the early 1980s, people were resistant to interact with computers. While its invention 'was trivial on one level', it is also true that it has contributed to people's mobility. By creating a cooperative network between banks, on a global scale, people are not tied down by having to visit their local branches. The ease with which people can now withdraw cash from anywhere in the world has contributed to their mobility and freedom (see Keen and Mackintosh, 2001).

The dangers of listening to the customer have not gone unnoticed. According to Anthony Ulwick, a consultant, 'there are several concrete dangers of listening to customers too closely. One of these is the tendency to make incremental, rather than bold, improvements that leave the field wide open for competitors' (Ulwick, 2002). Companies that decide to retreat from bold innovation, Ulwick suggests, can become more vulnerable to competition.

The Harvard Professor, Clayton Christensen, author of *The Innovators Dilemma*, has explored this theme more systematically than most. In his view, companies that listen to customers too closely end up stifling growth opportunities. It is precisely by listening to customers that companies find it difficult to escape from stagnating markets and pursue new opportunities (see Christensen, 1997). Despite his observations, and similar ones elsewhere, the obsession with the customer gets stronger and stronger however.

A fixation with loyalty

The quest for customer and brand loyalty, it should be underlined, is not just about a change in emphasis in corporate marketing. For instance, in the early 1990s, marketing gurus began to talk about *The One-to-One Future*, the title of a best selling book by Peppers and Rogers (1993). They suggested that companies could leave mass marketing behind and focus on building closer relationships with individual customers, building a 'share of customer' rather than a 'share of market'. The emergence of the Internet generated considerable excitement in the marketing world. Consultants began to dream of a new nirvana of customer relationships. The old, 'hit and hope' impersonal mass advertising and marketing approach could be replaced by a more reciprocal and productive relationship-based approach, using the Internet, the aspiration went. Customers could give firms feedback on what they wanted, and receive customized and personalized goods and services in return.

The obsession with customer loyalty, and building relationships, though, is not just a marketing obsession. It goes to the heart of how companies operate, impacting new product development. It involves a far more conservative approach to innovation and growth *per se*. This can be seen with the new brand fixation. Corporations pump more resources into brands because they want to create comfort zones of safety around them. Once they create a sense of brand loyalty among consumers, companies launch brand extensions as a way of reducing risk. At the same time, they pump more resources into protecting brands and preventing their 'dilution' in the eyes of consumers. In this sense, companies want to grow, but only through comfort zones created by brand loyalty.

Companies are organizing more around customer relationships of loyalty. Again, this is not just about marketing. Take the rise of something called 'customer relationship management', or CRM. According to one definition, CRM 'is based on the now well established premise that it costs less to keep the customers that you have than try to win new ones – five times less expensive in fact ...' (see Swift, 2001). In recent years, firms have spent large amounts of money on CRM. Total global spending on CRM is expected to rise to US $76.3bn in 2005, according to Gartner Research, up from US $23bn in 2000.[2] The rationale for this activity is the quest for greater customer retention and customer loyalty.

CRM systems allow companies to collect, store and analyse customer data – or so the hope goes. The aim of CRM is to create a single organizational view of the customer. Several employees can often deal with the same customer without knowing it, creating confusion and disorganization. CRM however makes use of databases to track information on customers, and systems to deal with the interface with customers.

There has been a great deal of soul-searching over CRM, partly because of the well-documented failure rates. According to Gartner, around 65% of CRM projects fail. It is evidently very difficult to build customer relationships of loyalty. At the root of this problem perhaps is the fact that many customer relationships, especially in consumer markets, are by their nature weak types of relationship. It is difficult to get an organic, spontaneous relationship of reciprocity going. As a consumer, the relationship one has with a firm is considerably weaker and lacking in substance than, say, a relationship with a work colleague, or family member. Even brand loyalties are considerably weaker and more ephemeral than other types of loyalty, such as loyalty to political beliefs, family, friends or religion. But whether it works or not, the CRM obsession shows that customer management has become far more of an obsession within companies today.

Once customers are satisfied, there is an endless attempt to improve customer satisfaction. Companies spend more resources on customer satisfaction audits in order to track customer satisfaction levels. Companies spend a great deal more effort working out which particular customers are loyal. A hefty percentage of total sales can come from a small percentage of customers. Once armed with this information, firms then lavish greater attention on particular customer segments.

Once firms have loyal customers, they then talk to them – endlessly. Marketing consultants today stress the need to establish interaction, dialogue and *reciprocity* between firms and their consumers. But if customers decide not to be loyal, then firms devote considerable resources to asking why. Why have they switched to another brand? Have they changed their lifestyle? Or have they moved house? Have they got a better job? Have we given them a bad customer service experience? Why are our customers loyal in the first place? Why do they emotionally bond with our brand?

Firms now actively encourage customers to complain. Sounds mad? Not from the perspective of the holy grail of customer relationship-building. One may feel sorry for the employees at the receiving end. But companies now take the view that the irritation or anger of a customer provides the basis for a 'deeper' customer relationship. Companies can relate to that anger. They can turn it around, and create more lasting relationships of loyalty – or so the hope goes. Various books are now written on the precise nuances of dealing with customer complaints.

Again, there is nothing wrong with wanting to develop sound customer relationships. But it is no exaggeration to say that the new obsession with the customer is bordering on paranoia. The starting point is a narrow defensive quest for customer loyalty, far more as an end in itself. The problem is that companies are trying to avoid the risks of creating new markets in a more dynamic sense. The irony is that while much is done in the name of the customer today, the defensive way that firms relate to customers does not serve them very well. Today's fixation with the customer is built on a low view of the customer. Rather than really developing exciting new products and services, and pumping more resources into radical innovation, there is an attempt to get the customer excited about a better *quality* service, a re-branding initiative, or a bland brand extension.

The greater desire for customer loyalty, at the expense of investing boldly in new markets and taking a lead, is having an adverse impact in business-to-business markets. This is where the bulk of constructive cooperation goes on in the economy. This cooperation, however, requires individual firms to take a lead while working on projects. Today, there is a greater tendency to be more preoccupied with losing business and customers, and 'pleasing' existing customers.

This can be seen all the time on individual projects. In an over-zealous effort to 'please', relationships can break down because nobody is prepared to take a lead. Suppliers end up hanging on the every word of their customers, afraid to make a bold move for fear of upsetting them. Those being supplied, for their part, resort to endless meetings in an attempt to gain assurances that everything is 'on track'. Risk aversion is having a negative impact on business-to-business relationships.[3]

The new fixation with brands: the corporate creation of comfort zones

The rise of branding is a clear expression that something fundamental has changed in the relationships companies have with their customers, and the world more generally. This section argues that the branding obsession expresses a risk-averse desire for greater customer loyalty. The notion of brands is not new, of course. Corporations have always valued brands to some extent. They have realized that the familiarity, reputation, credibility, image, tradition and trust they have, and their products have, is an asset. 'Goodwill' – the reputation of a firm – has long been recognized as having financial value in the balance sheets of companies.

Corporations such as Coca-Cola, Sony, IBM and Disney have enjoyed strong brands. They and their products enjoy a strong familiarity, reputation and so on in the marketplace. Firms and products have enjoyed these reputations for various reasons: value-for-money, technical excellence, customer service, association with youth and passion, to name just a few.

The concept of building a brand first developed around simple commodity products. Different firms that produced very similar products, such as bars of soap or drinks, recognized they needed a point of differentiation between them. Through advertising campaigns they sought to create unique associations and unique images around their particular product. When cigarette manufacturer Marlborough developed the concept of the Marlborough man, it was attempting to create a point of differentiation. The type of people who smoked their cigarettes were supposed to be uniquely cool. Through the creation of a brand, it was hoped, consumers would be attracted to their particular product rather than a rival's.

Traditionally, then, brands have been a mechanism to create loyal customers and fend off the competition. Brands can endow firms will competitive advantages. It is often said that brands help to 'de-commodify' products. That is, firms with strong brands do not have to compete on price. They enjoy greater pricing flexibility than firms with weak brands.

Today, for instance, it could be said that the Nike brand has a stronger image, reputation and meaning in people's lives, compared with other brands in the sector. As a result, Nike can add a premium onto the cost of its shoes. The product itself may not be that different to another shoe. It might use very similar materials. The costs of making it may be the same. But Nike can charge more to the customer because of the cache of the brand. People are willing to spend more.

Yet it was only in the 1990s that the concept of branding became so elevated in importance. Brands were not just seen as one asset among many. Brands were suddenly perceived to be the most important asset. Relatively suddenly, brands were perceived as containing far more value than before. As a result, brands, corporations told themselves, would require active management. Brands needed defending against the possibility of 'dilution'. Brand considerations became central to questions of growth, strategy, finance and investment. Companies saw brand extensions as the best way to pursue growth.

Brands also became central to manager–employee relations. If firms were to build strong brands, employees needed to 'live the brand'. Brand values needed to be inculcated into corporate culture. At the same time, they would help to bind people together in the workplace through a shared vision.

Corporations would also find it acceptable to undergo 'rebranding' exercises. Brands, strangely, seemed to somehow take on a life of their own, perfectly expressed in the notion that brands have *personalities*.

During the 1990s, branding became an industry-wide obsession. Traditionally, corporations in the hi-tech industries, such as drugs or aerospace, never saw brands as that important. Somehow, they would have seemed superficial in the past. Companies in these industries saw themselves as pioneers, and had different priorities. The important thing was science and technology. Get that into a product, and the product spoke for itself. It did not need whole new layers of dressing up through advertising campaigns.

Yet in the 1990s, as noted in the previous chapter, hi-tech firms took branding far more seriously. In 2000, Boeing for instance formulated its first ever brand strategy. For all firms today, a strong or weak brand is viewed as absolutely central to competitive success in the marketplace.

As mentioned above, brands increasingly mediate relations between managers and employees. Communicating the values of a brand is seen as a way to cultivate loyal employees and foster a shared corporate culture. At the same time, it is hoped that if employees really understand and personally believe in the brand values, they can convince customers to believe in the brand too.

According to Sir Martin Sorrell, chief executive of leading advertising agency WPP:

> Well over 50 per cent of what we do for our clients in advertising, media investment management, information and consultancy, public relations and public affairs, branding and identity, healthcare and specialist communications is now directed at internal audiences. Making sure that internal audiences are onside is critically important in ensuring strategic and structural messages are transmitted to customers, clients, suppliers, investors, journalists, analysts, governments and non-governmental organizations (Sorrell, 2002).

So why are brands *so* highly valued today? Put bluntly, brands are valued because they create a *comfort zone* around a firm and its products. Corporations and products with strong brands are unlikely to die out overnight. They enjoy greater permanence in the marketplace because of their reputation, image, familiarity, and so on.

So, underlying the high value placed on brands is a high value being placed on a particular conservative relationship with the world. Corporations with strong brands enjoy greater *customer loyalty*. Branding promises to connect up firms, products and customers and bind them together – often through emotion rather than reason. When firms proclaim that their brands are their greatest asset, what they are really saying is that their relationship with customers is their greatest asset. Their greatest asset, as they perceive it, is not the capacity to create new markets with radical new products. Rather, they see themselves as valuable if they have a strong connection with the customer.

Once corporations develop strong brands they have a kind of comfort zone – a familiarity, credibility and durability in the marketplace – in which to pursue growth. Here, corporations only feel comfortable launching new products that customers are already semi-familiar with – brand extensions. These are products that are closely tied into the core values of the brand.

Brands become a medium for companies to establish a dialogue, albeit ephemeral and lacking in meaning, with consumers. Again, the aim is to lock in a relationship and establish loyalty. The holy grail of brand building for consumer goods companies is to create 'lifestyle brands', according to brand consultants. If corporate managers really feel that consumers identify with a brand through their lifestyle pursuits, then, the hope goes, this is a more compelling case for a more durable rapport with the product.[4]

The brand obsession, then, has everything to do with corporate survival and risk avoidance. At the same time as brands were being feted, corporations in the 1990s began to tell themselves explicitly that retaining customers was far less risky and expensive than winning new customers. It is this same mentality of risk avoidance that motivates the financial community to place greater value on brands. When investment bankers declare that brands contain great value, what they are really saying is that customer loyalty is of great value. This goes for both old corporations and new start-ups.

When all those dotcoms exploded onto the scene in the mid-to-late 1990s, the financial community wanted to know whether they could build a strong brand – whether they could build a strong base among consumers in society. The huge amount of cash devoted to marketing and advertising to create a brand seemed to become the most important thing itself, not whether the company was actually doing much innovation, for example. As a result, huge amounts of venture capital went straight through these companies, like water in a sieve, into the marketing, advertising and consulting industries so that brands could be developed. When the dust settled after the end of the 1990s bull market, the innovation content of these companies seemed remarkably low. People scratched their heads and asked: What was the money really spent on?

What is the real problem with brands?

For commentators, the rise of the brand is often interpreted as a sign of corporate 'bullying'. Here, brands signify an excessive abuse of corporate power. For some, brands threaten free self-expression and cultural diversity. A world dominated by brands crowds out other cultures, the fear goes. (See Klein (2000) for a fuller discussion of these ideas).

Overwhelmingly, though, the rise of brand building is a defensive move by corporations. It stems from risk avoidance, not a grand plan to take over the world. Branding is intimately connected to the defensive relationship managers now have with the world, and their own feelings of powerlessness. Brands present a problem not because people are manipulated by adverts and logos. If anything, this is a patronizing view of people which tends to cast them in a victim-like role. Brands represent a serious problem because they reflect a highly conservative approach to markets. Corporations have become obsessed with securing customer relationships of loyalty, rather than creating new markets with new products.

Commentators who see branded corporations as 'bullies' sometimes note that branding expresses nervousness. Thus Naomi Klein, noting the new worries of corporations over whether they are perceived to be 'cool' or not, writes:

> The insecurities go round and round the boardroom table, turning ad writers, art directors and Ceos into turbo-powered teenagers, circling in front of their bedroom mirrors trying to look blasé. Do the kids think we're cool? They want to know. Are we trying too hard to be cool, or are we really cool? Do we have attitude? The right attitude?' The quest for cool, notes Klein, 'is riddled with self-doubt' (Klein, 2000, p. 69).

Unfortunately, Klein does not follow through this insight in her analysis. She tends to see branding as a symptom of corporate aggressiveness, rather than a symptom of risk aversion.

An important point is that the obsession with brands now dictates the paths of corporate growth. Companies seem more reluctant to grow by launching radical new products, for instance. They want to invest and grow, but without upsetting their existing relationships with customers. Or, in the language of branding, they want to grow, but by not diluting their brands. This impulse leads companies to the vehicle of the brand extension.

The rise of the brand extension

Executives and consultants see brand extensions as analogous to the concept of retail franchising. Say an entrepreneur was looking to open a new hamburger restaurant. He or she could try to create a new type of restaurant and do something original. Or, the entrepreneur could approach an existing franchise, such as McDonald's. They could open up a new store under the safety net of the McDonald's franchise.

According to brand consultants, new stores that open under a franchise are far less likely to fail. The same logic is then applied to individual products. If a new product is somehow tied closely to the 'core values' of the brand, snuggling underneath its safe umbrella, it has a likelier chance of success. Companies can reduce the risk of product launches. The trouble is, as such a strategy becomes generalized across the economy, it reduces genuine choice for consumers. The level of genuine change with new products is much reduced.

The philosophy of the brand extension, or brand stretching as it is alternatively known, has everything to do with customer retention and customer loyalty. According to another brand consultant: 'The philosophy of brand stretching should be about getting more from existing customers, under the reality that it is easier to get revenue from existing customers than new customers.' The brand extension is a way of growing in the safest possible way, securing revenues on safer ground.[5]

When managers go through the process for brand extensions, then, typically, they ask questions such as:

> Where does the brand have 'permission' to stretch? In other words, what is the brand credibility in the eyes of consumers? Does Marks & Spencer, for example, have the credibility to stretch into financial services? Second, what is the strength of competitors? Nike may have permission to stretch into sunglasses. But will it succeed with existing competitors in the same category?[6]

Companies need to think about where they have 'permission' to expand and grow. The worst thing a company can do is launch a product that is outside the 'core value' of the brand. Often, the rationale for this thinking is that customers could be confused, surprised and even angry.

When executives make strategic decisions today, therefore, uppermost in their mind is what existing customers already think about their company and their companies' products and brands. The new challenge for executives is how to grow a company but without diluting the brand – without disrupting existing customer relationships.

This attitude can be seen in attitudes to diversification. Industrial diversification has been out of fashion in recent times, as noted in Chapter 4. But it is more acceptable for companies to diversify if they have built up a strong brand. Here, companies can diversify within the comfort zone of the brand. An example is Richard Branson's Virgin empire. This has stretched from music to airlines to railways and to financial services, to name a few. In each case, Branson has tried to replicate the same brand values of fun, fashion, rebellion, and the 'we're on your side' anti-capitalist consumer-friendly approach.

Brand stretching is well known in sectors such as luxury goods and sport. So, Calvin Klein has stretched the brand from clothes to fragrances to eyewear, and so on. But because all companies see brands as central to their success or failure today, it is not surprising that the outlook of brand stretching has become generalized across industry.

For example, at the beginning of the new millennium, global mobile phone manufacturers were all carefully considering how to launch new products, but only in the guise of brand extensions. Believing they were stuck in mature and saturated mobile phone markets, they explored how to create new growth opportunities, but only in a way that would not dilute the brand. In other words, they were trying to grow, but in a way that would not risk disrupting the existing loyalty of customers.[7]

Sometimes, companies feel that their efforts to stretch brands do not work out. In the late 1990s, the Danish toy company Lego wanted to become the 'leading family brand' around the world. It wanted to emulate Disney's expansion into entertainment, films, television and the media.

Lego consciously attempted to stretch its brand into new areas. It created new types of robot toys, computer games, television programmes, and took part in merchandising. In 2000, however, the company posted a loss.

It confessed, defensively, and pandering to conventional wisdom, that it was getting into areas where it did not have expertise. Brand consultants and marketing specialists had a field day in criticizing the company. For them, Lego had committed the ultimate business *faux pas* of the modern age. Lego, they said, had been far too arrogant. But worse: Lego had diluted its brand. Consumers, they argued, had become far too 'confused' by Lego's empire building. Senior managers at Lego went through much breast-beating about the affair.

The branding and brand extension phenomena express the way that corporations have hemmed in their growth aspirations. They confine the scope of change in their product offerings to a narrower and narrower area in an attempt to avoid disrupting existing relationships of loyalty to the brand. Because of an intense desire for certainty, corporations often end up limiting themselves in what they feel they can do. Everything has to be filtered through brand considerations. This gets taken to a surreal level when companies with strong brands do not want to launch new products at all. Rather, they endlessly try to refresh the meaning of the brand.

This situation has arguably been reached with the US drinks firm Coca-Cola. While the essential product of Coca-Cola remains relatively static, its image, according to brand theory, has to be continually updated and refreshed. Coke's attempt to create a new product – New Coke – in the mid-1980s, was essentially seen as a blunder of the first order by itself and legions of management consultants. The company took a risk, but it did not work out. Coca-Cola could have damaged the brand, and done more harm than good.[8]

One lesson that emerged was this: it is much better to keep to the original product which people already like, but try to 'relaunch' it through the prism of new images and cultural associations. Here, nothing new is actually being created. Rather, the *meaning* of Coca-Cola is furiously recycled and refreshed over time.

Once companies have built up strong brands, they quickly become paranoid about 'brand dilution' – the possibility that consumers may perceive the brand in a negative light. In recent years, corporations have gone to extraordinary lengths to try to prevent the dilution of the brand in the eyes of the consumer.

The protection of intellectual property more generally is now a well-worn obsession in the corporate world. Intellectual property risk management has almost become a discipline in its own right. In-house lawyers of major corporations are now instructed by boards to 'defend the brand' at all costs. This can become an irrational pursuit, however. For example, in-house lawyers now report that they spend inordinate amounts of time prosecuting 'rogue traders'. This is motivated by the anxiety that such traders could 'contaminate the customer base'.

For example, lawyers of a US telecom firm now spend huge amounts of time worrying about the risk of ex-engineers who, upon leaving the firm, might try to operate sneakily under the brand name of the firm in an attempt to win customers for themselves. The worry is that if a customer were to be manhandled by that ex-engineer, this could 'contaminate the customer base' and damage the brand. An annoyed customer could make some kind of public complaint against the company, not knowing that the engineer had left the company and was trading illegally.

In the context of fears about brand dilution, the resources devoted to potential risks such as these can be out of proportion to the potential damage. According to one lawyer, the time she spends trying to identify such individuals is incommensurate with the risks they pose. In her opinion, the firm would be better off trying to go on the offensive with its intellectual property portfolio, such as using its patents to create more innovatory products.[9]

The re-branding fixation

The brand has become a broad vehicle to enable firms to deal with their anxieties. Re-branding exercises often are resorted to when firms experience identity crises. Part One of this book showed the way that self-regulation, from ethics committees to risk management procedures, reflects the defensiveness of corporations. So too with re-branding.

Literally every 'old school' British corporation in recent years, from British Airways (BA), to the British Broadcasting Corporation (BBC), to British Petroleum (BP), seems to have experienced an acute identity crisis. In all of these cases, corporations attempt to reconnect to people through re-branding exercises because of acute fears over how they are perceived.

The BBC underwent a swift re-branding exercise in 2002. Strangely, it felt its globe logo, which would pop up regularly on the television screen between programmes, was too exclusive. It replaced it with a series of multicultural images, including disabled basketball players, salsa dancers, rugby players and young dancers in nightclubs. Why? According to the controller of BBC1, Lorraine Heggessey, 'I'm very sensitive to suggestions that BBC1 is not an inclusive channel. I want to represent the diversity and totality of Britain.' Some people felt that the BBC did that quite well with the globe. After all, it is hard to think of a more inclusive and universal identity.[10] A few years before, BA had become afflicted with strikingly similar anxieties. It had replaced some of its Union Jack tailfins with ethnic designs.

It is not difficult to see that re-branding becomes the rearguard action of a business world that is suffering from low public esteem. British Petroleum (BP) re-branded itself with its slogan 'beyond petroleum', and issued an ethically and environmentally sensitive green and yellow logo. The cost of implementing the brand was estimated at £100m (see Boylan, 2000). This was clearly a highly defensive move in a context where all oil companies are now continuously anxious about their environmental and social impact.

The resources going into re-branding, in addition to brand extensions, could be spent on genuine innovation and serving the customer in a more substantial sense. Instead, resources are allocated on the basis of anxieties about perceptions and image.

The dumbing-down of innovation

So far, Part Two of this book has explored the way that managers see the marketplace – and the world more generally – as more unpredictable and risky. It has explored the more defensive way that corporations approach markets, whether consumer or business markets. The new obsession with customers today, and building relationships of loyalty, is a major illustration. Firms seem more reluctant to blaze a trail and take a lead. Rather, the risk of losing business, and damaging customer relationships, seems to loom large in the imagination.

Of course, customer loyalty can never become an end in itself – firms still have to make products after all. And, the ongoing reality of scientific and technological progress always gives rise to exciting new possibilities for new products. Here, companies are put in positions where they have to take risk and gamble on new developments.

What is new today is that customer loyalty considerations are now more fully factored into doing business. Corporations want to grow and go forward, but they only want to do so if they can hang on to existing customers and avoid disrupting relationships of loyalty. Hence, they plough more resources into brands, CRM, customer satisfaction and customer service. The survival of the company becomes more of an end in itself. Competition between firms takes a more defensive form. Firms try to compete by holding on to their existing customers, rather than creating new markets where they could sail away from the competition in terms of winning new revenues. Writ large: companies in the economy compete through customer loyalty, rather than expansion.

This is an irrational over-cautiousness, because there is no underlying reason to be so conservative. Managers tend to perceive greater commercial risk than there really is. There is a sense of being hemmed in by the competition. But the opening up of markets, and new technologies, warrants a bold approach. They expand the possibilities for firms, not close down options.

The next chapter looks at a related trend, the dumbing-down of innovation. The dumbing-down of innovation refers to a two-fold process. Corporations are retreating from radical innovation because of risk avoidance. Second, the innovation concept itself is being increasingly relativized.

The rise of risk-averse and relativist thinking are two sides of the same coin. On the one hand, managers are less comfortable with risk and uncertainty, and are less prepared to go for radical innovation where there are fewer guarantees of success. On the other hand, corporations are less prepared to uphold high standards in innovation and discriminate between different sorts of innovation. This should be understood as a paradoxical development. Technology is getting better. Organizations are becoming more sophisticated in their ability to innovate. Yet there is a retreat from ambitious thinking and practice.

Notes

1. Correspondence with Satkar Gidda.
2. See Gartner press release, 'Gartner says CRM spending to reach $76.3bn in 2005', 7 March 2001.
3. Correspondence with project managers.

4. Discussions with brand consultants.
5. Correspondence with brand consultant.
6. Correspondence with brand consultant.
7. The author worked on research for a brand-stretching project for a global mobile phone manufacturer.
8. The New Coke saga is told in Tibballs (1999, pp. 1–10). Another point that Tibballs notes is that the failure of New Coke ironically served as an affirmation of the Classic brand, so it was not a complete failure.
9. Correspondence with in-house lawyer, US telecommunications firm.
10. See 'End of the world for BBC branding', *The Observer*, 31 March 2002.

7

The Dumbing-Down of Innovation

At the end of the 1990s, *The Economist* commented that:

> Innovation has become the industrial religion of the late 20th century. Business sees it as the key to increasing profits and market share. Governments automatically reach for it when trying to fix the economy. Around the world, the rhetoric of innovation has replaced the post-war language of welfare economics. It is the new theology that unites the left and right of politics....[1]

Superficially, innovation appears to be a defining characteristic of our era. According to one popular economics writer:

> the modern economy's most impressive feature is its ability to create streams of new products and services. The spectacular growth of organized science, the consequent acceleration of technological change and the speed at which new ideas are translated into commercial products distinguish our era from previous ones (Leadbeater, 1999).

Superficially, innovation seems to be thriving. The number of inventions patented is on the rise. Certainly, corporations have spent huge amounts on IT.[2] At the same time, in the second half of the 1990s, there seemed to be a revival of R&D spending after a period of falling expenditure from the mid-1980s to the mid-1990s. In the second half of the 1990s, R&D spending in the United States climbed back to reach the level it was in 1990, around 2.63% of GDP in 1999.[3]

Yet while one group of people suggests we are living in innovative times, another group has consistently claimed that there is a retreat from genuine innovation within industry. The observation that corporations are retreating from radical innovation in their R&D efforts has proved remarkably stubborn. It is made by academics after in-depth studies of innovation within corporations, managers of R&D centres, engineers and scientists who have worked in R&D, and a range of other commentators.

For instance, Greg Blonder spent 16 years as a researcher and manager at AT&T Bell Laboratories between 1982 and 1998, and holds more than 70 patents. For him, the 1990s entrepreneurial goldrush served to mask a more intractable problem at the heart of the US innovation machine. 'It created a climate that was negative toward long-term thinking and work on long-range problems', he said in an interview with *Business Week* in July 2002. 'I don't think we realize how broken we are. And when we wake up, when the next crisis hits, it will be way too late. Innovations are built on basic research that was done long ago – 15 or 20 years ago for electronics and communications, and 20 to 30 years earlier for new materials.'

Blonder also argues that the rise in patent activity cannot necessarily be equated with greater innovation. 'Patents are issued much too readily, for really trivial ideas', he says. 'Patents should be reserved for the few critical inventions – and these occur rarely.'[4]

Blonder is not alone. Others have suggested similar trends are afoot. In another media interview, Ray Gehani, an assistant professor of management and international business at the University of Akron, suggested that firms are taking a far more cautious approach to innovation, investing only in incremental innovations with a high probability of return. 'It's happening at IBM, and GE and Lucent, which used to be the technological leaders that propelled the US economy to the next frontier', said Gehani. 'For years, these kind of companies were the pistons of economic growth.'

Here, large corporations prefer to stick with existing, hot-selling products, and give them cosmetic changes now and then in a bid to maintain sales. The aerospace industry is making bigger jets, but not passenger rockets that can fly passengers from New York to Hong Kong in a few hours. The computer industry focuses on making desktop machines with more memory, not bold, new network systems. The publishing industry could spend more on electronic books. 'If we continue to do only incremental improvements, we as a country are going nowhere', Gehani said. (see Russell, 2001.)

In the late 1990s it became common to hear similar comments elsewhere around the world. In the UK, according to one major public figure in the chemicals industry, '... the traditional emphasis on achieving organic growth, by discovering and developing new technology, may now have low priority'. And he added, 'as a consequence of sharper business focus, most effort is now given to providing customer satisfaction through technical services and incremental improvement to existing products and processes'.[5]

The retreat from radical innovation

Mark Rice has been studying the issue of radical innovation in depth for the last eight years. He is co-author of the book, *Radical Innovation: How Mature Companies Can Outsmart Upstarts*. The book presents the results of a five-year study of innovation in 10 American corporations (see Leifer et al., 2000). According to Rice, 'there is no question that the R&D activities of large technology firms have increasingly been directed towards incremental innovation. There has been increasing pressure on R&D to pay for itself, and an orientation towards the short term.'[6]

For Rice, this risk avoidance is linked to financial performance requirements. The financial markets drive large established companies in two competing directions, he says. Companies have been driven to grow their business in order to increase stock market valuations, and to meet expectations of growth. But at the same time, they face pressure to deliver predictable results every quarter (a trend examined in Chapter 4). Companies have attempted to reduce the prevalence of things that cause volatility and deviation from a plan. But that leads to risk avoidance. The managerial mindset that is created is one of rigid control, rather than tolerating an exploratory approach.

When these factors are put together, Rice believes that companies want to achieve growth but in the safest possible way – primarily through mergers and acquisitions and incremental innovation. But this can be self-defeating. There are limits to how much real 'growth' can take place through this route.

Rice's argument is that at the organizational level, companies approach radical innovation in an unsystematic, *ad hoc* fashion. Radical innovation requires long-term commitment. But the companies that Rice has studied are often tempted to give into short-term opportunism. If, say, the economy worsens, US companies often cut back on long-term projects to shore up profitability.

For example, a large chemicals company examined its internal commitment to radical innovation over many decades, discovering that commitment waxed and waned over a 17-year cycle. One innovation project was set up by senior managers who wanted to kick-start corporate growth and counter stagnation by focusing on innovation. However, more than eight years later the strategic message from senior management was to focus on the firm's core businesses and go back to basics. Researchers were told that their annual performance reviews would focus on the impact of their work on current lines of business. The technical leader of the innovation project commented that the new message was very de-motivating to him and the rest of the project team.

In newer industries such as IT, according to Rice, the pattern of cyclical commitment to innovation, followed by neglect and even obstructionism, can be much shorter – less than half the length of that observed in the 'old economy' industries, such as chemicals and materials. 'US companies tend to be cyclical in their commitment to radical innovation', says Rice. 'They never stay at it long enough to get good at it.'

Balancing the short and long term is never easy. It is idealistic to think that corporations in a market economy can pile endless resources into radical innovation. However, the balance has swung far too much in the direction of incremental innovation.

Mark Bernstein is acting CEO of the Palo Alto Research Center (PARC), formerly owned by Xerox but now an independent centre. He dates a move towards short-term thinking to the mid-1980s. Scientists and engineers at PARC were told for the first time to focus on projects with more certain pay-offs:[7] 'There has been a general trend in recent years to fine-tune businesses as financial engines', he says. 'Issues such as efficiency and quality improvement come to the fore. A large part of "managing for shareholder value" is the extent to which one can predictably create value for the company going forward. That has to be done by creating predictable purchasing decisions among consumers and predictable cash flows.' In this scenario, more radical innovation starts to be removed from the equation.

'With radical innovation, you just have to stick with it', says Bernstein. 'It becomes impossible if you let other forces such as globalization and competition stop you. Long time frames are always difficult to grapple with. There is always the reality of, "What did I really get accomplished today?" You have to stick to a long-term vision.'

It would be wrong to suggest that no long-term projects are taking place at all. In 2000, for example, Japanese firm Honda launched ASIMO, a new four-foot tall robot of human appearance. ASIMO stands for Advanced Step in Innovation of MObility. It is not the equivalent of an android that might grace the screen in an episode of *Star Trek* of course, but as a technological achievement for its times, it is pretty impressive.

Back in the mid-1980s, robots were largely confined to manufacturing and undersea exploration. Nobody had managed to create a robot with two arms and two legs that could walk upright like a human or do human movements, such as make a bow, walk backwards, climb a staircase and make a 360-degree turn. Given the complexity of human movement, this was no easy task to replicate. ASIMO however can do all these things on its own two feet. It took researchers and engineers at Honda around 10 years to develop.

According to Toru Takenaka at Honda, chief engineer and one of the key developers of the project, Honda established a basic research centre in 1986. Back then, they discussed a variety of long-term projects, and the idea of what they call a human robot cropped up. 'The aim was to create a robot that could perform tasks for humans, in order to increase human mobility. ASIMO ultimately should be a partner for humans. To reach that goal, there are many steps along the way.'[8]

At present, ASIMO is used for entertainment purposes, and reception-related and secretarial work, such as greeting guests and showing guests to particular rooms. The medium-term potential is a more sophisticated stage of 'partnering'. That could mean helping humans to do dangerous work, such as fighting fires. It could also mean carrying heavy loads over distances in particular situations. ASIMO could also help people with mobility impairments. There are many potential areas for creative cooperation.

Until recently, ASIMO was an underground project at Honda, according to Takenaka.

> Nobody in Honda knew about it. That is why it was potentially easy for Honda to erase it and quit the project. That is why I felt pressure to speed up the project and show results. Year by year, we had to show the output to our senior managers, showing every change in the technology to demonstrate the progress being made.

> Every company needs a short-term profit. But long-term research, from 10 to 20 years, is absolutely necessary. A company needs originality in its products and technologies for it to survive. The output from short-term research does not result in a competitive difference from another company.

Long-term projects have not completely disappeared off the map, then. But anybody looking at R&D trends in recent years would not be reassured that companies are becoming more pioneering in their approach to innovation. The comments earlier suggest the opposite – and in fact R&D departments have already restructured around shorter-term objectives.

In the early 1990s, R&D in the United States and Europe fell victim to a new bout of cost-cutting and downsizing. Managers explicitly wanted to make R&D more profitable and more productive in the shorter term. They wanted to make corporate research labs much more accountable to the bottom line. That meant cutting back in long-term areas and reorganizing. In particular, the type of research that could lead to more radical and break-through innovation was cut back.

At the same time, companies experimented with new organizational forms in a bid to speed up results. They decentralized R&D to business units to encourage these units to pay for their own R&D. Since these units are their own profit centres, and do not rely on a central budget, they tend to be more stringent and only fund projects with a more immediate chance of success.

Many firms also changed incentive schemes. Engineers would be paid according to short-term product development success. Others deliberately encouraged a high turnover of staff, limiting long-term contracts apparently in order to encourage fresh waves of new ideas. Companies have also looked for other ways to share costs and reduce risks – in particular entering into alliances with other firms. Such alliances have mushroomed in recent years.

The severity of the cut-backs in R&D prompted much debate in the United States, becoming a major business theme of the mid-1990s. One article in 1995 noted that corporations had become more interested in cutting costs and using available research money on projects with near-term payoffs. For John Gibbons, former White House Science Adviser, corporations' 'headlights are lowered, they can't look ahead so far' (see Boyd, 1995).

A speech given at the New York Academy of Sciences in 1995, called 'Innovation at risk: the future of America's research-intensive industry', suggested that R&D had become too one-sidedly oriented toward short-term product development.[9]

In 1996 an article in the *New York Times* suggested that 'many corporate executives have decided that basic research for tomorrow is simply too speculative'. It suggested that corporations now expected a return on investment in R&D to materialize in three years, and not much longer (see Uchitelle,

1996). Some academics argued that 'decentralization dynamics' in R&D 'tend to promote both short-termism in innovative efforts and a strong but risk-averse market orientation'.[10]

Other commentators accept that corporations have cut back on risk-taking R&D. But they then argue that this is some inevitable result of, you guessed it, globalization. An example of this mindset was expressed in the book *Engines of Tomorrow*, written by ex-*Business Week* technology editor, Robert Buderi, and published in 2000.

The book is a historical overview of corporate research in the United States. Buderi notes that more ambitious and speculative research has been scaled back in recent years. As he says, 'it's true in the face of new realities, including higher costs and stiffer competition, company research arms have had to scale back some longer-range projects. A hard line was especially needed in the ferociously competitive and tumultuous computer, telecoms and electronic industries.' Elsewhere, 'many of these pioneering investigations have also been phased out', of the sort, he notes, that led to the innovation of the transistor.

But essentially, according to Buderi, this is no one's fault. Managers have just had to confront 'the new realities'. Here, the essential retreat from radical innovation – which is what is taking place – cannot be helped. As he says, 'some things are outside anyone's control – and the changes in corporate research have proven so universal that it's hard to simply blame management. Even if companies made serious mistakes – and many did – it doesn't alter the fact that corporations must adapt to a rapidly evolving world (Buderi, 2000, ch. 1).

But this logic does not stack up. Essentially, the decline of a pioneering spirit is blamed on external events. Why should the 'new realities' automatically lead to a decline in radical innovation? One could argue that firms that take a more pioneering spirit equip themselves better to deal with the pressures of the marketplace. A firm that does ambitious long-term R&D and product development ends up having more choices, not less. As a result, it equips itself with more choices in being able to adapt to circumstances. Giving up on radical innovation in order to be reconciled with 'the new realities' has dangers of itself. It can leave firms more at the mercy of external forces and, paradoxically, leave them less able to adapt to change.

The reluctance of firms to do radical innovation is strange because the potential for organizations to innovate has never been better. Rice and his co-authors point out that 'a large firm is an amazing storehouse of accumulated knowledge, which can be tapped through informal networks that bring together scientists, business unit managers, sales people, marketers, and people who control financial and laboratory resources'. No one can doubt that corporations today are far more sophisticated than those of 30 or 50 years ago.

Process innovation

Schematically, innovation can take place in two major overlapping ways. Institutions and industries can devote resources to creating new products. They can also use technologies, and new products, to make working practices more efficient, and innovate at the level of processes – ways of doing things.

In the broadest sense, all processes – all human activities – can be done in a quicker, easier and more productive way by using new technology. In this sense technology helps overcome natural limitations. A primitive hunter–gatherer can use a bow and arrow to kill an animal rather than using his bare hands. People in their houses can use a washing machine and tumble dryer with electric motors to wash and dry their clothes. Office workers using the Internet can instantly send all sorts of information to people on the other side of the world rather than using mail by land or sea. In myriad ways, process innovations therefore lead to productivity gains.

Traditionally, firms have always created new products through R&D and other means. At the same time, factories and offices have used new products, in the form of new technology, to make themselves more efficient. The next section will examine how innovative firms have been with regards to IT and process innovation. To get a perspective on IT today, it is important to backtrack several steps to look at how industry has used technology more broadly, looking at the factory and the office.[11]

Technology in industry – a brief history

Industry first began in the nineteenth century to use technology for substantial efficiency gains. That century was witness to a plethora of innovations in machine technology to manufacture goods, such as new forms of energy to power machines, and new materials to improve cutting speeds.

In the interwar period of the twentieth century, the possibility that machinery could replace human labour more systematically gave rise to a discussion on 'automation' in the workplace. In the 1950s books started to appear on the subject, such as John Diebold's *Automation: The Advent of the Automatic factory* in 1952, and the 1958 study *Automation and Management* by James Bright, which charted the historic transition that had been made from the basic hand tool to programmable machines.

The potential for automation in manufacturing industry began in the 1950s, with a new technology that generated much excitement, 'numerically controlled' systems. Through these systems, the movement of a drill head or cutting tool could be programmed based on holes punched in a paper tape. In the early 1960s, computer numerical control machines were invented, creating more flexibility because different programs could be stored in memory, giving rise to the possibility of producing a range of goods on one machine.

In the early 1960s, a whole new host of other technologies began to emerge, such as robots, computer-aided design (CAD), computer-aided manufacturing (CAM), and flexible manufacturing systems. The first industrial robot appeared on the manufacturing scene in 1961, in a General Motors factory in New Jersey. Robots could do dirty and repetitive industrial work, such as welding, paint-spraying, grinding, molding and casting. By 1981, 4100 robots were in use in US industry.

Early CAD/CAM systems helped computerize the process of drawing and design. The first such system was launched in 1969 by Computervision Corporation. CAD established itself in the car and aerospace industries, as designers could design onto the screen directly, and use the computer to simulate the performance of a product. This eventually made it possible to bypass the lengthy process of making and testing a physical prototype. Finally, manufacturing systems became flexible enough to allow firms to create 'economies of scope' – the production of different goods in smaller batches, rather than having to rely on the production of one product.

Mechanization of the office also began in the nineteenth century, at first in a very basic fashion. Offices made use of typewriters, for instance. The first commercial sale of the typewriter was in 1873. By 1900 sales had reached 100 000. In 1935 the first electronic typewriter was introduced.

The automation of the office, however, relied on progress in IT. In 1947 the transistor was invented in Bell Labs. The transistor – a device that acts as an electrical switch and is able to encode information in binary form – was considerably built upon in the late 1950s, when the integrated circuit was invented. The microprocessor of 1971 was a further advance. In the 1960s, Gordon Moore predicted that the number of transistors that could be fabricated on a microchip would double every 18 months – today known as Moore's Law. In 1971, the first microprocessor had 2300 transistors. The Pentium 4, released by leading semiconductor manufacturer Intel in November 2000, had 42 million.

IT in the shape of mainframe computers began to permeate offices after the invention of the transistor in the late 1940s. The number of computers in the US federal government grew from 2 in 1950, to 45 in 1955, 531 in 1960, and 2188 in 1965 (see McLaughlin, 1966). In the business world, General Electric was the first US firm to install a mainframe in 1953.

By the 1960s, the bulk of large organizations had developed data-processing centres to deal with the payroll, issue invoices and control inventory. In the late 1960s, writers were already heralding the importance of IT and were discussing the imperatives of using IT for strategic competitive advantage – a contemporary theme. In 1969 one author wrote:

> Today a company's competitive survival may well hinge on the way in which it manages information – on the sureness with which it maintains control over production, inventory and other costs and the speed with which it reacts to shifts in demand, moves by competitors, emergency needs of customers, and development in its own technology.

He noted that information processing had become a 'major preoccupation' and a 'top management' concern (Heyel, 1969).

A whole new range of devices for the office emerged with the advent of the microchip in the early 1970s: programmable calculators, word processors, fax machines, copiers, electronic switchboards and micro- and mini-computers. In the 1970s and 1980s, companies such as Xerox, Wang, Exxon, ITT, Olivetti, Siemens and Philips, as well as IBM, Apple and AT&T, attempted to sell various visions of 'the office of the future'. *Business Week* published an executive briefing on 30 June 1975, called *The Office of the Future*. It included a discussion on the theme of the 'paperless office', now heavily debunked, a vision where paper would become obsolete because of IT.

In 1981, IBM launched what it called a personal computer (PC), after Apple had launched various forms in the 1970s. In the same year, IBM licensed the MS-DOS operating system from Microsoft. When Microsoft launched Windows as the new operating system in 1985, the basic framework for today's computer systems was established.

Progress in computing technology was accompanied by progress in telecommunications. In the 1970s, packet switching routers were developed, which enabled data to be sent in digital form down a telephone wire. This laid the foundation for progress to occur in the 1990s, with the convergence of computer and telecommunications technology in the form of the Internet. This convergence has facilitated enormous progress in processing, manipulating, storing and moving information. More recently, the ability to transmit data over cellular networks to mobile phones and devices means that people will be able to access networks while on the move.

Thinking about the Internet: the potential and the barriers

The reason for giving this history is to make a simple point about the Internet today. In the past, the technologies available to firms were fairly limited in what they could offer in terms of process innovation. Mainframe computers could process data far more efficiently than the machines beforehand. But IT was limited to creating efficiency gains in particular niche areas.

IT today has become infinitely more sophisticated. There are many more tools available to process, manipulate, organize, store and transfer information in digital form. What is really new about the Internet is the potential to create efficiency gains in a huge number of areas. Standardization in the underlying network and computer language has become an enormous benefit and the basis for collaboration – anyone in the world, for instance, can send a Word document to another person through email.

In the coming period, it is likely that firms will make use of wireless technology as an extension of their existing IT systems. To increase productivity, employees on the road, or on the move anywhere, can be given access to existing IT tools and networks. By using mobile devices, they can access different sorts of information bound up in a firm – information related to stock availability and the supply chain, different customers, finance and so on. Also, firms will be able to track an employee's location using wireless technology, leading to a sophisticated communication of data between individuals on the move and in offices.

The Internet and other developing tools surrounding it, therefore offer a kind of standardized foundation on a global level to communicate, collaborate, solve problems, centralize resources, speed things up, become more efficient and so on. In theory, as some economists have pointed out, IT tools today 'can affect every economic activity in which organization, information processing or communication is important – in short, every single economic activity' (see Cohen et al., 2000).

The sophistication of IT has therefore given rise to the possibility that literally *any* kind of activity, any human process, can be made more efficient using computers and the Internet. Arguably that is what is new about it.

For individual firms, there is great potential to use the Internet in a whole range of processes: selling more goods online; attracting new customers online; purchasing supplies online; connecting up with suppliers to improve inventory control and providing a service online. With intranets – Internet technology used to create an internal organizational network – companies can reduce the cost of printing and distributing corporate literature, speed up employee communication, facilitate information sharing, and so on.

However, there is a caveat. One of the myths about the Internet is that it will bring great transformation to the world. That is wrong. The Internet offers a huge number of ways to do things more efficiently, but it will not transform the physical world on its own. The Internet has arrived in a physical society that was not designed for it. In order to get the best out of the Internet, the physical world requires modernization and transformation.

Take e-commerce as an example. It is great being able to order a physical book over the Internet. But the service obviously cannot take place without physical warehousing and delivery systems. And, a whole range of other so-called 'old economy' limitations have to be overcome, some very basic but highly annoying. At present, many consumers have to be in their houses to take a delivery, because the postman cannot get goods through small letterboxes. If the parcel has to be taken to a collection point half an hour away, the buyer could have gone to her local bookshop to buy the book.[12]

Another example is logistics. It is great being able to track goods through the Internet as they move across the world – a development that has increased coordination and sped up the process. But many logistics providers complain that the process of going through customs at national borders is cumbersome, slowing everything down. The physical and the virtual need changing at the same time – not one or the other.

This is why the discussion about the 'old' and 'new' economies ironically poses a major barrier to the Internet's progress. During the 1990s, it became fashionable to believe that if you were left in the 'old' economy, you were somehow left behind. But to get the best out of the Internet, the so-called old economy has to be modernized at the same time. Seeing them as separate arenas only reflects the narrowness of the vision of change on offer today.

On its own, the Internet offers incremental innovation

It is not surprising that corporations use the Internet in a huge number of ways to become more efficient. The business case for doing so is compelling. Use of the Internet fits into a very familiar pattern outlined by the brief history of technology in the workplace above – using technology to become more productive. When firms use the Internet, they are not being innovative *per se*, any more than it was particularly innovative on the part of offices in the late nineteenth century to use typewriters for the first time.

The business case for using the Internet is probably more compelling than previous technologies. History shows that there always is a certain amount of initial resistance to new technologies. The author Tom Forester notes that, in the early 1980s, only a small percentage of firms in countries such as Britain were bothering to use some of the new technologies that had emerged in the post-war period, such as CAD/CAM and robots. Governments launched awareness campaigns in a bid to speed up their use (Forester, 1987).

But it is comparatively easy, using the Internet, to make immediate efficiency gains. Corporations spend billions on procurement every year, for example. By employing the Internet to cut out paperwork and enter into markets for supplies where prices are bid down, they can make immediate savings. Corporations take to the Internet because it offers them *incremental* improvement in existing processes. Using the Internet is part of a longer historical process of improving the efficiency of existing processes. This is the least exciting aspect of the Internet. Many areas that the Internet helps with are not very exciting. Just as mainframe computers introduced in the 1950s to 'number-crunch' data in various industries, such as banking, were not very exciting, buying corporate supplies such as paper clips over the Internet in 'e-marketplaces' is not very exciting either.

Some firms have been imaginative in using the Internet to make incremental improvements in business processes. WebCor is a Californian construction business that has attempted to incorporate the Internet, and mobile devices, into its basic operations, using them for communication and co-ordination. One problem in construction involves coordinating the many different teams on a project, from architects to plumbers and electricians. The firm has used the Internet to centralize information and plans. It has encouraged architects to stop using physical blueprints that have to be commercially printed, packaged and delivered to all the participants on a project. It has encouraged everyone to have electronic access to the drawings. This means that the electricians, plumbers and other subcontractors can work around each other better. If any changes occur, the architects, engineers and owners can approve them more quickly. WebCor also encourages different groups to communicate data using mobile devices on sites. In various ways, using the Internet can speed up the time it takes to complete a project. It usually takes two months to start a project for example, once approved by the local building department. Using the Internet, WebCor has reduced that to around 20 days.[13]

The Internet is used heavily in logistics and the supply chain. The logistics providers run many of the supply chains for large corporations, and claim to have speeded up product delivery times. By using the Internet, the provider UPS claims it has sliced four days off the average time it takes to deliver a Ford car from factory to the dealer. Corporations use the Internet to share information in various ways. Sigma-Aldrich, the life sciences company, has built a content website for its partners which shows the attributes of chemicals, and holds related documents on purity, safety and usage. Similarly, Boeing uses the Internet to share information with airlines. It has posted an estimated 122 000 aircraft maintenance documents online for airlines to use. Firms such as General Electric use intranets for internal knowledge management purposes. General Electric has something called the Support Central initiative. Employees give details of their area of expertise so that other people can find them and ask them questions.[14] Other corporations, such as 3M in the United States, the diversified manufacturer, uses its intranet to connect up its 750 manufacturing engineers around the world in order to swap ideas and take product ideas from the research stage to manufacturing (see Marsh, 2001).

Corporations in all industries now experiment with mobile devices to make processes more efficient and work more productive. Some pharmaceutical firms encourage employees to use mobile devices to communicate data in clinical trials. Some aspects of the experimentation process can be sped up using wireless technology. Elsewhere, shipping ports such as France's Le Havre have now equipped employees with wireless devices for data communication. Broadly, they are used to help coordinate ships leaving and docking, and the loading and unloading of cargo. If plans change, staff on the quays can be sent new information to their screens. In retail, UK supermarket Tesco and IBM have been testing a wireless system that equips staff with hand-held devices. This is a stock management system that provides data about goods on the shelf and in the storeroom. The productivity gain is that staff do not have to trek back and forth to the storeroom to check the availability of goods. They can use the mobile device to see what is on the shelves and in storage.

The introduction of so-called 'web services' in the coming years will offer more possibilities in using the Internet. There are several interrelated aims of web services. The hope is to create common technology standards for different systems to work together, so that more ambitious online services can be bundled for businesses and consumers. At the same time, an aspiration is to transform the user interface of the web into a dynamic medium, where the web becomes more akin to an operating system on which to run programs. The web may become more like Microsoft's Windows, i.e. a foundation to lay applications on, rather than a static display for information and a medium for fairly limited tasks such as ordering goods online (see Harvey, 2002).

Transforming the physical – a more radical task

The Internet is used to make existing processes more efficient. But one could argue this is the easy part. It follows a well-trodden path. Of course, IT systems implementation can be notoriously difficult, but in many of the above examples the business case is compelling, and the gains often immediate in the form of savings.

To get the most from the Internet often requires a more transformative approach to the physical world. Unfortunately this is precisely the area where firms start to go wobbly. The reluctance to change the physical world can be seen all the time in individual IT projects. Take one example. In the late

1990s, a major US food company began an IT project in its grain division, with an estimated final cost of US $100–200m. The project began to create a new IT systems infrastructure around its grain elevators, huge silos that store grain before being transported around the world. The central objective was to create an infrastructure where information could be centralized, so managers could tell instantly how much grain had been sold, for a particular price. The firm invested in building a new software program, PCs, servers and networks.

The project replaced a legacy system and was expected to reduce the administration required to run the system. But the project had conservative aims. First, the company wanted real-time information so that it could coordinate its risk management efforts, namely hedging price volatility by using derivatives. Second, it wanted to coordinate data in order to improve customer service and customer satisfaction. If, for instance, a customer wanted to go to a different elevator than usual, the company could provide the appropriate information to the customer on that particular site.

The project was not built around more fundamental changes to the unloading and transportation of grain, or the automation of the elevators. There was no intention to conduct a more thorough standardization of practices. This would mean taking the argument to customers and suppliers as to the new benefits of such a move.

The firm ended up with more information about its business, but the business itself was fundamentally untouched. One consequence was the creation of more complexity in the system. For instance, different businesses had many different ways of doing business, and were not standardized. Because the firm did not want to address this issue, because it would require a more thorough standardization process and radical change, the new IT systems had to accommodate all the different requirements and standards. For the technical staff working on the project it became a nightmare to try to accommodate the different requirements while building the software program.[15]

Using the Internet to avoid risk

The Internet does not lead to innovation itself. If companies are innovative, they will find a way to use the Internet in an innovative way. But if they are trying to *avoid* risk, then they will find a way to use the Internet for that too.

The Internet can be used to pursue highly conservative goals. For example, lazy journalists use the Internet to write articles. Articles can quickly be patched together through an imaginative assembling of the thousands of other people's articles available on the Internet. Rather than go out into the world to interview people and get first-hand quotes, they turn to the Internet.

Governments believe, somewhat optimistically, that by employing the Internet as a medium to allow people to vote online, democracy will be magically restored and low election turnouts can be reversed. Rather than go out into the world to win the hearts and minds of citizens through bold ideas, governments are falling back on the Internet.

Unfortunately, one of the major reasons the Internet is eulogized in business is that it actually allows firms to avoid some of the major risks they have always faced. Of course, nobody quite puts it like this. What they tend to say is that the Internet allows firms to pursue a business model based on the 'virtual company' or some variant of it – a business model where supply chain risk is much reduced, companies are light on assets, and use the Internet to 'get close to the customer'.

The classic example is the US computer manufacturer Dell, founded in the 1980s by the entrepreneur Michael Dell. It is significant that Dell is held up as a highly innovative firm and a great example of the new economy at work. Dell is an interesting company, and it is very good at what it does. But Dell's whole business model, more than other hi-tech companies, is built around avoiding risk. It uses the Internet to fine-tune a business model where revenues can be won in a low-risk fashion.

What Dell does is very simple. It specializes in assembling computer components into a final product, which it delivers direct to the customer – an example of a manufacturer bypassing the retail stage. It does not make computers, nor, to be fair, is really contributing to progress in computing technology. It does do R&D, but far less than other hi-tech companies. As one commentator puts it, Dell 'have never really had to develop their own cutting-edge products or take a gamble on technology choices'.[16]

Dell's main area of innovation is customer service. Its proposition is that it delivers a finished product to the consumer far faster, and more efficiently, than its competitors. Since people and companies understandably want their computers to be delivered quickly, it has thrived in recent years. Dell uses the Internet to advance this particular business model even further. It uses the Internet to speed up coordination in the supply chain, and network with semiconductor manufacturers, disk drive producers and others, such as television monitor manufacturers, so it can assemble computers quicker and reduce its inventory. According to one estimate, Dell held 32 days of inventory in stock in 1995, but only four days in 2002.[17]

Tying up capital in the form of inventory has always been a major area of risk for companies. No company – especially in a fast moving environment such as computers – wants to be caught with old computers because they will be obsolete when the next generation of better, faster chips, and therefore better, faster computers, hits the shelves. At the same time, Dell uses the Internet to 'get closer to the customer'. It sells a huge amount of its product online, increasing its own coordination and further speeding up the process of computer delivery to the customer.

Michael Dell has called this model 'virtual integration'. Dell uses the Internet to become a kind of 'virtual company' that has avoided the risks associated with the physical world. Dell carries no final goods inventory, so it does not run the risk of being caught with unwanted stock. It does not manufacture many computer components itself. But, more significantly, Dell does not do much risk-taking R&D. All it does is assemble and deliver computers. It does this more efficiently than anyone else by using the Internet.

Commenting on Dell in July 2002 in the magazine *Wired*, the innovation writer Michael Schrage made some perceptive points:

> Almost uniquely among high tech firms, Dell forbids internal subsidies. No loss leaders, no prolonged grace periods, no long bets on trends yet to emerge. Michael Dell is too smart to think he's smart enough to predict the future . . . let others dream up products never before imagined and risk their futures on that vision. Dell is content to ask consumers what they want and then sell it to them (Schrage, 2002).

In other words, Dell's whole attitude is, let other companies take risk. Let others try to shape the future. As Schrage adds, Dell 'doesn't even pretend to be an innovator. Instead the company uses its clout to get early access to its partners' most innovative products and components . . . .'

From this perspective, it is possible to understand why the Internet is so liked in the business world, and why companies such as Dell are so eulogized. Many of the so-called 'new economy' companies that are held up as great business models are not actually taking that much risk at all, but using the Internet to fine-tune a business model of low risk, high return. In today's cautious business world, the ultimate business model seems to be one where firms use the Internet to tap into a huge market, often as an intermediary, and lower the traditional business risks they have faced.

For the entrepreneur seeking a high return at a low risk, the Internet offers a host of opportunities. The ultimate business model in this scenario would be one where firms could leverage the global reach of the Internet to tap into a newly global online market, to provide an online service, but avoid any physical risk in the form of goods delivery.

This is precisely why the US firm eBay, the online auction site that matches buyers and sellers in second-hand goods, has been so feted. At the height of the financial bubble in the late 1990s, eBay was receiving among the highest valuations on the stock market. Why? It was perceived to have a particular business model. It had positioned itself in a large global market (second-hand goods exchange), and therefore was facing certain revenue streams and strong cash flows. But it was also deemed to be low risk, for the simple fact that it had few physical operations such as warehouses, and no inventory which could lead to problems of over-capacity and the risk of unsold and rapidly depreciating assets. Investors and analysts tend to get very excited about companies that are very well positioned in growth markets, but face little risk in their operations and markets going forward.

The virtual business model is only for the lucky few, however. Not everybody can become a virtual intermediary in this fashion. All sorts of companies can certainly use the Internet to reduce inventory and improve customer service. But it is not difficult to see that the Dell or eBay models cannot be generalized across the economy. Schrage notes that while Dell is seen as the ultimate 'new economy' business model, it is remarkable how so few firms have managed to emulate its way of operating. Significantly, one reason is that firms 'innovate too much', according to Schrage. They are still engaged in the messy business of initiating R&D projects and taking bets on new technologies.

It is not an exaggeration to say that behind the eulogizing of companies like Dell is a desire to retreat from traditional business risks. If only we could escape to the virtual world of the Internet, people seem to think, and avoid all this horrible physical stuff. Unfortunately, this is slightly idealistic. The rest of the economy is still out there – a physical economy of people messing about with test tubes, making things, travelling on transportation systems, and so on. And, somebody still needs to do the real innovating. Only a very few firms can position themselves as virtual intermediaries.

The narrow way in which the Internet is often conceived, as a vehicle to avoid risk, is not encouraging. Genuine innovation lies in the opposite direction – taking a radical approach to transforming the physical world, to restructure around the Internet. By virtue of its nature, the Internet calls out for restructuring of the physical world in a way that previous information technologies did not. In the past, for instance, it would have made no sense to restructure around mainframe computers – they did not offer that kind of potential. The Internet, alongside other technologies and tools such as wireless, is different. It provides a socialized network with huge potential for efficiency gains in all kinds of area. It provides a standardized foundation on a global level to communicate, collaborate, solve problems, centralize resources, speed things up, become more efficient, and so on. The challenge for institutions and society is not to use the Internet to retreat into the virtual, as a way of cleverly avoiding risk in the physical world. Rather, the challenge is to take a bolder approach to innovating in the physical world in order to maximize the potential of the Internet.

The relativization of the innovation concept

So far this chapter has argued that firms are retreating from radical innovation, even though technology offers more potential today. A parallel problem is the relativization of the innovation concept.

While everyone talks more about 'innovation' today, as mentioned in the introduction, it is becoming more and more unclear as to what they are talking about. Rather oddly, everyone seems keener to stress that innovation is not necessarily about R&D, technology or investment. It can be about culture, employees, competitiveness. It is about creativity, thinking on the left side of the brain, being inspirational.

Take some examples. Roundtable discussions among business leaders reflect the new way that innovation is defined. In July 2001, the US magazine *Fast Company* held a special roundtable, asking business leaders from 10 major companies to discuss innovation. What was clear from the discussion was that innovation for them really equated with any kind of creative approach to business, and any notion of change. 'It's important to recognize that innovation is relative', said Simon Jeffrey, Chairman and Chief Operating Officer of LucasArts Entertainment, in one contribution to the discussion. 'It happens in companies of different sizes, at different levels. Innovation can be a clerk who finds a way to make filing 20% more efficient. It's important that we notice innovation, nurture it, and reward it.'

A survey conducted in the late 1990s by Mori for 3M UK, asked British executives to name the most important 'drivers of innovation'. Interestingly, R&D, new technologies and investment were not rated all that highly. In this survey, executives identified four key issues behind success in innovation: competition, customer requirements, employee development, and organizational culture (see Brown, 1999).

Global consulting firms make numerous studies of innovation. Consultants are often very keen to stress that innovation is not just about R&D. It can be anything. In some companies, 'innovation' is thriving everywhere – at the level of brand marketing, the creativity of office workers, and in the supply chain. Cultural definitions of innovation have become considerably dumbed-down. For instance, in March 2002, a magazine of a British Sunday newspaper published its guide to the Innovation 100 – a list of, supposedly, the major innovations since 1990. Dolly the Sheep, stem cells, genetically modified food, nanotechnology and hydrogen engines were rightly included. But also in the list were 'patient power', the 'coffee culture', not to mention women-friendly bars, supermalls, lad mags, reality TV, pet passports, boutique hotels, designer books and loyalty cards.[18]

It may seem strange, but discussion on innovation today often has little to do with innovation! As innovation has become elevated in importance in the business world, it is increasingly associated with ever more nebulous notions of creativity and adaptability. The idea that innovation might mean introducing something genuinely new is confined to a shadowy existence.

Since concepts of innovation have become so dumbed-down, it is not surprising to discover that anyone can become an innovator. Small companies are innovative by virtue of being small. Brand managers are innovative. Designers are innovative. One does not need a science or technology doctorate, training or even experience to be innovative these days, it seems. Rather, for managers and consultants, all employees can contribute to innovation.

In this context, the key to encourage innovation within the firm is not to invest more in R&D, take a long-term approach, restructure operations or use technology in a bold way. Rather, everyone stresses the importance of creating the right 'culture' of innovation, the right psychological mindset within the company, where everyone can contribute ideas. Hence, innovation is often seen as a matter of having the right values or vision.

So what is going on? Put bluntly, in a world where there is a new unwillingness to take risk and define high standards, the concept of innovation can only take on a nebulous, vacuous existence. It becomes an increasingly abstract concept, empty of meaning. Innovation becomes reduced almost to a matter of psychology – somehow having the right attitude or mindset.

Just as politicians talk more and more vacuously about the importance of missions and values, the business world talks about culture and creativity. As people in the real world evade taking risk, the concept of innovation becomes ever more elusive. To be innovative is not to put four billion dollars into a new type of IT network, aircraft or drug project. Rather, it is an ongoing process of creativity and adaptation, which helps you survive in a more unpredictable world.

Employees are encouraged to be innovative – they just need to 'unleash' their creativity. The flaw with these ideas is that innovation cannot just be 'unleashed', like some kind of frustrated dog that has not been out of the house for a while. The saying that inspiration is 99% perspiration is probably closer to the truth. The people who genuinely innovate tend to be those who have trained in a specialist field, have a full knowledge of past achievements, and toil and experiment over a long period of time. This is not elitist. It simply recognizes that genuine insights that advance knowledge tend to come out of this process, not from people suddenly attempting to use the 'left side of their brain'.

There is a darker downside to the relativization process. The trouble with failing to uphold some kind of standard and high aspiration for proper innovation means that, inevitably, inferior and trivial forms of innovation can quickly become vaunted as breakthrough innovation. This is happening now all the time.

Take an example. In the summer of 2002, General Motors launched a new advertising campaign on British television to promote the Vauxhall Vectra car. Ed Harris, the dynamic American actor well known for roles in films such as *Enemy at the Gates* and *The Abyss*, had become co-opted in this endeavour.

In one particular advert, Harris was cast trying to convince a jury – symbolizing the TV audience – that 'this car is a phenomenon'. 'Ask yourself this', he said to the jury, 'is your automobile a new piece of thinking?' And then came the punch line: 'Let me put it another way. How many new cars do you know where the indicators get louder the faster you go . . . so if on a noisy motorway you don't forget to turn them off.'

The startling innovation at the heart of the Vauxhall Vectra had been dramatically unveiled: slightly louder indicators. The background music suddenly became all thoughtful and mysterious. The jury feigned a look of deep wonderment at this revelation. As the advert came to a close, viewers were left with the impression that something profound had been uttered. And all this without a hint of irony.

This one advert sums up the way that the concept of innovation has become dumbed-down. No doubt, the Vauxhall Vectra has lots of wonderful new features. But the idea that these constitute a radical leap forward in the history of the automobile, as implied without irony in the advert, stretches credibility. If Vauxhall had unveiled a car powered by a completely new energy source, a completely new design, or one that could fly, then perhaps these claims could be justified. But slightly louder indicators?

The problem is this: once institutions and society fail to define standards in innovation, it then becomes possible to pretend that naff innovation is really great innovation. Rather suddenly, rather small leaps forward are suddenly presented as great leaps forward. This is a slippery slope which then leads to all sorts of other problems. What emerges is a kind of Orwellian world of innovation double-speak. Corporations are already very uncomfortable with taking risk. They now approach markets far more conservatively, wanting to get closer to the customer at every opportunity, and only engaging in incremental innovation. But once the innovation concept becomes relativized, corporations can justify incremental innovation on the grounds that, in fact, it is something great after all.

From timid innovation to timid growth

The paradox about the dumbing-down of innovation is that it coexists with genuine progress in science and technology and organizational capability. As technology improves, and organizations become more sophisticated, the business world seems less and less willing to engage in radical innovation and uphold high standards in innovation.

The final chapter in Part Two examines the strange nature of growth today. In a world where the marketplace is seen as more unpredictable and risky, the nature of 'growth' has been redefined.

Notes

1. See 'Innovation in industry: a survey', *The Economist*, 20 February 1999.
2. In Britain a survey of manufacturers in 1999 by the Bourton Group, a management consultancy, found that manufacturers spent as much on IT as other equipment for the first time since they began the survey 12 years earlier (see Guthrie, 2000).
3. Statistics from the US National Science Foundation.
4. See 'Everyone wants to be a VC', *Business Week Online*, 2 July 2002.
5. See Inch (1999). At the time of writing, Inch was the secretary general of the Royal Society of Chemistry.
6. The following remarks all come from correspondence with Mark Rice.
7. The following remarks all come from correspondence with Mark Bernstein.
8. Correspondence with Toru Takenaka.
9. This speech was given by J.Ian Morrison, President, Institute for the Future, and William Pietersen, Chairman, 7 November 1995.
10. See the paper, 'The dynamics of the diversified corporation and the role of central management of technology', by Jens Frřslev Christensen, 12 December 1996, available on the Internet.
11. Many of the facts in the following section are taken from the excellent historic overview by Tom Forester, *High-Tech Society: The Story of the IT Revolution* (Forester, 1987).
12. According to one expert, 'fulfilment levels in home delivery are very unsatisfactory. There is a 60 per cent failure rate at the first time. It's a huge cost to business' – James Bates, marketing director, Bear Box, quoted in 'Is this tomorrow's letterbox', *The Observer*, 22 July 2001. In 2001 the British Post Office launched an initiative to place boxes outside homes to allow parcels to be deposited.
13. See www.webcor.com for news stories on the company.
14. See the magazine *Smart Business* for examples of how companies such as Ford, Sigma-Aldrich, Boeing and General Electric use the Internet.
15. This case study has come from correspondence with an IT consultant working on the project.
16. Adrian Slywotzky, author of *How Digital is Your Business?*, quoted in Carlos Grande, 'Facing up to the new computer world', *Financial Times*, 16 February 2001.
17. See 'Special report: the future of e-business', *Business Week*, 13 May 2002.
18. See *The Observer* Magazine, 31 March 2002.

8

Fear of Growth

During the 1990s a range of economic commentators in the United States believed that the US economy was experiencing a new renaissance. This was a 'new economy', they suggested, a nirvana of low unemployment, low inflation, high growth, high productivity, dynamism and impressive innovation. But with the slump in technology stocks in Spring 2000, the minor downturn of 2001, and the business scandals of 2001–2002, a feeling developed that the 1990s were not all they were cracked up to be.

Many corporations that were deemed to be new economy dynamos have experienced problems of growth. Some now question the nature of 'growth' in the 1990s. Many corporations, from Enron to WorldCom and others that have not experienced scandals, such as Cisco Systems, appeared to be very dynamic and fast growing. But today the nature of that growth appears more flimsy than ever. Many corporations were in fact 'growing' through mergers and acquisitions rather than developing new products for new markets. They were also creating an appearance of dynamism through burgeoning stock market capitalizations.[1]

This chapter examines the very peculiar nature of growth in the 1990s. The whole nature of growth took a decidedly different direction in the 1990s, and produced patterns that were unique in the history of capitalism. The divergence between the appearance and reality of growth was never greater.

It was a period when, for the first time, corporations grew profits faster by cost-cutting than by selling things; when corporations invested far more in each other, and their own shares, than new productive capability; and when global 'expansion' (both in developed and developing nations) was often a kind of global swapping of assets, rather than 'greenfield' investment – investment in new assets.

When the decade is taken as a whole, it was a period when fast growth in profits, rapidly changing ownership of assets, corporate investment in financial assets and rapidly rising stock prices created an appearance of dynamism. Not surprisingly, with less actual growth going on, economists recognize that the 1990s was actually the worst economic performance in America's post-war history.

The 1990s reconsidered

The historic emergence of capitalism led to an unprecedented new dynamic for economic growth. Yet growth can be a confusing concept in the context of a capitalist economy. Since the late nineteenth century, economic growth has been mediated through large institutions: corporations that organize production and distribution, and financial institutions, such as banks, that channel savings to fund development, and stock markets.

A lot of activity in these institutions can make things appear very dynamic on the surface. Investment bankers can return home exhausted after working all night on merger deals. Consultants can enthuse about burgeoning stock market capitalizations. Academics can get very excited about the levels of trade in financial securities. Companies can buy existing assets from each other in the form of acquisitions. Firms can restructure internally, and resort to outsourcing, 'delayering' middle managers and other forms of cost-cutting. Thousands of employees can be downsized. Employees can suddenly leave large firms to set up small firms and become entrepreneurs.

But if little is happening underneath, if firms are not investing in new assets, creating new products, and creating new markets both domestically and internationally, then something is not quite right. An appearance of dynamism on the surface coexists with a reality of stagnation and risk avoidance.

The nature of 'growth' in the 1990s took place in a peculiarly defensive and superficial way. The way that firms increased their profits over the 1990s was unusually defensive. In fact, something happened that had never happened before. Very basically, there are two ways to increase profits. Firms can either cut back on costs, and make immediate savings compared with the prior period, or they can increase sales and win a larger share of profits in markets. But the 1990s as a decade was characterized by a faster rate of profit growth than sales growth for corporations. When profits are growing faster than sales, it tends to mean that firms are 'growing' by cost-cutting and rationalization, rather than by actually investing and selling more products.

According to James Paulsen, economist and chief investment officer for Wells Capital Management, 'although profits and sales had grown at about the same rate over the previous four decades, profits grew almost twice as fast as sales in the nifty '90s' (see Welling, 2001). There is nothing wrong in cutting costs *per se*, of course. But it is a major problem when it becomes a substitute for investment.

A second related point is that firms were growing far more through mergers and acquisitions (M&A) than organic growth – new investment in productive capability. M&A activity rose to record levels. Continuing with the United States, from the mid-1990s the number of M&A deals rose massively to an unprecedented high level. The year 1997 saw the most deals ever in US domestic and US cross-border transactions – 7848 deals, beating the previous record in 1969 of 6107 deals. Then, the record was smashed again in 1999 and 2000, where the number of deals shot up to around 10 000. Even in 2001 and 2002, supposedly depressed years for M&A activity, deals were still at historically high levels.[2]

The increased tendency to rely on M&A as a form of growth expresses a peculiar mixture of defensiveness and short-term opportunism. Mergers are often seen as a bid for global domination. Critics look at the process of monopolization through the prism of immoral behaviour, discussed before. Here, managers are on some kind of manic ego-trip to dominate the world.

Yet as *Financial Times* commentator Peter Martin perceptively noted in 1998, just before the height of the merger boom, 'many of today's mergers represent weakness rather than strength, a huddling together for defensive purposes rather than as an aggressive bid for global domination (Martin, 1998).

It is arguable that mergers are more motivated by fear of the future, especially today where competition and the pace of change is always said to be 'increasing'. Managers are often explicit in telling themselves that 'they cannot go it alone' and out-compete their peers. Surveys capture this element of 'huddling together'. A survey by a professional services firm in 2001 revealed an interesting finding in the financial services industry. Of the 300 executives

interviewed, 41% replied that 'defending their position' was the most important external factor for undertaking a merger. In a world that is considered
to be far more risky and turbulent, managers resort to more defensive forms
of growth, rather than take a risk.[3]

M&A activity is a perfect investment choice for managers who might feel
that they should defend their position, and grow without taking risks. M&A
activity eliminates competition for individual firms. There is a defensive element. At the same time, M&A give firms instant access to assets. In particular, firms gain access to the highly prized asset of a competitors' customer base,
leading to instant new revenues and marketing opportunities. Firms have a
chance to 'get closer' to what were previously their competitors' customers.

It could be said that M&A are challenging and risky because of the possibilities that integration will not work out. But on the whole, they are far less
risky than organic growth. An organic investment runs the risk of committing capital upfront before a return can be guaranteed. M&A, however, offer
a more instant return on investment. Once one firm buys another, they have
instant access to customers and revenues.

M&A activity has also been a route for immediate cost-cutting and profit
gains. When oil companies BP and Amoco announced a merger in 1998,
they estimated the cost savings to be US $2bn a year following 6000 job
losses. When fellow oil companies Exxon and Mobil announced a merger
later that year, they went one better, and announced they would be able to
cut US $2.8bn a year in costs and eliminate 9000 jobs. In the same year,
Deutsche Bank's purchase of Bankers Trust was accompanied by a plan to
cut 5500 jobs. In the pharmaceutical sector, 6000 job cuts would be made
from UK firm Zeneca's purchase of Swedish firm Astra.

It is through the process of consolidation and cost-cutting that growth
has taken a peculiar form. This process of continual cost-cutting would have
been untenable were it not for M&A. For any one firm, there are limits to
how far cut-backs can go. Firms would have no business to speak of, having
downsized all employees and sold off all assets. As one executive has put it,
'you cannot shrink to greatness'.

But if firms are consolidating with each other through M&A, then the
process can continue for a while longer. Here, a strange pattern of 'growth'
occurs. Firms become 'mean and lean' by cutting costs in various ways. Many
large corporations have reduced their labour force over the last decade or
two, and have resorted to measures such as outsourcing non-core activities.

But firms 'grow' by buying up each other, either in the form of acquisitions or by merging.

All this has a global expression. It is significant that much more of investment abroad, foreign direct investment (FDI), takes the form not of 'greenfield' investment, which is investment in new productive capability, but through consolidation on a global level. The proportion of FDI taken up by M&A accelerated during the 1990s. Cross border M&A have been the major force behind the growth of FDI in the last decade.

The United Nations states in its *World Investment Report 2000* that: 'most of the growth in international production has been via cross-border M&As...rather than Greenfield investment'. The ratio of the value of cross-border M&A to world FDI flows in 1999 reached over 80%, according to the UN. Interestingly, in the developing world, the value of M&A made up a tenth of the value of FDI at the end of the 1980s, but a third at the end of the 1990s. The character of global expansion today is actually very weak. The market for buying and selling existing companies and assets is thriving on the surface, but corporations do not often try to create new assets, new products and new markets when entering other countries.

It is interesting that the United Nations in their analysis resort to the idea that the pace of change is speeding up. Here, in a world where managers feel that everything is speeding up, they want instant access to foreign markets. Rather than go through the messy and risky process of making a proper investment, they would rather simply buy another firm. This way they can get instant access to their competitors' customers.

As pointed out in an earlier chapter, this notion of 'speed' is very misleading. It is not that the world is speeding up but rather that the global business community has become more insecure about the future and less willing to take risk. In a world that has seen increased liberalization in the last decade, everyone seems scared of having to compete with new entrants. A kind of 'huddling together', to use Peter Martin's phrase, is taking place on a global level (see United Nations, 2000).

A final point is that the attempt to grow through M&A often backfires. It is well known that a large proportion of mergers, for instance, do not work out. There has been much discussion of why, but a basic problem seems to be, not surprisingly, that mergers do not compensate for a lack of genuine growth and investment. For instance, according to one commentary on why mergers fail, 'too many companies lose their revenue momentum as they concentrate on cost synergies or fail to focus on postmerger growth in a systematic manner. Yet in the end halted growth hurts the market performance of a company far more than does a failure to nail costs' (Bekier et al., 2001).

Why the move into services is risk-averse

It was noted in Chapter 4 that corporations are far keener on 'capital efficient' growth. That is, they are looking for areas to grow their business, but invest as little capital as possible. At the same time, and linked, they are looking to grow into areas where they can 'get closer to the customer' and develop more reliable and predictable customer relationships.

Consumer-, business- or technology-related services fit this agenda perfectly. The trend for industrial companies to move into services, either by developing their own or, more likely, by acquiring firms in services, has occurred regardless of sector. It has happened in the automobile, aerospace, engineering, electronics, IT, travel and retail industries, to name a few. It has been a marked trend in the United States, Europe and Asia during the last decade or so.

The recent move into services by large industrial corporations should not be confused with the way that services now make up an increasing portion of developed economies, especially in the United States and Britain. That trend has to do with a historical transition from manufacturing to services that began in the 1960s. In the United States, the jump in the percentage of people employed in social services – medical and health services, hospitals, education, government and so on – rose the most from 1950 to 1970, from 12.4% to 22%. Producer services – banking, insurance, real estate, legal and business services – grew from 4.8% of the population in 1950 to 14% in 1990. Part of the same trend was the decline in the number of people in manufacturing, from around 28% in 1960 to 18% in 1990 (figures taken from Castells, 2000, pp. 304–305).

The trend for non-service corporations to diversify into services, however, has been a phenomenon of the mid-1990s onwards. It has more to do with a conservative approach to using capital, and a risk-averse approach to competition, than anything else. The move into services is often motivated by the idea that the core products of corporations are becoming commodities. That is, firms say they are experiencing slower growth in product markets as these markets mature, and therefore have no choice but to enter services.

But there is no such logical relationship. It is perfectly understandable that firms want to escape from slow growth markets, of course. But by escaping into services, firms are arguably putting off the risks of restructuring and creating new markets with new products. They are shying away from innovation. Services provide two things for corporations: they allow them to grow without investing much capital, and they allow them to 'get closer to customers'. Rather than transforming the existing landscape, through product and process innovation, these companies appear more motivated by playing it safe and avoiding risk. This can be clearly seen when examining particular firms and their motivations for entering services.

IBM became one of the largest consulting firms in the world by investing in IT-related services during the 1990s. In the last few years, the firm has signalled its intentions to move even more into services. What is the rationale? According to Lou Gerstner, speaking as chief executive in 2001, 'you are headed for commoditization hell if you don't have services'. For Gerstner, the services market is more 'recession proof' than other markets. Service companies, he commented, tend not to become obsolete. They can adapt to new technologies and business models more easily (see Cowley, 2001).

What is being said here? There is an old joke that those in the business and financial services sector – financiers, accountants, lawyers and consultants – benefit from both boom times and bust times. In the boom times, they can provide advice on matters of growth. In bust times, they can help with bankruptcy proceedings.

The same logic applies to other services. In the IT world, IBM can help companies with cutting costs if they want to outsource any of their activities. Or, if they want to spend more money on computers, IBM can help them with that too. Here, services are conceived of as a kind of foolproof business model. Companies do not take the risks of more fundamental innovation, but can get closer to the customer by adapting to all situations and circumstances. The core product – that companies need various business services – does not have an obvious life cycle.

Again, consulting provides a great example. One moment, one consulting service is all the rage, such as business process re-engineering, offering bountiful fees. The next moment there is a counter-reaction, and the adoption of another fad, such as 'customer relationship management', offering equally bountiful fees for the service providers. And if CRM does not work (as it has not been, apparently, in recent years), then service providers can move on quickly to something else. That model can continue indefinitely, especially in a context where corporations, the clients, are keen to cut costs and adopt new management techniques. The key idea, then, is that once a customer relationship is established, service providers can pursue a high return, low risk agenda and business model.

Many corporations are jumping on the services bandwagon. Services now account for around a fifth of the revenues of Siemens, the German electronic and engineering group. Of particular growth in recent years has been Siemens Business Services (SBS). SBS was founded in 1995 as a subsidiary of Siemens. It started with 2100 employees. Two years later, it had 16 700 employees and had diversified more into IT services. In late 1998, it won a £1bn contract with the UK government to run its back office functions. In 2000 Siemens merged its Business Services and IT Service group. It began to focus more heavily on e-business and mobile business, offering services in areas such as supply chain management, enterprise resource management, business information management, customer relationship management and electronic commerce. By then, the group's employees had increased to 36 000. It has developed into one of the world's largest suppliers of IT services in general, including management consulting, system integration and courses and training.

Other firms are eyeing up business services. Proctor & Gamble, in 2001, formed a new marketing consulting company called Project EMM (Enterprise Marketing Management), signing up clients such as Coca-Cola and Philips. In 1999, Boeing set up a division to service its customers, the airliners. Car firms such as Ford have entered the services business in a big way, often through acquisitions.

Services account for a growing proportion of General Electric's (GE) business. In 1995, services based around jet engines and medical equipment accounted for 8% of revenues. In 2000 they accounted for 17%. Considering that financial services account for around 40% of GE's revenues, GE is fast becoming a service company, rather than a manufacturer. ABB, the Swiss–Swedish heavy equipment group, extended the service element of its business from 10% at the start of the 1990s to around 25% at the end of the decade. The financial services division of ABB accounted for half of the group's US $32bn assets and around a third of its profits in 2002.

The largest blue chip Internet companies are trying to reorient themselves to services. In November 2001, Amazon.com announced that it was reorganizing its business operations into five departments, partly because of an increased emphasis towards the provision of third-party services. According to one analyst observing this move, 'services is not nearly as capital intensive' and the profits are higher. With services, he added, the company does not have to sell a physical object. It can therefore avoid capital investments in the area of e-fulfilment – delivering the physical product, e.g. the book, compact disc, etc. to the customer. Like many other companies, Amazon.com is looking to grow but without investing much capital (see Weisman, 2001).

In Britain, many corporations began to invest in financial services from the mid-1990s on. Travel operator Thomas Cook built up its financial services division over the 1990s, and sold it in 2000 for £440m. British Airways announced a further expansion into financial services in 1998, offering credit cards, travel insurance and foreign currency. Supermarkets have been especially keen to offer financial services. In 1996, major UK supermarket Sainsbury's for instance announced plans to set up its own bank in partnership with the Bank of Scotland. Since then, it has got into insurance, mortgages and savings products.

Growth at the macro level

The peculiarly risk-averse nature of growth, explored at the micro level so far in this chapter, is perfectly mirrored in the way that whole economies, at the macro level, performed extremely badly over the 1990s. Economists now realize that the 1990s were a period of sluggish economic growth overall.

The 1990s was supposed to be about an economic miracle in the United States. But in the cold light of the new century, many economists realize that the 1990s were actually the opposite. According to figures from the US Bureau of Economic Analysis, average annual increase in real GDP for the 1990s was the worst since the 1930s. Over the 1990s, it averaged only 2.84%, compared with 3% for the 1980s, 3.22% for the 1970s and 4.15% for the 1960s.[4]

According to economist James Paulsen again, 'the "miracles" of the '90s – central to which was the phenomenon of "real growth with falling inflation" – did not reflect a booming economy, even if it was the longest uninterrupted expansion in US history' (see Welling, 2001). Another highly regarded US economist, Dean Baker, has argued a similar line. Baker writes that 'even the most cursory review of the data shows that the "new economy" was mostly hype'. The New Economy was supposed to be about high levels of investment. But this is another myth. According to Baker, 'it was not an investment boom that spurred the economy forward in the last half of the decade, but rather a stock market driven consumption splurge. This consumption splurge sent savings rates to record lows and levels of consumer indebtedness to record highs' (Baker, 2001).

The economic commentator Anatole Kaletsksy suggested in 2002 that 'outside the computer and telecoms sectors American industry actually invested much less than in the late 1990s than it had in previous economic booms' (Kaletsky, 2002a). He has argued the same line for the British economy. According to him, '. . . the sums of money actually spent on investment by British industry were lower in the late 1990s than at the top of any previous economic cycle' (Kaletsky, 2002b).

The economist Jeff Madrick noted at the height of the boom in 1998 that

> the US remains a complacent country. Little new money is spent on education or several other kinds of investment that will improve productivity over the next decade, whether in physical infrastructure, day care or basic research. Self-congratulation about the current state of the economy is distracting the public and politicians from addressing what remains to be done to raise America's rate of growth (Madrick, 1998).

In Britain, economists wondered why investment appeared to be so low even at the height of the recovery in the mid-to-late 1990s. A *Bank of England Quarterly Bulletin* flagged this point in February 1998. It suggested that: 'investment has grown less rapidly in this recovery than during the previous ones, despite a relatively low user cost of capital, high levels of profitability, and high stock market valuations of capital'.

Unlike in the previous recovery period, from 1981 to 1986, the study found that whole economy investment had declined as a percentage of GDP. It explored the notion that this might have something to do with high costs of finance for firms. But it argued that the cost of finance had not increased, but decreased compared with the 1970s and 1980s, taking into consideration both the cost of equity and debt. It was perplexed why investment should be so low.[5]

Many others at the time noted the trend. As one manager of a British investment fund put in, again in 1998, 'there's this rather perverse thing. We have these historic returns on equity, and low costs of capital – and nobody's investing'.[6]

To conclude here, then: genuine investment in the US and UK economies was poor in the previous decade.

The financialization of economies

The nature of 'growth' was peculiar in the 1990s. Another main reason concerns the way that economies became increasingly 'financialized'.

Today, corporations in the 'real' economy – the economy where goods and services are produced – engage far more in financial activity than in the past. That can mean that companies invest in other companies' shares, rather than new assets that lead to production of goods. It also means that companies invest in their own shares – a practice known as share buybacks, explored in Chapter 4.

Corporations also buy and sell shares in smaller companies, a practice known as 'corporate venturing'. Here, large companies become venture capitalists – buying a share in a start-up company, building up its value, and realizing a profit when the company is floated on the stock market for a higher value.

Companies have reported huge one-off gains from financial activity. In January 2000, US airline Delta Airlines disclosed that it made US $596m from selling its equity holding, or its shares, in company Priceline.com, more than three times the US $175m it made in flying aeroplanes. In May 2000, Japanese optical-fibre company Furukawa Electric announced that it had earned ¥100bn – around $760m – from a sale of its shares in Canadian fast-growth firm JDS Uniphase. In the first quarter of 2000, before the slump in technology stocks in Spring of that year, the chip maker Intel made $640m through investment in equity. Microsoft reported nearly a billion dollars, US $885m, of income made in the same way.

Increased financial activity of firms takes place against the backdrop of an unusual historic trend. In the post-war period, the ratio of the stock market's value in the US economy was about 50% of the value created in the real economy. In other words, the value of all investment and consumption in the productive economy was around twice as much as the paper value of the stock market. The year 1990 was significant. For the first time, the entire paper value of the US stock market was worth more than the value created in the real economy. By 1999, the ratio of the stock market's value to GDP stood at 150% (see Ben-Ami, 2001).

As is well recognized, the market values of companies now significantly diverge from their book values, even in the context of the bear market of the new millennium. That is, market capitalizations of companies, their market values, as measured by the value of the share price multiplied by shares in circulation, is far greater than their book values – the value of their physical assets.

The rise of the value of stock markets in the 1990s did not relate to 'fundamentals'. That is, stock market rises were not reflecting increases in the underlying profits of firms. Standard & Poor's Composite index increased by 570% from 1981 to the end of 1999. But the earnings of companies in this index only increased by 61% over this period (see Ben-Ami, 2001).

The main point here again is that an increase in financial activity can give the appearance of dynamism. But again, appearance and reality diverge. Evidence suggests that the growth in financial activity is related to stagnation and risk aversion at the level of the real economy and productive investment. This can be grasped at the micro level when companies refuse to invest in productive assets and instead invest in their own shares or other companies' shares, boosting stock market values further. At the macro level, as the author and financial journalist Daniel Ben-Ami notes, 'history shows us that the growth in global finance has occurred at precisely the time when economic growth is relatively stagnant'.

For Ben-Ami, during the post-war period, real economies experienced record levels of growth. But financial economies – the activities of stock markets, banks, investors and so on – were far more marginal to the economy compared with today. The main role of the financial sector, banks in particular, was to channel funds to companies for investment in productive assets.

During the 1970s, he writes, the relationship between the real economy and the financial economy began to change. The intervention of governments was crucial in building up institutions and activity in the modern financial sector. In responding to economic slowdown, governments began to encourage competition in financial sectors in order to loosen up credit to an ailing economy. At the same time, they wanted to find a way to reduce taxation on the private sector, to help it restore profitability in the wake of the slowdown.

Governments took a fresh look at their welfare commitments, such as pension provision, and encouraged individuals to save for their pensions so that they could reduce their own welfare spending and lower taxation. Corporations were encouraged to run pension funds for their employees. This process was instrumental in leading to the rise of the fund management industry, and the rise of new types of fund, such as mutual funds.

By the turn of the 1990s, financial sectors had mushroomed. New types of financial institution had grown, new markets had emerged and were thriving, such as derivatives, and more liquidity had found its way into the stock market. Companies took advantage of rising bull markets by engaging more in financial activity, which became a source of profits. Over the 1990s as a whole, however, growth in the real economy was not that impressive. While financial economies have boomed, with rising stock market values, greater trading activity, new markets, and so on, real economies have stagnated.

The myth of the entrepreneurial revolution

Economies during the 1990s were supposed to be highly dynamic for another reason – the greater prevalence of nimble risk-taking entrepreneurs. The arrival of the new economy, it has been said, with its potent combination of abundant capital and new technology, had profoundly empowered the individual. It laid the foundation for a new 'entrepreneurial revolution'. Literally everyone, anywhere in the world, could become the next Bill Gates – overnight.

'America's new emblem is the footloose, independent worker – the tech-savvy, self-reliant, path-clearing micropreneur', writes Daniel Pink, author of *Free Agent Nation* (Pink, 2001). For him, 'the individual, not the organization, has become the economy's fundamental unit'. 'Free agents' – individual entrepreneurs in control of their destiny – were to be the new revolutionary vanguard of change. The corporation, with its bureaucracy and 'organizational man', was on the verge of becoming an endangered species. Just look at all those nimble dotcoms, it was said, dancing around the marketplace and running rings around the corporate dinosaurs.

Elsewhere, business writers observed that 'this is the era of the entrepreneur. What began in the melting pot of Silicon Valley as a dream for a select few has become a worldwide phenomenon. For growing numbers of young people, creating a business has become a calling; a vocation; a mission. It is the spirit of the age. The new zeitgeist' (Crainer and Dearlove, 2000, p. 3).

For the Global Entrepreneurship Monitor (GEM), which conducts an annual global survey, 'around the world, entrepreneurship is at the top of the social, political and economic agenda. Fuelled in part by the rash of Internet start-ups in the late 1990s, and the associated increase in venture capital investment and stock market values, the process whereby individuals create and build new firms has captured the public imagination.'[7]

The entrepreneur was back. This was the rhetoric of the late 1990s. But then, in 2000, the bull market abruptly came to an end. The 1990s seemed to be cast in a new light, and rather suddenly, being an entrepreneur was out of fashion again. The term 'dotcom' became a term of abuse overnight, and venture capitalists were reluctant to finance start-ups.

But the entrepreneurship movement will not lie down. Business writers, not to mention governments and corporations, are becoming increasingly enamoured with entrepreneurs and small businesses. The world of fast change and technological obsolescence is said to favour the small and nimble, not large bureaucracies. For entrepreneurship enthusiasts, individuals are far more likely to be more inventive, creative and sensitive to the needs of customers than large corporations. Rather than entertaining grand strategies or elaborate plans, it is said that the 'new pioneers' just get on with it. (See Petzinger, 1999, for a discussion of this type.)

Similarly, individuals and small businesses have never been more courted by economists. Small businesses, it is now frequently said, are responsible for much of the risk-taking, growth, employment and innovation in an economy. For governments everywhere, the concept of entrepreneurship is becoming central to economic policy.

Is this a new era for the entrepreneur?

The trouble with the entrepreneurship thesis is that it makes an optimistic generalization from what are very disparate and distinct activities going on in the economy. For instance, a very tiny proportion of individuals were able to make a fortune from floating Internet businesses on the stock market, in the narrow window of opportunity that was the mid-to-late 1990s. That is one thing. Another group in the economy, different again, in the hi-tech sectors, are genuinely innovative. These companies, led by fairly dynamic individuals, pursue worthwhile experimentation and innovation. But the vast bulk of individual and small business activity, the largest group, is the very opposite of risk-taking, creativity and innovation. It seems strange to suggest that there is something great about individual and small business activity *per se*.

The 1990s did throw up some novel conditions. In the midst of the financial bubble, even cunning schoolchildren and pensioners seemed to be on their way to becoming millionaires after creating specialist Internet businesses that nobody had thought of before. For one brief moment in time, roughly around mid-1999, everyone seemed to have ambitions to set up an Internet business, exploit a gap in the market, and make their fortune. Being an entrepreneur was in fashion. At the same time, more capital was available to individuals. Venture capital investment increased.

But the dotcom phenomenon, which only benefited a lucky few anyway, is a world away from the rather grubby reality of the self-employed and small business. It remains the case that the vast bulk of individual and small business activity is highly unglamorous. When people start up businesses, what areas do they tend to go into? In 1996, in the United States, the most popular start-ups were builders, restaurants, corner shops, cleaners and estate agents (see Bhide, 2000, p. 30).

Entrepreneurship enthusiasts are keen to reinterpret the self-employed as glamorous 'soloists' or 'freelancers'. Yet even according to *Inc.* magazine, the bible of entrepreneurship, 'the solo-operator segment of the business world, despite the glossy images in magazines, does not consist of mainly good-looking thirtysomethings working on laptops beside the pool'. So what does it include? 'Plumbers, landlords, hairstylists, and lawyers.' *Inc.* adds that 'it's a safe bet that most of the statistics for 1997 haven't changed much' in 2001.[8]

It is hard to see why small business *per se* excites the imagination and is considered special or innovative. There were around 5.5m small businesses with 500 or fewer employees in 1997. Of these, 40% are in services, 27.4% in retail and wholesale trade, 12% in construction, 8% in finance, insurance and real estate (FIRE), and the rest in manufacturing, transport and communications, utilities, and agriculture. About 1% of these firms are involved in computers. Even here though, this includes 'computer services' which most likely includes relatively non-innovative activities.

In the services category, the most popular services were health services such as doctors' offices and nursing facilities (20% of the 40% noted above), business services (16%) and personal services (8%). Building cleaning and maintenance services are the most popular business service, followed by computer programming. Again, an even tinier percentage of services can be said to be 'hi-tech'.[9]

The trouble with today's commentary on entrepreneurship, however, is the belief that there is something great about small business *per se*. For a popular business writer such as Larry Farrell, for example, the 'entrepreneurial revolution' is 'a new page in economic history'. Why? It 'welcomes the participation of everyone, from welfare-to-work graduates starting private day-care centers, to university scientists becoming biotech CEOs...' (Farrell, 2001, p. 4).

Another point is that there is no evidence to support the idea that structurally the economy is being reshaped around the individual, rather than organizations. Self-employment as a percentage of total employment actually declined in both the United States and the United Kingdom over the 1990s. In the United States, according to the Bureau of Labor Statistics, those who were self-employed in the civilian workforce declined from 8% in 1990 to 7% in 2000, and decreased consecutively from 1994 onwards.[10]

The *New York Times*, picking up on this development, ran an article in December 2000 entitled 'Entrepreneurs' "golden age" turns out to be mythology'. It pointed out that the 1994–1999 period was the first five-year period that self-employment had consecutively declined since a similar period in the 1960s (see Leonhardt, 2000).

In the United Kingdom, the story seems to be similar. As the *Financial Times* commented in 2002, 'writers such as Charles Handy...and Daniel Pink...may have fed an understanding that a generation of "new alchemists" was going it alone, shaking off the shackles of wage-slavery and turning freelance – or e-lance. The statistics suggest otherwise.' The British government's Labour Force Survey shows that around 10% of the workforce was self-employed in 1992. By 2002, however, that had shrunk to 8.8% (see Overell, 2002).

There is little other evidence to suggest that economies are restructuring around individual, or small business, entrepreneurial activity. For instance, one might think that the US economy has been composed more of highly dynamic, fast growing companies in recent years. Yet this is not the case. Gazelles, a term coined by leading entrepreneurship researcher David Birch, describe those companies that have grown their revenues by more than 20%

for a period of four consecutive years, from a base of at least US $100 000. In the United States at the end of the 1990s, these firms numbered 352 000, roughly 6% of the total number of firms in the economy. This percentage has remained fairly static since gazelles were first counted around 20 years ago. Also, a fifth of all gazelles have been in existence for over 30 years. So, in other words, not all the fastest growing firms in the US economy are new start-ups. Only a very small proportion of these fastest growing firms in the US economy are hi-tech. In 2000, research conducted by Birch's firm, Cognetics, found that around 30% are in the wholesale and retail trades, with another 30% in services, with only a very small proportion of those services relating to hi-tech fields. Ten percent are in manufacturing, 5% in FIRE, with the rest making up miscellaneous industries (about 25%).[11]

It is possible to say that a very small proportion of small businesses create a large proportion of new jobs. According to David Birch, 3% of all companies in the US economy account for around 70% of job growth, and most of them are small when they start growing very fast, and start hiring staff (see Webber, 1998). But again, this does not mean that all small business is dynamic and fast growing. Only a very small minority of small firms are fast growing and create new jobs. The vast majority of small business does not grow at all in any dynamic sense.

The 'myopic opportunism' of small business

There is nothing special about small business *per se*, then. It is revealing that one of the world's foremost authorities on entrepreneurship, Amar Bhide, has also been one of the most sceptical about the claims made of small business. In a recent study, one of the most exhaustive to date, Bhide suggested that small business on the whole is characterized by 'myopic opportunism', not 'risk taking, breakthrough creativity, vision and foresight or grand ambition'. He also suggests that most entrepreneurs modify or copy someone else's ideas when they start a new business (see Bhide, 2000).

Small companies, he points out, are highly constrained in what they can do. They often have severe capital constraints that make it difficult to plan ahead. They are dependent on many variables in their environment – the whims of their customers, the demands of their financiers, and so on. They tend to be opportunistic to the moment. Some almost completely change their business model and market positioning if old markets dry up or if new opportunities present themselves.

Small businesses are often lauded because they can 'adapt' to change. But they are powerless to do much else. This so-called strength comes from necessity, not choice. They do not have the resources to initiate ambitious projects of their own. They are highly dependent on the environment around them. Bhide finds that 'opportunistic adaptation' is the most accurate way to describe how small companies operate.

Small businesses therefore do not have power and choice. They tend to change their business model depending on change in the market. They may start off with a particular goal, but move substantially in another direction if the market changes. Large corporations are better able to pick and choose between different directions.

In this context the idea that small business is better at adapting to the environment than large companies also contains a fatal conceit. Large corporations can 'adapt' far more effectively by mobilizing considerable resources and networks to enter brand new markets and achieve new revenue streams. And that is exactly what they have done in recent years, as the dotcoms in the meantime went out of business.

Small business is often seen as more 'creative' than other sectors of the economy. But again, as also suggested above, this does not square with reality. Gordon Moore, co-founder of Intel, and founder of Moore's Law, makes a crucial distinction. 'It is often said that start-ups are better at creating new things', he says. 'They are not; they are better at exploiting them.' He adds that 'successful start-ups almost always begin with an idea that has ripened in the research organization of a large company. Lose the large organizations or research organizations of large companies, and start-ups disappear' (Moore, 1996).

Entrepreneurs then often specialize in commercialization, marketing and often, downright opportunism. There is absolutely nothing wrong with a bit of opportunism and making money. But it is important not to confuse opportunism with genuine risk-taking and innovation.

Conclusion

Perceptions and reality can be two different things. The 1990s appeared to be a time when a great deal of dynamic growth was taking place, a time of frenzied M&A activity, burgeoning stock market capitalizations and new company listings. In reality, the nature of growth has changed. Corporations arguably have never been more risk-averse when it comes to genuine investment and the creation of genuinely new products and new markets. The 1990s was a period when companies became more fearful of growing in a dynamic sense.

From cautious growth to a crisis of belief

Through self-regulation, and cautious commercial behaviour, risk aversion has become institutionalized in business. That is, it has become far more of a permanent mindset and mode of operation for corporations. By all accounts, this is a peculiar development. So how can it be better explained?

Risk aversion is not an economic phenomenon. Nor is it a new kind of psychological condition. It is bound up with a wider social and political trend. The belief systems that used to drive capitalism forward in the past have broken down. Unwilling to shape change in any meaningful sense, individuals and institutions have, over time, come to see themselves as the victims of external forces. Today, rather than act on positive beliefs of what might go right, institutions are more prone to act on fears of what might go wrong. Part Three examines this process in more depth, and proposes some ways to challenge it.

Notes

1. *The Economist* in 2001 explored what it called the 'illusory' nature of growth in the US technology sector. 'Much of the growth in technology spending turns out to be a product of the stockmarket bubble', they noted. See 'That falling feeling', *The Economist*, 17 March 2001.
2. Figures from Mergerstat, www.mergerstat.com
3. See 'Organic growth neglected as financial services companies combine to defend themselves', *AccountancyMagazine.com*, 26 February 2001.
4. Figures from the Bureau of Economic Analysis, interpreted by Ted Bos, professor of quantitative methods in the Department of Finance, Economics and Quantitative Methods at the School of Business at the University of Alabama at Birmingham. See Ben-Ami (2001).
5. See 'Investment in this recovery: an assessment', *Bank of England Quarterly Bulletin*, February 1998, by Simon Whitaker of the Bank's Structural Economic Analysis Division.
6. Michael Taylor, director of UK equities at Threadneedle Investment Managers, London, quoted in 'So much cash, so few options', *CFO Europe*, June 1998.
7. See Global Entrepreneurship Monitor, 2000 Executive Report.

8. See Small Business Report, *Inc. Magazine*, May 2001.
9. See Small Business Report, *Inc. Magazine*, May 2001.
10. Statistics of the Bureau of Labour Statistics, taken from 'Small Business Economic Indi-cators for 2000', see www.sba.gov/advo/stats
11. See Corporate Almanac, Cognetics, 2000.

PART THREE

Explaining and Challenging Risk Aversion

9

A Crisis of Self-Belief

The American intellectual Russell Jacoby characterizes the current era as *The End of Utopia* (Jacoby, 1999, Preface). 'A utopian spirit – a sense that the future could transcend the present – has vanished', he writes.

Particular new social and political trends have emerged in the last decade or so. For centuries, people have always retained a basic belief that the future could be better than the present. Through individual initiative and the purposeful action of institutions, people believed they could shape the future. A basic positive orientation toward change and the future was taken for granted.

Conservative impulses in society have often been strong, of course, and people have often expressed a desire to return to the past. But these were contested by other forward-looking beliefs. Since the eighteenth century, society has had some conception of left and right political positions, and different visions of organizing the world and shaping the future. In recent years, these positions have rather suddenly collapsed and now mean little.

Politicians today are routinely seen as timid, on both sides of the Atlantic. It is not difficult to see why: they are very uncomfortable with taking risk. The new way to survive in politics, it seems, is to actively avoid putting forward a strong belief. Many politicians seem to cling to the safety zone of the centre ground. Politics is now dominated by a bland pragmatism.

As many realize, there has been a narrowing of the political agenda. In the last British election of 2001 the whole election was fought on which party would manage schools and hospitals the best. In the United States, things are worse, it seems. There, elections are now fought on issues of ethics: who appears to be the more ethical, or nicest, presidential candidate. At the same time, politicians have shifted the political agenda to issues of corruption, or in Britain, 'sleaze'. It is no exaggeration to say that bereft of strong ideas, the only way politicians can galvanize a sense of purpose for themselves is to moralize about each other's behaviour.

It is not just that those in authority lack strong beliefs. The very notion of having a strong belief is under considerable attack. Strong ideas are interpreted as 'ideologies'. Take a contemporary example. In recent years, it is striking how those who profess to believe strongly in the free market have suddenly been labelled 'market fundamentalists'. The underlying message is that they must be naïve and even mad to believe strongly in free enterprise.

The more substantial underlying message is that strong beliefs are dangerous. They lead to dangerous things, such as mad dictatorships. Critics look at the twentieth century and draw the conclusion that society would be much better off without strong principles. Look at what has happened, they say. A strong belief ends up in totalitarianism or fascism. Human beings should be more humble. They should drop this stupid and dangerous arrogance that they can shape the future.

A lack of faith in strong ideas goes hand in hand with a lack of faith in institutions. There is a lack of belief in institutions to shape the future in any meaningful way. It was once believed that the state could affect change, or that relying on the free market would lead to a better society. Strong opinions were put forward on both sides.

However, what is uniquely new is that there is neither a belief in the state nor the market. The validity of state intervention was attacked during the 1970s and 1980s, along with the other institutions of the post-war arrangement, such as trade unions. But since then there has not been a resurgent belief in the free market.

There tends to be a consensus that 'there is no alternative' to the market. But nobody really believes strongly in the market. The market has been interpreted through the prism of an anxious society. Leaving the market alone, without constant re-regulation, is often seen as far too dangerous. It is interesting to note that when cases of privatization or liberalization have gone wrong, either in Britain or the United States, such as the British railway industry, or the Californian energy industry, few have been prepared to put a strident case for free market principles of organization. In fact, the free market is frequently seen as compromising human safety in various ways, and people of all political persuasions feel comfortable with the state taking control again. The notion of the 'third way' in politics sums up a situation where nobody really believes strongly in either the state or the market, a contrast to the past.

Belief in the corporation has suffered a noticeable battering. It is surely no exaggeration to say that hardly anyone has anything positive to say about the corporation as an institution. More significantly, the people *running* corporations are far more cynical about them. Talk to executives today, and even their own lack of faith in big business becomes clear. Those at the top often express feelings that corporations are places of great stress, wrecking their own work–life balances.[1]

Many people are suspicious of strong beliefs. But what is not often realized is that having no beliefs causes serious problems. In this respect politicians have been hoist by their own petard. 'There are few spectacles quite so sad in politics as that of Tony Blair trying to explain what New Labour stands for – five years after coming to power', writes the *Financial Times*.[2] Having turned their back on strong principles, politicians are now suffering from a crisis of ideas.

One of the problems British Prime Minister Tony Blair has had in office is redefining New Labour's mission. Blair has admitted that many New Labour supporters do not know what the government stands for. After five years, a vision to excite people has remained elusive. A refusal to take risk and say anything exciting simply results in the most spectacular blandness. What happens is that political debate is reduced to a kind of series of vacuous nonsense concepts. When ministers make speeches, it has become common to hear talk of values, the third way, fairness and, elsewhere, the mouth-watering vision of 'quality public services'. It could be argued that these concepts are really attempts to evade saying anything of substance.

The refusal to put forward bold ideas for change has horribly rebounded on politicians. For a start, the electorate are massively turned off. This then makes it very hard for politicians to actually conduct politics. It is difficult to engage people when their eyes glaze over in indifference. Politicians are then tempted to blame the voters. They must be 'apathetic' for not turning out to vote, goes the theory.

The point of taking a detour into politics is to contextualize the same process of change in industry and the business world. In business, strong beliefs and a faith in the future are also on the wane. In the last decade or so, it is striking how people working in industries as diverse as IT, movies, aerospace, drugs, chemicals and consumer products report that the pioneering spirit that used to exist in the past has somehow vanished. There does not seem to be the excitement about the future that there once was.

As documented earlier, many corporations themselves are retreating from radical innovation. When it comes to really daring innovation, there is often a sense of, 'What is the point in doing this?' Managers often justify this move on the grounds of pragmatism. They fall back to the safety ground of 'shareholder value'. What they often say is something like, 'our shareholders will not tolerate experimentation that may benefit society but not us. They want to see value.'

Unfortunately, this position obscures the real trend. The decline of a pioneering spirit in industry, a loss of belief in the future, and a breakdown in trust between managers and shareholders has led managers to embrace financial principles far more rigidly than in the past. These principles – which are really new forms of self-regulation – appear to provide guidance and moral certainty in a world where managers have little moral authority and are more intolerant of risk and uncertainty.

Such a position often contradicts the fact that corporations are in a far better position to do ambitious things than in the past, because of technological and organizational progress. This is perhaps why engineers working in R&D labs often feel so aggrieved when senior managers tap them on the shoulder and say, sorry, we cannot do this anymore.

It is not the case that R&D in the past was some kind of altruistic gesture on the part of corporations to society. Business leaders did not interpret it through some kind of prism of social responsibility. Rather, elites in society themselves, including leaders of industry, had strong beliefs in science and technology and breaking new ground. The very attempt to be pioneering is often reinterpreted as foolish and 'arrogant'. Firms with research centres that supposedly did too much experimenting, and not enough commercialization of products, are used as cautionary tales of the dangers of pioneering. For instance, various debates around the Palo Alto Research Center (PARC), set up by Xerox, often fall foul of these assumptions. PARC has been, and continues to be, one of the most pioneering research centres in the world.

Established in 1970, PARC pioneered the first personal computer and the graphical user interface that was the precursor for the Macintosh and Windows interfaces today. It is well known that Xerox was unable to capitalize commercially on these innovations. Others, most notably the computer firm Apple, beat them to it.

Yet examples such as these are quickly used as an excuse to argue that pioneering itself is too 'arrogant'. Critics ask, 'What is the point in pioneering, if products cannot be commercialized?' They suggest that corporations should be far more pragmatic in how they proceed with R&D. As the writer Michael Hiltzik puts it, 'PARC today remains a convenient cudgel with which to beat big business in general and Xerox in particular for their myriad sins, including imaginary ones, of corporate myopia and profligacy.'

The reality is more complex. For a start, as Hiltzik points out, a 'great myth' about PARC is that Xerox never profited from it. Yet it is often forgotten that PARC pioneered the laser printer. 'The truth is that its revenues from one invention alone, the laser printer, have come to billions of dollars – returning its investment in PARC many times over' (Hiltzik, 2000, p. 397 and Introduction).

Ambitious research is often reinterpreted today through a moralistic outlook that has more to do with low aspirations than anything else. Of course, some corporations in the past have had problems commercializing products. Elsewhere, some corporations have patented many inventions but have been slow off the mark in commercializing products from those patents.

But these examples do not provide a sound reason to avoid radical innovation. The real crime is allowing particular failures to be used as an excuse for not even bothering to try. In any process of experimentation, mistakes will be made, and money lost. But it is far better to have lots of mistakes occurring, and a few real genuine hits, then no mistakes occurring and no hits. The latter is a grim scenario where anxiety about what might go wrong quickly swamps considerations of the prize to be won for ambitious thinking and practice.

A pioneering spirit seems to be on the wane in business; but just as profound, business is not driven forward by a strong belief in the private mission of business. Rightly or wrongly, those running private enterprise have tended to believe traditionally that the self-interested actions of private individuals would benefit society. As mentioned in the introduction to this book, Milton Friedman's dictum was that the only social responsibility of a private enterprise was to make a profit. As long as business complied with the law, a strongly held view was that it was important to maximize the freedom of business to operate, and give free expression to self-interest. Of course, individuals in business today still pursue self-interest and make personal fortunes. But the belief that business as a whole should be given as much freedom as possible to operate has taken a battering. There is more ambivalence and conflict about the idea of self-interest. For example, with the corporate governance codes of conduct, the business world does not want to give a freer expression to the self-interested actions of executives. Rather, there is a fear that self-interest could lead to all sorts of problems, such as 'autocratic' leaders or greediness, and self-restraint needs to be imposed. In this context, the reality of self-interest and free enterprise, which rightly or wrongly is simply integral to capitalist society, now coexists with a greater ambivalence about it.

The rise of 'mission' and 'vision' statements in the workplace, a 1990s phenomenon, reflects the way that organic beliefs have broken down, but with little to replace them in driving things forward. These statements are pieces of paper that spell out a firm's mission or vision for the future. What these express is that, in an age where strong beliefs have broken down, attempts to create a 'mission' and 'vision' tend to be highly contrived and artificial. Although well meaning, even the people writing such statements sense that they are glib. In the past, those running business would have felt a sense of mission in a more organic way, connected to wider beliefs around them.

Similarly, it is only in a period where leadership is genuinely difficult because of a lack of strong beliefs that management education schools report that courses on 'leadership' are full to bursting point. Although well intentioned, such classes forget that leadership is a fairly organic process that cannot really be taught in the classroom. Genuine leadership is bound up with strong beliefs, passions and convictions. It involves individuals taking the initiative in a fairly organic way by responding to the world around them. The belief that leaders can be created in a classroom is really a kind of hidden statement of what leadership has become. In the absence of genuinely strong convictions, the notion of leadership becomes more of an empty concept, reduced almost to the status of a management fad.

A risky future

The loss of strong convictions across society, and a loss of faith in institutions, does not just result in a bland pragmatism. The assumption that human beings cannot shape their future has a more disturbing consequence. If individuals and institutions in society do not have confidence in themselves; if they do not believe they can shape the future in any meaningful sense; then, eventually, they tend to see themselves as victims of forces outside their control. The sense that the world is more risky and unpredictable does not correspond to an actual increase in risk and unpredictability. Rather, society tends to perceive it as such, because society lacks the confidence to affect change and shape the future, based on strong beliefs. A breakdown of belief, and faith in institutions, goes hand in hand with a perception and suspicion that the world is more risky.

Today, it is simply amazing how the future is conceived of almost wholly in negative terms. Relatively suddenly, positive views of the future seem to have dried up. The future, it seems, is one of grave dangers, threats, risks and problems. It has almost become impossible it seems to put forward a positive counterbalance. First of all, there are the usual environmental catastrophes that humanity is said to be facing. Global warming with its rising sea levels, floods, freakish weather conditions, and so on, awaits us. But of course, loss of biodiversity, resource depletion and pollution are never far behind. The ongoing spectre of overpopulation is always there. Then we have the theory that the future will be characterized by ethnic conflict and a clash of civilizations. New forms of international crime are not far behind, added to the list in recent years by new forms of international terrorism. Then we must not forget the ongoing theme of financial markets meltdown which periodically pops up in the business world, accompanied by a close colleague, the global collapse of information systems.

The concept of globalization captures the way that developments are interpreted through the prism of an anxious world. The end of the cold war should, in theory, have ushered in a period of capitalist self-confidence and pride. During the cold war the future was uncertain. Which was going to triumph, communism or capitalism? In the end, capitalism won the day. Finally, after all these years, the market was triumphant.

Soon after, an optimistic discussion of globalization began. The extension of market principles would bring about a new global prosperity. But before long, something odd happened.

During the early 1990s, discussions of globalization were increasingly about the destructive impact of the global market. Globalization, it was said, had rendered the nation state powerless. Corporations had entered a new era of intense competition where more was unpredictable. Individuals too were facing an uncertain, more alienated future, the victims of new global forces beyond their control.

Take the title of one account, *Runaway World: How Globalization is Reshaping Our Lives* (1999), written by the academic Anthony Giddens. He writes that 'we face risk situations that no one in previous history has had to confront – of which global warming is only one. Many of the new risks and uncertainties affect us no matter where we live, and regardless of how privileged or deprived we are. They are bound up with globalization . . . .' He adds that globalization 'brings into play other forms of risk and uncertainty, especially those involved in the global electronic economy . . .'.

It is often very hard to find strong positive beliefs in today's discussion of globalization. One might think that, for business, the opening up of markets is an unparalleled entrepreneurial opportunity. One could also make the argument that globalization brings new opportunities for human beings to cooperate, and share knowledge and experience.

A few make these points, but they tend to be in the minority. On the whole, the opening up of markets, and greater integration of economic activity, tend to be interpreted through the prism of risk, and various problems. Globalization has led to new risks and new forces that are dominating people's lives, it is assumed.

Defensive relations

When institutions are not driven forward by the strong ideas of the past, and see the future as more risky, then their relationships with the world around them begin to change. Put simply, they begin to relate to the world in a far more defensive manner and seek protective measures. In a world where strong beliefs have receded into the darkness, and where ideas of risk come to the fore to dominate, it becomes almost natural to be more defensive.

For example, without strong ideas, and a strong relationship with society, political institutions now tend to behave far more defensively in relationships with the world around them. It becomes hard for them to take a lead because there is no framework of ambition and sense of purpose. What happens is that politicians end up asking 'the people' what they want.

So, in recent years, politicians on both sides of the Atlantic have dabbled with focus groups. Unfortunately, in the absence of any proper rigorous debate, voters tend to articulate their own fears about the world around them. Politicians regurgitate those fears back to them, often proposing new types of regulation to try to address those fears.

The defensiveness of political institutions is captured by the new obsession with public relations, or in Britain, what is called 'spin'. Politicians suffer from anxiety attacks about their image and the press they are getting. It is not surprising that the phrase, 'more spin than substance' has come to define New Labour's term in office. Soon after winning the second term in office in 2001, Alastair Campbell, the British Prime Minister's director of communications and strategy, widely seen as the party's arch 'spin-doctor', made a confession. Surprising nobody, he admitted that the New Labour party had too often been 'more worried about what kind of press we were going to get than what a policy was going to do over time'. Rather than acting on strong beliefs, the New Labour government has been acting on fears of what might go wrong (see Baldwin, 2002).

In the business world, it is no coincidence that, without a strong agenda of their own in shaping the future – such as creating new markets with new products – corporations have rather suddenly expressed a desire to 'listen to society' and 'listen to the customer'. The attempt to listen to society and the customer, however, causes serious problems. This is because society and the customer tend to be more fearful of the future, and lack strong positive beliefs.

For instance, many NGOs are at the forefront of expressing these fears and anxieties, as they campaign against genetically modified organisms, or try to convince everyone that environmental catastrophe is just around the corner. When businesses 'listen to society' they end up just doubling their own fears about the future, and end up institutionalizing an irrational caution and restraint.

Business leaders, feeling defensive about the institution of business, and unwilling to uphold wider principles, use self-regulation as a way to try to establish some moral legitimacy in society. Self-regulation takes on a logic of its own, because it becomes a key vehicle for business to relate to the world around it.

Rather than taking a leadership role by pumping resources into radical new products to create new markets, corporate leaders turn to 'the customer' and ask them what they would like. Unfortunately, they do much more than that. As a previous chapter showed, corporations are hoping to hang onto existing customers for dear life. Corporations have a new mission in life. They are attempting to create more stable customer relationships, through brands and 'customer relationship management', in the hope that such relationships will create a comfort zone from the many uncertainties and anxieties that they have.

A jittery attitude toward change

When institutions lack a strong purpose, are trying to avoid risk in the future, and are in defensive relations with the world, unexpected change is quickly reinterpreted as a major source of anxiety. Without a framework of self-confidence and belief, it becomes very difficult to get problems in perspective, however minor. There is a tendency to over-react to change in a pessimistic fashion.

As mentioned in the introduction, the last few years have been witness to an 'irrational pessimism'. It is not that 11 September and the various business scandals have 'caused' this pessimism. Rather, business leaders are far more prone to react in an anxious fashion to new developments. In the past, new unexpected changes might have been interpreted more confidently. Business leaders might have felt they could overcome new shocks. Today, unexpected shocks can quickly become major crises that throw an already uncertain future into considerable doubt. As a result, it is possible for the business world to suffer from prolonged periods of pessimism, even though the underlying economy is relatively sound. A theme of the irrational pessimism of recent years is that economists are more optimistic than businesspeople, because they realize that the pessimism is not warranted objectively by economic developments.

Events such as the stock market slump in 2000, 11 September, and Enronitis seem confirmation of the anxieties and prejudices that the business world already has: that the world is more out of control, complex, chaotic, unpredictable, risky and uncertain. In this context, it is not surprising that a new phenomenon has emerged in recent years: the phenomenon of 'talking oneself into a recession'. The fears that managers have about the future have, on the one hand, led to an institutionalization of caution and restraint. This book has explored the major expressions of this process – self-regulation and new commercial risk-averse practices. But on the other hand, managers react to new developments and changes in a far more jittery fashion. This then reinforces the institutionalization of risk aversion.

It is worth remembering the reaction to the Asian crisis of 1997–98. For one thing, a large reason for the crisis itself was the panic reaction by Western investors, who suddenly withdrew capital from the region, fearing the worst after Asian nations devalued their currencies. But even more telling was the more general panicky reaction to the whole event. Many Western politicians and industry leaders actually feared that the Asian crisis might plunge the world back to the severity of the economic problems of the 1930s. In the wake of the troubles, it soon became second nature for a variety of commentators to make doomsday analogies with the 1930s, even though the comparisons were always tenuous. There was grave talk of the contagion effect, the idea that problems in Asia might engulf Western economies. At the same time, a huge new call for regulation ensued, and a one-sided discussion began on the corrupt 'crony capitalists' of Asia.

In society more broadly, without a strong framework of beliefs and confidence in the future, problems and uncertainties can easily be blown out of proportion and take on a significance they do not merit. Individuals now tend to interpret isolated incidences of immoral behaviour as something they are not, as a decline in moral standards across society. There is now a belief that somehow, behaviour across society, in professions and institutions is more unethical, reckless, destructive, corrupt and abusive than in the past. At the same time, relatively minor risks and uncertainties suddenly become major threats to humanity.

Today's perceptions of the corporation feed off a new sense of powerlessness

It is a major irony that, just at a time when managers and corporations see the world as more risky and unpredictable and are more defensive, a range of commentators view corporations as wanting to aggressively 'take over' the world.

Academics, journalists and demonstrators attack brands as being symbols of 'frightening' corporate power, not realizing that brands are the defensive response of a business world newly obsessed with 'getting close to the customer'.

Anti-capitalists believe that corporations want to evade regulation all the time, not realizing that one of the most significant trends of the last decade has been the new willingness of managers and corporations to regulate their own behaviour. A world where executives wrap themselves up in ethical codes of conduct or trot off to ethical training courses, just to pick two examples, is hardly the world of the robber barons of the past, after all.

The people who run corporations have power, of course. They have the power to hire and fire. They have the power to choose which products get made. They have power in the marketplace over smaller companies. They have the power to sue individuals in society. There is a great deal of talk about corporate power today, but commentators tend to miss the really new development: managers and corporations have power, but they feel more *powerless*. They have a diminished sense of their own power because the beliefs that used to drive them forward in the past have broken down, and the world seems a more risky place.

With such a diminished sense of using power, corporations want to listen to society and listen to the customer. Corporate leaders exercise power in a far more anxious and defensive way today.

An odd development is that anti-capitalist academics and business leaders have far more in common than they would like to believe. What they both have in common is an outlook of powerlessness. For anti-capitalists, globalization is a 'frightening' development. And in the business world? For business, too, globalization has meant that the world is more chaotic, complex, uncertain, risky, turbulent and volatile.

It is arguable that today's criticisms of the corporation by radical thinkers tend to express their own feelings of powerlessness. Those with left-wing views used to believe they could change the world. In recent years older radical traditions and aspirations have collapsed. Radical thinkers have much lower aspirations. Increasingly, they tend to see themselves as victims of external forces beyond their control. They want corporations to be re-regulated. Rather quickly, they have come to see themselves as being *dominated* by corporations. This feeling of domination and powerlessness before the almighty corporation comes across strikingly in today's so-called 'anti-capitalist' literature.

For instance, Charles Derber, author of *Corporation Nation* (1998), is one of many to use the phrase 'take over' to describe corporate behaviour today. (See also Hertz (2001) and Monbiot (2000)). Derber writes that 'the personal identity of today's worker, consumer and citizen is becoming a corporate construction'. This is a striking thing to suggest. The underlying assumption is not that individuals shape the world around them but rather that individuals are being shaped by the will of corporations. They have lost control even of their own personal identities! These identities, it is assumed, are being shaped and constructed by corporations. The world of 2001, writes Noreena Hertz, 'is getting dangerously close to the apocalyptic visions of *Rollerball*, *Network* and *Soylent Green*'. These are futuristic films where corporations dominate and even murder the population (see Hertz, 2001, p. 3).

Elsewhere, in the literature on brands it is assumed that brands have destroyed free cultural and individual expression. Brands are seen as swamping individuals, dominating them, manipulating them. Individuals are quickly reinterpreted as lifeless puppets of 'evil' corporations pulling the strings.

The anti-corporate, anti-capitalist perspective manages to reinterpret everything through the prism of a victim mentality, and in doing so distorts reality. So, in this topsy-turvy world of the anti-capitalist, brands are symbols of greater corporate oppression, not a risk-averse, defensive response to customers and markets. Everything is somehow perceived to be less regulated compared with the past. Somehow, the increase in competition regulation, labour regulation, financial regulation, health and safety regulation, environmental regulation, data protection and privacy regulation, the rapid proliferation of codes of conduct, not to mention the huge increase in ethical self-regulation, risk management, corporate governance, sustainable development and corporate social responsibility, not to mention the new fixation with accountability, responsibility, transparency and disclosure, is somehow not really happening.

An increasingly common fear expressed by commentators is that multinational corporations are on the verge of 'taking over' from governments and states, degrading democracy in the process. This is a world where governments have ceded power to huge corporations, and pander to their every need, instead of addressing the needs of citizens. This is viewed as a 'frightening' development that could leave individuals at the mercy of unaccountable corporations. The balance of power has shifted too far in the direction of corporations. For instance, in *The Silent Takeover* Noreena Hertz suggests that 'the state has been stepping back, and the market has been taking over', that 'the balance of power between politics and commerce has shifted radically' and that the 'power and credibility of politicians wanes and the power of corporations and international organizations grows'.

Is this an accurate picture of reality, however? As a concept it certainly attracts attention. In reality, though, the so-called power shifts that are supposed to be taking place between corporations and states are not really happening. This seems to be a very inaccurate way of understanding the world. Modern capitalist economies and states are so inextricably bound up with each other that, with the exception of a change to a radically new type of society – not on the cards at the moment – they will continue to need each other in various ways. Historically, states and businesses have tried to serve each other's interests as new circumstances have unfolded. This happens on so many levels it would take another book to detail them all.

For instance, when the private sector was suffering from poor profitability in the wake of the 1970s economic slowdown, states stepped in to restructure labour relations and dismantle the post-war industrial relations framework. This action was instrumental in making it easier for business to deal with labour.[3] In recent cases of liberalization and privatization that went wrong or had unintended consequences, such as the Californian energy crisis, and in Britain the privatization of the railway system, states have had to step in to oversee the restructuring of industries. The tragic events of 11 September brought into focus the ongoing role of governments in supporting civil aviation. US airlines suffered billions of losses on international scheduled services because of the reluctance of the population to fly, and the US government stepped in and handed US $5bn in cash grants to US airlines, while making a further US $10bn available in state loan guarantees.

States regulate business in myriad ways, and, this book has argued, regulation is increasing. On the other hand, states rely on the income of taxes from the private sector. Corporations turn to states to seek protection for their intellectual property, such as patents. In times of war, states need the private sector in various ways, and the private sector needs the state. These examples only scratch the surface of how states and corporations and the private sector are enmeshed.

Commentators tend to look at particular trends and then make sweeping generalizations. For instance, there is an idea that bigger and bigger monopolies challenge the power of states. Yet the developed nations with the largest monopolies and greatest concentration of economic power have the strongest states – just think of the United States, Germany, Japan, France and Britain. Also, governments and states have benefited from multinational corporations. The profits corporations earn from overseas activities help create stability in domestic economies, ensuring the survival of companies and jobs, and making life easier for governments. States reciprocate, by promoting the interests of their multinational corporations in foreign policy. Yes, large corporations often lobby governments to pay less tax. But this has hardly undermined the power of states, and is only one facet of the many relationships between the two.

The idea that state and government roles are being taken over by subversive, outside forces in the shape of corporations can only be a misleading conception of the real relationships between them. In a capitalist society, states and corporations have evolved as part of the same system.

Certainly, politicians increasingly *see* themselves as powerless, and perceive the state to be less able to affect economic change. They espouse the view that 'there is no alternative to the market'. This trend is related to the one outlined in this chapter. Political parties have shed their traditional beliefs, but with little to replace them. Because of a universal retreat from strong ideas and visions, democracy has become degraded. Democracy means little when all political parties offer no genuine choice to the electorate. But this does not mean that states are less powerful, or that big business is more powerful, or that states are handing over power to corporations. States and corporations exist as part of the same system. Both politicians and corporations tend to see themselves as more powerless. Defensive political and economic institutions today relate to a more anxious society.

Summarizing *The Timid Corporation*

The trends discussed in this chapter help to explain how risk aversion has become institutionalized in industry and the business world. Business is not propelled forward by the strong belief systems that existed in the past, such as those based around pioneering, or free enterprise. Over time, business leaders and corporations have come to feel less able to shape the world around them, and that, rather, they are the victims of external forces. They have come to reorient themselves more defensively to the world, and to change, and have ended up taking on board the fears and anxieties of society. Rather than act on positive beliefs of what might go right, business leaders increasingly act on fears of what may go wrong. Through this process, risk aversion has become institutionalized, expressed in self-regulation and cautious commercial behaviour.

The problem with self-regulation, in the business world and elsewhere, is that it internalizes and entrenches a society-wide desire for caution and restraint in behaviour. Here, the 'code of conduct' is the tip of the iceberg. Decisions are needlessly pushed through ethics departments, which deliberate endlessly on the morality of particular actions. Employee decisions are subject to authorization under new risk controls.

Elsewhere, managerial decisions are pushed through elaborate risk assessment practices. Corporations tell themselves they must be sustainable in their thinking and practice, because of fears they have a damaging impact. This leads to further self-regulation, caution and restraint. So far, self-regulation has been most insidious in the way that it affects finance and investment – and therefore strategy and growth. Here, many corporations have effectively installed a business version of the 'precautionary principle'. Companies become reluctant to invest unless risks and returns can be quantified beforehand.

Managers are much more conscious of what could go wrong in commercial behaviour. Rather than act on positive beliefs, such as creating new markets and taking a pioneering role, they orient themselves far more defensively to markets. Building relationships of customer loyalty has become more of an end in itself as companies spend more and more on brands and 'customer relationship management'. Companies are increasingly reluctant to pioneer in their innovation efforts, and worry more about the dangers of not commercializing products. At the same time, they are often reluctant to take a bold view of new technologies such as the Internet. Finally, corporations try to avoid the risks of investment, preferring comparatively safe routes of growth.

Today's risk aversion is not just a mood that, with luck, might go away in a few years time. There is a more entrenched basis for its existence: the breakdown of strong beliefs, the tendency to view the world as more risky and institutional defensiveness. The problem with the institutionalization of risk aversion is that caution becomes more of a permanent way of thinking and acting. In this context, when new opportunities do come along – perhaps in the form of new technologies, new growth industries or the opening of new markets – they are interpreted through an existing, entrenched mindset of caution and restraint. Here, risk aversion becomes difficult to shake off. This is a paradoxical situation because there are so many opportunities today for dynamic innovation and growth.

To conclude then: the institutionalization of risk aversion does not mean that economies will never see periods of dynamic growth again, or that new industries will never emerge. Rather, when economies enter growth phases and opportunities present themselves, there will always be a greater sense of caution dragging things back. There is a tendency to react to new change in a jittery, anxious fashion. Capitalism goes forward, but wrapped in more regulation and self-regulation, attempting to make profits, products, innovate and grow in the safest way possible.

Because risk aversion is not a psychological condition, an appeal to the business world to 'get a grip' is not going to restore a sense of risk-taking that easily. However, the final chapter offers two main ideas to challenge risk aversion. The first is to take a far more critical attitude toward regulation and self-regulation. The second is to raise expectations of technological progress, and take a more ambitious view of innovation.

Notes

1. Correspondence with executives.
2. See 'Blah Blah Blair', Editorial, *Financial Times*, 13 March 2002.
3. Stewart (1993, p. 91) notes that the curtailing of union power 'made it easier for employers to reduce restrictive practices, eliminate over-manning and generally introduce changes that significantly raise productivity'.

10

Conclusion: Challenging the Culture of Risk Aversion

It is worth bearing in mind three major points about today's culture of regulation and self-regulation. The first is that the new dynamic of regulation is based on an increasingly one-sided view of the world: a world where unethical and damaging behaviour, and risk, are exaggerated and inflated.

The second is that regulation will not 'restore trust', a much hoped-for objective. This is because mistrust is not caused by a lack of regulation. A culture of mistrust, or a 'culture of suspicion', relates more to the breakdown of commonly held beliefs and faith in institutions. Rather than challenging a culture of suspicion, regulation acquiesces to it and actually reinforces it.

Finally, it is important to realize that regulation often proceeds in a euphemistic fashion, especially in the business world. There is a tendency by corporations to see self-regulation as an 'opportunity' in various ways. The danger in this development is that caution and self-restraint, although not fully consciously, become reinterpreted as positive values, as values to aspire to.

An exaggerated sense of damage and risk

One could at least say that regulation in the past had a rational component if it responded to a real problem. For example, for a long time, industrial accidents were unacceptably high. It was important to address the problem. The attempt to improve safety standards and conduct in unsafe workplaces was not based on fear and anxiety, an over-reaction or an unrealistic desire to reduce risk and be safe – but on a real problem. People in the workplace were needlessly losing their lives and something needed to be done.

Today, however, we live in a society where perceptions of risk, and damaging behaviour, are often out of kilter with reality. Society tends to view behaviour in a more one-sided way. Commentators recognize that we now live in 'a culture of suspicion' and a 'culture of fear'. Here, there is a tendency to inflate and exaggerate scandal, corruption, and unethical, damaging, risky, excessive and reckless behaviour.

An expression of how irrational regulation has become is the fact that when governments and institutions try to re-regulate, they actually discover, in the process, that there is a poor case for regulation. This was a theme of Part One.

So, government regulators perceive that corporations abuse their power in various ways. Yet when they investigate, they find little evidence of wrongdoing. Corporate governance committees fear that corporations are badly run and that fraud is increasing. Yet when they investigate, they conclude that most corporations are run fairly well, in a responsible, competent manner and with integrity. Directors themselves sense that the world has become more risky. They fear that corporations are more exposed to risk, and are not managing risk very well. They instruct other managers to create elaborate new risk management frameworks. Yet when risk managers respond, investigate and take a hard look at employee behaviour, they find that risk is already fairly well managed.

One problem is that because fears have become so strong and detached from reality, and because re-regulation has taken on a logic of its own, there is often little attempt to seriously question whether re-regulation is really necessary. So, governments often find no wrongdoing when they investigate corporations for alleged abuse. Yet they still feel the urge to increase regulation. Corporate governance committees admit that most companies, on the whole, are well run and adequately managed. Yet they still feel that more regulation is needed. Risk managers find that companies are not more exposed to loss than before, and manage risk fairly well. But they feel that, to be on the safe side, it is important to filter every decision through elaborate new risk assessment schemes.

In this climate, one suggestion is to adopt a more questioning attitude, and challenge perceptions and suspicions. Do corporations really need yet more ethical codes of conduct? Are corporations really damaging the environment? Are they really socially irresponsible in the way that is suggested? Are corporations inefficient with their use of capital? Could we not do with more risk-taking investment?

Regulation does not restore trust

The creation of more rules, guidelines, codes of conduct, committees, audits and so on is often motivated by a desire to 'restore trust'. However, this is fundamentally misguided. Trust or mistrust has little to do with regulation in the first place. It involves deeper issues of how society has lost its traditional beliefs and faith in institutions that used to bind people together and give them a sense of purpose in shaping the future. For the same reason, a related point is that regulation does not allay fears about risk. Perceptions of risk today have little to do with the presence or non-presence of regulation.

Serious scholars of regulation make the point time and time again: regulation does not restore trust. Regulation has increased over the past 10 years, but at the same time, so has mistrust. Thus, in the field of ethics, the writers Peter Morgan and Glenn Reynolds note that ethics rules over the last few decades were supposed to increase public confidence in institutions, but ironically, public confidence has decreased in institutions over the same period (see Morgan and Reynolds, 1997).

In her discussion on the new regulation affecting public life in Britain, and the new obsession with accountability, the philosopher Onora O'Neill says that 'new legislation, regulation and controls...require detailed conformity to procedures and protocols, detailed record keeping, and provision of information in specified formats and success in reaching targets'. She adds that 'all institutions face new standards of recommended accounting practice, more detailed health and safety requirements, increasingly complex employment and pensions legislation, more exacting provisions for ensuring non-discrimination, and, of course, proliferating complaint procedures'.

She then asks: Do we see indications that public trust is reviving? In fact, she suggests, the situation is the opposite.

In the very years in which the accountability revolution has made striking advances, in which increased demands for control and performance, scrutiny and audit have been imposed, and in which the performance of professionals and institutions has been more and more controlled, we find in fact growing reports of mistrust.[1]

Regulation cannot restore trust, because it is intimately bound up with the dynamic of mistrust. Increased regulation and self-regulation is the logical extension of a society that mistrusts individual and institutional behaviour, and desires greater rules, regulations, checks and balances, measures of accountability and disclosure, and so on. Regulation entrenches mistrust. Once it is in place, by its nature it seems to confirm to society that unethical, irresponsible and damaging behaviour is really a new problem.

Self-regulation often proceeds in a euphemistic fashion

Voluntary regulation often proceeds in a euphemistic fashion. It does not herald itself as such. In fact, corporations now tell themselves that regulation and self-regulation is an *opportunity* for competitive advantage.

So, by disclosing information about risk to shareholders, companies feel they have an opportunity to increase shareholder trust. This might lead to further opportunities. It is hoped that firms may get cheaper capital because of increased trust and lower risk perceptions among investors. By posting privacy statements on websites, and installing chief privacy officers, not to mention completely re-regulating the interface between themselves and the customer, corporations hope to restore consumer trust. That may lead to opportunities. It may increase customer loyalty and enhance the brand. By creating sustainable development and CSR frameworks, corporations hope to generate opportunities. They hope to attract employees, for instance. The hope is that employees will see them as more responsible in their dealings with the world, and may become more loyal to the brand.

Unfortunately, the attempt to transform voluntary regulation into a new kind of business opportunity is an act of self-deception. For a start, as we have seen, attempting to restore trust in this way fails miserably because it does not challenge a culture of suspicion in the first place. Rather, it panders to it, and reinforces it. The most likely outcome is a downward spiral of behaviour, where society increasingly mistrusts corporations, and corporations increasingly impose voluntary regulation on themselves. In the process, corporations will become even more risk-averse.

After a while, there is a danger that the burden self-regulation imposes is no longer seen as such. The self-restraint imposed by ethics committees, boardroom rules and codes, risk controls, responsibility and sustainability criteria, capital efficiency measures, and so on, begins to be seen in a positive light. Essentially, risk-aversion, caution and restraint are repackaged as positive forms of behaviour.

A more ambitious view of innovation

A major paradox about risk aversion is that our capacity to innovate is better than ever before. Technology is far more sophisticated. Organizations are far more sophisticated. Our knowledge base is deeper. Yet our view of innovation has become diminished. This is an age where corporations are retreating from radical innovation, and where the innovation concept has become relativized.

The first objective is to restore an idea that corporations can create genuinely new products and services, and that not everything will end in failure. Sure, mistakes will be made and money lost. But the unwillingness to try should not be an option. One remedy could be to 'tolerate mistakes'. However, this was a view that was heard during the late 1990s, when venture capitalists poured investment into dotcoms. The trouble with the 'tolerating mistakes' slogan is that it does not raise expectations of ambitious innovation.

A better formulation is to advocate 'purposeful experimentation'. That is, where possible we need to define tangible ambitious goals and outcomes to achieve in the future. We also need to remind ourselves that purposeful experimentation always has a benefit, even where the outcome is not well defined. In the course of ambitious experimentation, new insights and unexpected benefits often arise. For organizations, trying to reach for the stars has its own rewards in terms of increased confidence and knowledge.

Innovation needs to be conceived in a more holistic way. That means taking a more socialized view of innovation. The Internet raises some interesting issues about the nature of innovation in our society. It reveals the fact that, as society becomes increasingly sophisticated in its ability to create new information technologies, it then begins to make sense for the first time to take a more ambitious view of modernizing the society around that technology. So, the Internet allows us to speed up things, make other things more efficient, solve problems, bring together people, communicate, and so on, on a global level. There is a lot more that can be done to pull out its potential, but that requires a bolder approach to innovation in the physical world as well.

The physical and the virtual overlap in so many ways, from the laying of cables and infrastructure, to the delivery of goods ordered online, from the people that dream up the content for the Internet, to the operating practices that surround the Internet in the workplace, and even the aeroplanes that people email from. The IT tools available will be held back if institutions are afraid to innovate and change the world around them.

In this context it is important to raise expectations about genuine change. We hear so often that change is very fast today. In fact, change is far too slow in so many areas. We need to speed up change, and raise expectations of innovation. When will we see new types of aeroplane that can take us from New York to Hong Kong in a matter of hours? When can we have universal broadband connections for the Internet? When can we have drugs to cure our most intractable diseases? How can we use new technology to automate processes and eliminate tedious jobs?

Integral to this is taking a less patronizing view of 'the customer'. The business world is keen to do a lot for 'the customer'. Yet surely the irony about the new obsession with the customer is that the customer is not served very well by it. Customer needs are arguably best served through new radical products that excite the imagination, rather than re-branding exercises, bland brand extensions, customer loyalty initiatives and automated telephone systems that irritate the hell out of people. It is worth remembering that consumers did not take to the radio, car, aeroplane, television, computer or mobile phone because they were branded products. Rather, these products were able to give fuller expression to human needs in some way.

The challenge above all is to reverse a culture of low expectations. This is a world where risks apparently proliferate, and where human behaviour is thought to be out of control. A world where we seem almost enthusiastic about regulating our own behaviour. Where failure to adopt a 'code of conduct' is viewed with suspicion and where our behaviour must be 'ethical' at all times. This is a world where growth can only be 'sustainable'. Where our actions must be highly 'responsible'.

This is a world of safety, security and 'risk management'. It is a world of gradual innovation, and 'getting close to the customer'. A world where risk aversion has become institutionalized.

In this world, it is worth bearing in mind that a society that does not try to shape its future ends up being dictated to by its own anxieties.

Note

1. See the Reith Lectures 2002, A Question of Trust, presented by Onora O'Neill.

Bibliography

Aaker, David (1991) *Managing Brand Equity*. New York: The Free Press.

Aaker, David and Joachimsthaler, Erich (2000) *Brand Leadership*. New York: The Free Press.

Albert, Michel (1993) *Capitalism Vs. Capitalism*. New York: Four Walls Eight Windows.

Ansoff, Igor (1988) *Corporate Strategy*, revised edition. Harmondsworth: Penguin.

Baker, Dean (2001) *The New Economy Goes Bust: What the Record Shows*. Centre for Economic Policy Research, October.

Baker, George and Smith, George (1998) *The New Financial Capitalists*. Cambridge: Cambridge University Press.

Baldock, Robert (2000) *The Last Days of the Giants?* Chichester: Wiley.

Baldwin, Robert and Cave, Martin (1999) *Understanding Regulation*. Oxford: Oxford University Press.

Baldwin, Tom (2002) 'I spun too much repents Campbell.' *The Times*, 9 May.

Baran, Paul and Sweezy, Paul (1966) *Monopoly Capital*. New York: Monthly Review Press.

Barnes, James (2001) *Secrets of Customer Relationship Management*. New York: McGraw-Hill.

Barnouw, Erik et al. (1997) *Conglomerates and the Media*. New York: The New Press.

Barron Baskin, Jonathan and Miranti, Paul (1997) *A History of Corporate Finance*. Cambridge: Cambridge University Press.

Basel Committee on Banking Supervision (1988) *International Convergence of Capital Measurement and Capital Standards*. July.

Beatty, Jack (ed.) *Colossus*. New York: Broadway Books.

Beaumont, Rupert, Duffett, Christopher and Leahy, Gerald (1998) *Non-executive Directors – A Risky Business*. London: The Association of Corporate Treasurers.

Bekier, Matthius, Bogardus, Anna and Oldham, Tim (2001) 'Why mergers fail.' *The McKinsey Quarterly*, no. 4.

Ben-Ami, Daniel (2001) *Cowardly Capitalism*. Chichester: Wiley.

Berle, Adolf and Means, Gardiner (1999) *The Modern Corporation and Private Property*. New Brunswick, NJ: Transaction Publishers.

Bernstein, Peter (1996) *Against the Gods*. New York: Wiley.

Bhide, Amar (2000) *The Origin and Evolution of New Businesses*. New York: Oxford University Press.

Bijker, Wiebe, Hughes, Thomas and Pinch, Trevor (1987) *The Social Construction of Technological Systems*. Cambridge, MA: MIT Press.

Black, Andrew, Wright, Philip and Bachman, John (1998) *In Search of Shareholder Value*. London: Pitman.

Blair, Margaret (1995) *Ownership and Control*. Washington: The Brookings Institution.

Bonardi, Jean-Phillipe (1999) 'Market and non-market strategies during deregulation: the case of BT.' *Business and Politics*, 1, no. 2, August.

Bookchin, Murray (1995) *Re-enchanting Humanity*. London: Cassell.

Booker, Christopher and North, Richard (1994) *The Mad Officials*. London: Constable.

Boyd, Robert (1995) 'R&D cuts, corporate focus on near-term payoff could test health of US economy.' *Knight-Ridder Newspapers*, 23 April.

Boylan, Brian (2000) Viewpoint. 'Brand new direction.' *Financial Times*, 9 August.

Braithwaite, John and Drahos, Peter (2000) *Global Business Regulation*. Cambridge: Cambridge University Press.

Brealey, Richard and Myers, Stewart (2000) *Principles of Corporate Finance*, 6th edition. Boston: Irwin/McGraw-Hill.

Brown, Kevin (1999) 'Innovation top 10 lists four British companies.' *Financial Times*, 25 January.

Brown, Kevin (2001) 'Ministers strain to hold the middle ground.' *Financial Times*, 31 January.

Brown, Kevin and Peel, Michael (2001) 'Blueprint to help bring business into 21st century.' *Financial Times*, 27 July.

Buderi, Robert (2000) *Engines of Tomorrow*. New York: Touchstone.

Burgess, Adam (2001) 'Flattering consumption: creating a Europe of the consumer.' *Journal of Consumer Culture* 1, no. 1.

Burnham, James (1941) *The Managerial Revolution*. London: Putnam.

Cameron, Doug (2002) 'Barclays chief denies that Big Four make excessive profits from small business banking.' *Financial Times*, 15 May.

Cappelli, Peter (1999) *The New Deal at Work*. Boston: Harvard Business School Press.

Cassis, Youssef (1997) *Big Business*. Oxford: Oxford University Press.

Castells, Manuel (2000) *The Rise of the Network Society*, 2nd edition. Oxford: Blackwell.

Castells, Manuel (2001) *The Internet Galaxy*. Oxford: Oxford University Press.

Chancellor, Edward (2002) 'Perverse incentives.' *Prospect*, June.

Chandler, Alfred (1977) *The Visible Hand*. Cambridge, MA: Harvard University Press.

Cherney, Andrei (2000) *The Next Deal*. New York: Basic Books.

Chew, Donald (ed.) (1998) *Discussing the Revolution in Corporate Finance*. Malden, MA: Blackwell.

Christensen, Clayton (1997) *The Innovator's Dilemma*. Boston: Harvard Business School Press.

Clarke, Michael (2000) *Regulation*. Basingstoke: Macmillan Press.

Cohen, Stephen S., DeLong, J. Bradford and Zysman, John (2000) 'Tools for thought: what is new and important about the "e-economy".' BRIE Working Paper 138, 27 February.

Conger, Jay, Lawler, Edward and Finegold, David (2001) *Corporate Boards*. San Francisco: Jossey-Bass.

Cope, Nigel and Grice, Andrew (2001) 'MPs call for windfall tax on oil firms after BP Amoco reports £9.8bn profit.' *Independent*, 14 January.

Corbett, J. and Jenkinson, T. (1997) 'How is investment financed? A study of Germany, Japan, the United Kingdom and the United States. *The Manchester School*, 65, 69–93.

Cowley, Stacy (2001) 'IBM will rule the services roost.' *InfoWorld*, 11 May.

Crainer, Stuart and Dearlove, Des (2000) *Generation Entrepreneur*. London: Pearson Education.

Dahms, Harry (ed.) (2000) *Transformations of Capitalism*. London: Macmillan Press.

Daniell, Mark (2000) *World of Risk*. Singapore: Wiley.

Daniels, P.W. and Lever, W.F. (1996) *The Global Economy in Transition*. Harlow: Longman.

Davis, Stan and Meyer, Christopher (1999) *Blur*. Oxford: Capstone.

Denton Wilde Sapte (2000) *The ART survey 2000*. London: Denton Wilde Sapte.

Derber, Charles (1998) *Corporation Nation*. New York: St Martin's Griffin.

Dertouzos, Michael, Lester, Richard and Solow, Robert (1990) *Made In America*. New York: HarperPerennial.

Dicken, Peter (1999) *Global Shift*, 3rd edition. London: Paul Chapman.

Drucker, Peter (1959) 'Long range planning means risk-taking.' *Management Science*, April.

Drucker, Peter (1999) *Innovation and Entrepreneurship*. Oxford: Butterworth–Heinemann.

Duetsch, Larry (ed.) (1998) *Industry Studies*, 2nd edition. New York: M.E. Sharpe.

Durodie, Bill (2002) 'Why I think a dialogue with the public will undermine science.' *The Times Higher*, 12 April.

Eccles, Robert, Herz, Robert, Keegan, E. Mary and Philips David (2001) *The Value Reporting Revolution*. New York: Wiley.

Ehrbar, Al (1998) *EVA*. New York: Wiley.

Elkington, John (1997) *Cannibals with Forks*. Oxford: Capstone.

Elkington, John (2001) *The Chrysalis Economy*. Oxford: Capstone.

Eller, Claudia and Bates, James (1999) 'In Hollywood, more business than show.' *Los Angeles Times*, 13 August.

Farrell, Larry (2001) *The Entrepreneurial Age*. Oxford: Windsor.

Fingleton, Eamonn (1999) *In Praise of Hard Industries*. London: Orion Business Books.

Finke, Nikki (2002) 'Who would have guessed? Moguls scarce in Hollywood.' *Business News*, NYPost.com, 18 February.

Fligstein, Neil (1990) *The Transformation of Corporate Control*. Cambridge, MA: Harvard University Press.

Fombrun, Charles (1996) *Reputation*. Boston: Harvard Business School Press.

Forester, Tom (1987) *High-Tech Society*. Cambridge, MA: MIT Press.

Fradette, Michael and Michaud, Steve (1998) *The Power of Corporate Kenetics*. New York: Simon & Schuster.

Francis, David (2002) 'Big business races to reform itself.' *The Christian Science Monitor*, 2 August.

Freemantle, David (1998) *What Customers Like About You*. London: Nicholas Brealey.

Friedman, Milton (1962) *Capitalism and Freedom*. Chicago: The University of Chicago Press.

Frost, Chris, Allen, David, Porter, James and Bloodworth, Philip (2001) *Operational Risk and Resilience*. Oxford: Butterworth–Heinemann.

Fukuyama, Francis (1996) *Trust*. New York: Free Press Paperbacks.

Furedi, Frank (1997) *Culture of Fear*. London: Cassell.

Galbraith, John Kenneth (1958) *The Affluent Society*. Harmondsworth: Penguin.

Galbraith, John Kenneth (1967) *The New Industrial State*. London: Andre Deutsch.

Gallagher, Russell (1956) 'Risk management: a new phase in cost control.' *Harvard Business Review*, September–October.

Garfinkel, Simson (2000) *Database Nation*. Sebastopol, CA: O'Reilly.

Gavron, Robert, Cowling, Marc, Holtham, Gerald and Westall, Andrea (1998) *The Entrepreneurial Society*. London: Institute for Public Policy Research.

Giddens, Anthony (1999) *Runaway World*. London: Profile Books.

Giddens, Anthony (2000) *The Third Way and its Critics*. Cambridge: Polity Press.

Goodchild, John and Callow, Clive (eds) (2001) *Brands Visions and Values*. Chichester: Wiley.

Gray, Colin (1998) *Enterprise and Culture*. London: Routledge.

Gray, John (1998) *False Dawn*. London: Granta Books.

Greider, William (1997) *One World, Ready or Not*. London: Allen Lane The Penguin Press.

Guthrie, Jonathan (2002) 'Industry spends as much on IT as on equipment.' *Financial Times*, 31 July.

Gunnell, Barbara and Timms, David (2000) *After Seattle*. London: Catalyst.

Hall, William (2002) 'Misunderstood units hold the key to ABB.' *Financial Times*, 18 March.

Hamel, Gary (2000) *Leading the Revolution*. Boston: Harvard Business School Press.

Hammer, Michael and Champy, James (1993) *Reengineering the Corporation*. London: Nicholas Brealey.

Harney, Alexandra (2000) 'Cracks widen in Japan's commercial code.' *Financial Times*, 17 August.

Harris-Jones, Judith and Bergin, Louise (1998) *The Management of Corporate Risk – A Framework for Directors*. London: The Association of Corporate Treasurers.

Harrison, Bennett (1994) *Lean and Mean*. New York: Basic Books.

Harvey, Fiona (2002) 'Into the age of the living page.' *Financial Times*, 15 May.

Hawken, Paul, Lovins, Amory. B and Lovins, L. Hunter (2000) *Natural Capitalism*. London: Earthscan.

Heartfield, James (1998). *Need and Desire in the Post-Material Economy*. Sheffield: Sheffield Hallam University Press.

Heath, Robert. (1998) *Crisis Management for Managers and Executives*. London: Financial Times Professional Limited.

Heilbroner, Robert (1975) *The Making of Economic Society*, 5th edition. Englewood Cliffs, NJ: Prentice-Hall.

Heller, Robert (1995) *The Naked Manager for the Nineties*. London: Warner Books.

Henwood, Doug (1997) *Wall Street*. New York: Verso.

Hertz, Noreena (2001) *The Silent Takeover*. London: William Heinemann.

Heyel, Carl (1969) *Computers, Office Machines and the Information Technology*. Washington: Business Equipment Manufacturers Association.

Hill, Andrew (2000) 'Oil giants roll out their share-buyback barrels.' *Financial Times*, 6 August.

Hilmer, Frederick and Donaldson, Lex (1996) *Management Redeemed*. New York: The Free Press.

Hiltzik, Michael (2000) *Dealers of Lightning*. London: Orion Business Books.

Hobsbawm, Eric (1975) *The Age of Capital*. London: Weidenfeld & Nicolson.

Hobson, Dominic (1999) *The National Wealth*. London: HarperCollins.

Homer-Dixon, Thomas (2001) Personal view. 'A world that turns too fast.' *Financial Times*, 2 January.

Hoskyns, John (2000) *Just in Time*. London: Aurum Press.

Howard, Philip (1994) *The Death of Common Sense*. New York: Warner Books.

Hunt, Ben (ed.) (2001a) *Risk Management Guide 2001*. London: White Page.

Hunt, Ben (2001b) 'Issue of the moment: the rise and rise of risk management.' In: J. Pickford, ed., *Financial Times Mastering Risk. Volume 1: Concepts*. London: Financial Times/Prentice Hall.

Hutter, Bridget and Power, Michael (2001) 'Risk management and business regulation.' In: J. Pickford, ed., *Financial Times Mastering Risk. Volume 1: Concepts*. London: Financial Times/Prentice Hall.

Hutton, Will (1996) *The State We're In*. London: Vintage.

Hutton, Will (2000) Personal view. 'The buck stops with big corporations.' *Financial Times*, 28 February.

Hutton, Will and Giddens, Anthony (eds) (2000) *On the Edge*. London: Jonathan Cape.

Inch, Tom (1999) Technology viewpoint. 'Getting the measure of innovation.' *Financial Times*, 11 August.

IPCC (2001) Technical Summary of the Working Group 1 Report.

Jacoby, Russell (1999) *The End of Utopia*. New York: Basic Books.

Jenkins, Patrick (2002) 'The bosses who are jumping to smaller ships.' *Financial Times*, 28 March.

Jensen, Michael (1986) 'Agency costs of free cash flow, corporate finance, and takeovers.' *American Economic Review (Papers and Proceedings)* 76, 323–329.

Jensen, Michael and Meckling, William (1976) 'Theory of the firm: management behaviour, agency costs and ownership structure.' *Journal of Financial Economics*, 3, 305–360.

Jensen, Michael and Smith, Clifford (1984) 'The theory of corporate finance: a historical overview.' In: M. Jensen and C. Smith, eds, *The Modern Theory of Corporate Finance*. New York: McGraw-Hill.

Johnson, Hazel (1999) *Determining Cost of Capital*. London: Pearson Education Limited.

Jones, Ian W. and Pollitt, Michael G. (2001) 'Who influences debates in business ethics? An investigation into the development of corporate governance in the UK since 1990.' Working Paper no. 221. ESRC Centre for Business Research, University of Cambridge, December.

Kaletsky, Anatole (2002a) 'Is America's ascendancy on the wane?' *The Times*, 30 April.

Kaletsky, Anatole (2002b) 'Chancellor plays a dangerous game.' *The Times*, 26 March.

Kaufman, Allen, Zacharias, Lawrence and Karson, Marvin (1995) *Managers Versus Owners*. Oxford: Oxford University Press.

Keen, Peter and Mackintosh, Ron (2001) *The Freedom Economy*. New York: Osborne/McGraw-Hill.

Kennedy, Allan (2000) *The End of Shareholder Value*. London: Orion Business.

Klein, Naomi (2000) *No Logo*. London: Flamingo.

Kreitzman, Leon (1999) *The 24 Hour Society*. London: Profile Books.

Kuttner, Robert (1996) *Everything for Sale*. Chicago: The University of Chicago Press.

Larkin, Judy (2001) 'Rethinking crisis management.' In: B. Hunt, ed., *Risk Management Guide 2001*. London: White Page.

Leadbeater, Charles (1999) *Living on Thin Air*. London: Viking.

Leifer, Richard, McDermott, Christopher, Colarelli O'Connor, Gina, Peters, Lois, Rice, Mark, and Veryzer, Robert (2000) *Radical Innovation*. Boston: Harvard Business School Press.

Leonhardt, David (2000) 'Entrepreneurs' "golden age" turns out to be mythology.' *New York Times*, 1 December.

Lester, Richard (1998) *The Productive Edge*. New York: W.W. Norton.

Lewis, David and Bridger, Darren (2001) *The Soul of the New Consumer*. London: Nicholas Brealey.

Lomborg, Bjørn (2001) *The Skeptical Environmentalist*. Cambridge: Cambridge University Press.

Madrick, Jeff (1998) 'Computers: waiting for the revolution.' *The New York Review of Books*, 26 March.

Maitland, Alison (1999) 'The value of virtue in a transparent world.' *Financial Times*, 5 August.

Malone, James (2002) 'Confidence goes bust.' *spiked-online.com*, 2 July.

Mandelson, Peter and Liddle, Roger (1996) *The Blair Revolution*. London: Faber & Faber.

Marr, Jeffrey and Walker, Steven (2001) *Stakeholder Power*. Cambridge, MA: Perseus Publishing.

Marsh, Peter (2001) 'Joined up information.' *Financial Times*, 3 August.

Martin, Peter (1998) 'Gorging on mergers.' *Financial Times*, 22 December.

Marx, Karl and Engels, Friedrich (1967) *The Communist Manifesto*. Harmondsworth: Penguin.

Matthews, Virginia (2002) Inside track. 'Caution versus creativity.' *Financial Times*, 17 June.

McChesney, Robert, Meiksins Wood, Ellen and Bellamy Foster, John (eds) (1998) *Capitalism and the Information Age*. New York: Monthly Review Press.

McIntosh, Malcolm, Leipziger, Deborah, Jones, Keith and Coleman, Gil (1998) *Corporate Citizenship*. London: Financial Times Professional Limited.

McLaughlin, John (1966) *Information Technology and the Survival of the Firm*. Homewood, IL: Dow-Jones Irwin.

Meadows, D.H., Meadows, D.L., Randers J. and Behrens, C.W. (1972) *The Limits to Growth*. New York: Universe Books.

Micklethwait, John and Wooldridge, Adrian (1997) *The Witch Doctors*. London: Mandarin.

Micklethwait, John and Wooldridge, Adrian (2000) *A Future Perfect*. London: William Heinemann.

Mills, Roger (1998) *The Dynamics of Shareholder Value*. Lechlade: Mars Business Associates.

Minford, Patrick (1998) *Markets not Stakes*. London: Orion Business Books.

Mintzberg, Henry, Ahlstrand, Bruce and Lampel, Joseph (1998) *Strategy Safari*. London: Prentice Hall.

Monbiot, George (2000) *Captive State*. London: Macmillan.

Moore, Gordon (1996) 'Some personal perspectives on research in the semiconductor industry.' In: R. Rosenbloom and William Spencer, eds, *Engines of Innovation*. Boston: Harvard Business School Press.

Morgan, Peter and Reynolds, Glenn (1997) *The Appearance of Impropriety*. New York: The Free Press.

Morita, Akio (1987) *Made in Japan*. London: HarperCollins.

Morris, Julian (ed.) (2000) *Rethinking Risk and the Precautionary Principle*. Oxford: Butterworth–Heinemann.

Moschella, David (1997) *Waves of Power*. New York: American Management Association.

Moss Kanter, Rosabeth (1983) *The Change Masters*. New York: Touchstone.

Mowery, David and Rosenberg, Nathan (1998) *Paths of Innovation*. Cambridge: Cambridge University Press.

Nader, Ralph (1976). *Taming the Giant Corporation*. New York: W.W. Norton.

Neal, Mark and Davies, Christie (1998) *The Corporation Under Siege*. London: The Social Affairs Unit.

Nicoll, Alexander (1999) 'Defence giants under fire.' *Financial Times*, 21 July.

O'Reilly, Brian (2001) 'There's gold in them thar pills.' *Fortune*, 23 July.

Ormerod, Paul (1994) *The Death of Economics*. London: Faber & Faber.

O'Sullivan, Mary (2000) *Contests for Corporate Control*. Oxford: Oxford University Press.

Overell, Stephen (2002) 'The workplace revolution that never happened.' *Financial Times*, 27 May.

Oxelheim, Lars and Wihlborg, Clas (1997) *Managing in the Turbulent World Economy*. Chichester: Wiley.

Packard, Vance (1957) *The Hidden Persuaders*. Harmondsworth: Penguin.

Peppers, Don and Rogers, Martha (1993). *The One-to-One Future*. New York: Doubleday.

Peters, Tom and Waterman, Robert (1982) *In Search of Excellence*. London: HarperCollins Business.

Petzinger, Thomas (1999) *The New Pioneers*. New York: Simon & Schuster.

Pickford, James (ed.) (2001) *Financial Times Mastering Risk Volume 1: Concepts*. London: Financial Times/Prentice Hall.

Pink, Daniel (2001) *Free Agent Nation*. New York: Warner Books.

Plender, John (1997) *A Stake in the Future*. London: Nicholas Brealey.

Porter, Michael (1980) *Competitive Strategy*. New York: The Free Press.

Power, Michael (1997) *The Audit Society*. New York: Oxford University Press.

Prechel, Harland (2000) *Big Business and the State*. Albany, NJ: State University of New York Press.

Putnam, Robert (2000) *Bowling Alone*. New York: Simon & Schuster.

Race, Tim (2002) 'Ashamed to be an executive.' *New York Times*, 1 July.

Raddock, D. (1986) *Assessing Corporate Political Risk*. Totowa, NJ: Rowman & Littlefield.

Rappaport, Alfred (1998) *Creating Shareholder Value*. New York: The Free Press.

Rich, Ben, and Janos, Leo (1995) *Skunk Works*. London: Warner Books.

Riechmann, Deb (2000) 'High Midwest gas prices fuel gouging investigation.' *Honolulu Star-Bulletin*, 16 June.

Rosenbloom, Richard and Spencer, William (eds) (1996) *Engines of Innovation*. Boston: Harvard Business School Press.

Roy, William (1997) *Socializing Capital*. Princeton, NJ: Princeton University Press.

Rugman, Alan (2000) *The End of Globalization*. London: Random House Business Books.

Rushe, Dominic (2002) 'Battle of the sequels, Part 1.' *The Sunday Times*, 24 March.

Russell, John (2001) 'Economy, companies affected greatly by expectations of shareholders.' *Akron Beacon Journal*, 9 July.

Sampson, Anthony (1996) *Company Man*. London: HarperCollins Business.

Saxenian, AnnaLee (1994) *Regional Advantage*. Cambridge, MA: Harvard University Press.

Scherer, F.M. (1999) *New Perspectives on Economic Growth and Technological Innovation*. Washington: British-North American Committee/Brookings Institution Press.

Scherer, F.M. (1992) *International High-Technology Competition*. Cambridge, MA: Harvard University Press.

Schnaars, Steven (1989) *Megamistakes*. New York: The Free Press.

Schrage, Michael (2000) *Serious Play*. Boston: Harvard Business School Press.

Schrage, Michael (2002) 'The Dell curve.' *Wired*, July.

Schumpeter, Joseph (1975) *Capitalism, Socialism and Democracy*. New York: HarperPerennial.

Schwartz, John (2001) 'Chief Privacy Officers forge evolving corporate roles.' *New York Times*, 12 February.

Scott, William B. (1999) 'Industry's hire-and-fire paradigm is obsolete.' *Aviation Week and Space Technology*, 21 June.

Scott, Mark (1998) *Value Drivers*. Chichester: Wiley.

Seely Brown, John and Duguid, Paul (2000) *The Social Life of Information*. Boston: Harvard Business School Press.

Sennett, Richard (1998) *The Corrosion of Character*. New York: W.W. Norton.

Shimpi, Prakash (1999) *Integrating Corporate Risk Management*. New York: Swiss Re New Markets.

Shulman, Larry (2000) 'Freedom from shareholder tyranny.' *Financial Times*, 25 July.

Shutt, Harry (1998) *The Trouble with Capitalism*. London: Zed Books.

Simons, Robert (1995) *Levers of Control*. Boston: Harvard Business School Press.

Skapinker, Michael (2000) 'How to bow out without egg on your face.' *Financial Times*, 8 March.

Smith, Adam (2000) *The Wealth of Nations*. New York: The Modern Library.

Smith, Alison (2000) 'Carnival pledges $1bn buy back to boost shares.' *Lloyd's List*, 1 March.

Smith, Douglas and Alexander, Robert (1999) *Fumbling the Future*. New York: toExcel.

Sorrell, Martin (2002) Viewpoint. 'Consumer is king as producers fight it out.' *The Times*, 20 February.

Sparrow, Malcolm (2000) *The Regulatory Craft*. Washington: The Brookings Institution.

Stapenhurst, Frederick (1992) *Political Risk Analysis around the North Atlantic*. New York: St Martin's Press.

Steiner, George and Steiner, John (2000) *Business, Government, and Society*, 9th edition. Boston: Irwin McGraw-Hill.

Stern, Carl and Stalk Jr, George (eds) (1998) *Perspectives on Strategy*. New York: Wiley.

Stern, Joel and Chew, Donald (eds) (1998) *The Revolution in Corporate Finance*. Malden, MA: Blackwell.

Stewart, Michael (1993) *Keynes in the 1990s*. Harmondsworth: Penguin.

Strange, Susan (1996) *The Retreat of the State*. Cambridge: Cambridge University Press.

Sutton, Brenda (ed.) (1993) *The Legitimate Corporation*. Cambridge, MA: Blackwell.

Swedberg, Richard (ed.) (2000) *Entrepreneurship*. Oxford: Oxford University Press.

Swift, Ronald (2001). *Accelerating Customer Relationships*. Upper Saddle River, NJ: Prentice Hall.

Thomson, Kevin (1998) *Emotional Capital*. Oxford: Capstone.

Thurow, Lester (1999) *Creating Wealth*. London: Nicholas Brealey.

Tibballs, Geoff (1999) *Business Blunders*. London: Robinson.

Ting, W. (1988) *Multinational Risk Assessment and Management*. New York: Quorum.

Uchitelle, Louis (1996) 'Corporate outlays for basic research cut back significantly.' *New York Times*, 8 October.

Ulwick, Anthony (2002) 'Turn customer input into innovation.' *Harvard Business Review*, January.

United Nations (2000) *World Investment Report 2000*.

Vaughan, Emmett (1997) *Risk Management*. New York: Wiley.

Vernon, Heidi (1998) *Business and Society*, 6th edition. Singapore: McGraw-Hill.

Vogel, Harold (2001) *Entertainment Industry Economics*, 5th edition. Cambridge: Cambridge University Press.

Vogel, Steven (1996) *Freer Markets, More Rules*. New York: Cornell University Press.

Ward, Ralph (1997) *21st Century Corporate Board*. New York: Wiley.

Waring, Alan and Glendon, A. Ian (1998) *Managing Risk*. London: International Thomson Business Press.

Warren, Richard (2000) *Corporate Governance and Accountability*. Wirral, UK: Liverpool Academic Press.

Webber, Alan (1998) 'Business race isn't always to the swift.' *USA Today*, 2 March.

Weisman, Jon (2001) 'Amazon reorganizes, emphasizing third-party services.' *E-Commerce Times*, 16 November.

Weiss, Linda (1998) *The Myth of the Powerless State*. Cambridge: Polity Press.

Weizsacker, Ernst Von, Lovins, Amory B. and Lovins, L. Hunter (1997) *Factor Four*. London: Earthscan.

Welling, Kathryn M. (2001) 'No fan of 90s miracles.' *Traders Magazine*, August.

Winston, Brian (1998) *Media Technology and Society*. London: Routledge.

Winter, Matthias and Steger, Ulrich (1998) *Managing Outside Pressure*. Chichester: Wiley.

Yergin, Daniel and Stanislaw, Joseph (1998) *The Commanding Heights*. New York: Touchstone.

Zadek, Simon (2001) *The Civil Corporation*. London: Earthscan.

Index

Index compiled by Annette Musker